TEXTBOOK OF PHARMACOLOGICAL AND TOXICOLOGICAL SCREENING METHODS-II

PCI M.PHARMACY (MPL 202T)

DR. ARAVINDA REDDY PURMA,
DR. B. SURYAPRAKASA RAO

Contents

PREFACE

The science of toxicology has long played a pivotal role in safeguarding public health and the environment by elucidating the adverse effects of chemical substances on living organisms. As the field evolves, driven by advancements in technology and an ever-increasing understanding of biological systems, there is a critical need for comprehensive and up-to-date resources that cater to the demands of modern toxicological research and practice.

Textbook of Pharmacological and Toxicological Screening Methods-II is crafted with the intention of bridging the gap between traditional toxicological methods and contemporary advancements. This book aims to provide a thorough and detailed overview of the various toxicological screening methods, encompassing acute, sub-acute, and chronic toxicity studies, reproductive and genotoxicity assessments, investigational new drug (IND) enabling studies, safety pharmacology, and toxicokinetics. Each chapter is meticulously structured to ensure that readers gain a deep understanding of the methodologies, regulatory guidelines, and practical applications essential for conducting high-quality toxicological research.

The motivation behind this textbook stems from the recognition of the critical role that robust toxicological assessments play in the development and approval of pharmaceuticals, cosmetics, chemicals, and other products that interact with biological systems. By adhering to rigorous testing protocols and regulatory frameworks, toxicologists can ensure the safety and efficacy of these products, ultimately protecting public health and the environment.

Throughout the chapters, the authors have endeavored to present complex information in a digestible and accessible manner, without compromising on the depth and detail required by professionals in the field. The inclusion of case studies and real-world examples further enriches the content, providing practical insights and illustrating the application of various toxicological methods in real-life scenarios.

This textbook is not only a valuable resource for students pursuing studies in toxicology, pharmacology, and related disciplines but also serves as a comprehensive reference for professionals, researchers, and regulatory bodies involved in the safety assessment of chemical substances. The collaborative efforts of Dr. Aravinda Reddy Purma and Dr. B. Suryaprakasa

Rao, both esteemed experts in their respective fields, ensure that the content is both authoritative and relevant to current toxicological practices.

In conclusion, Textbook of Pharmacological and Toxicological Screening Methods-II aspires to equip readers with the knowledge and tools necessary to navigate the complexities of toxicological assessments. It is our hope that this book will inspire and guide the next generation of toxicologists in their quest to advance the field and contribute to the protection of public health and safety.

Dr. Aravinda Reddy Purma
Professor
Mother Teresa College of Pharmacy
Ghatkesar, Hyderabad
Dr. B. Suryaprakasa Rao, M.D.
Professor
Dept of Pharmacology
Andhra Medical College (Rtd)
JULY 2024

TEXTBOOK OF PHARMACOLOGICAL AND TOXICOLOGICAL SCREENING METHODS-II

PCI M.Pharmacy (MPL 202T)

AUTHORS

Dr. Aravinda Reddy Purma

Professor

Mother Teresa College of Pharmacy

Ghatkesar, Hyderabad

Dr. B. Suryaprakasa Rao, M.D.

Professor

Dept of Pharmacology

Andhra Medical College (Rtd)

Published by Notion Press

Notion Press, Inc.

800, West El Camino Real #180,

California, USA 94040

Notion Press Media Pvt Ltd

#7, Red Cross Road,

Egmore, Chennai, Tamil Nadu 600008

Email ID: publish@notionpress.com

Phone Number: +91 44 46315631

July 2024

AUTHORS PROFILE

Dr. Purma Aravinda Reddy

Dr. Purma Aravinda Reddy is the esteemed principal of Mother Teresa College of Pharmacy, with a remarkable background in academia and leadership. He pursued higher studies at Kakatiya university where he earned a Bachelor's degree in pharmaceutical sciences and obtained a Master's degree in pharmaceutical chemistry from The Tamil Nadu Dr. MGR Medical university, during this time that he discovered a passion for research and teaching. Dr Aravinda Reddy pursued his Ph.D. at Acharya Nagarjuna University. His leadership skills and ability to effectively navigate complex academic environments. Dr Aravinda Reddy has held various academic positions, demonstrating a strong dedication to teaching, research, and administrative excellence. Prior to assuming the presidency at Mother Teresa College of Pharmacy, he served as Asst. Professor at Govt. Medical college at RIMS- Kadapa. Dr. Reddy is known for visionary leadership, unwavering commitment to educational excellence.

Dr B. Suryaprakasa Rao

Dr. Betha Suryaprakasa Rao worked as a professor at Andhra medical college with a remarkable background in academia and leadership. He pursued his MBBS and MD from Andhra medical college. He was member board of studies at NTRUHS, vice principal at RIMS Medical college, NCC naval officer at Andhra medical college and head at the Gayatri Parishad medical college. Dr Prakasa Rao was examiner at different universities in India and ethics committee chairman at Vishaka institutional review board from 2010 to 2019. He is the life member in Indian pharmacology society and Indian society of toxicology. Dr. Suryaprakasa Rao is known for his unwavering commitment to educational excellence.

I

Introduction to Toxicology

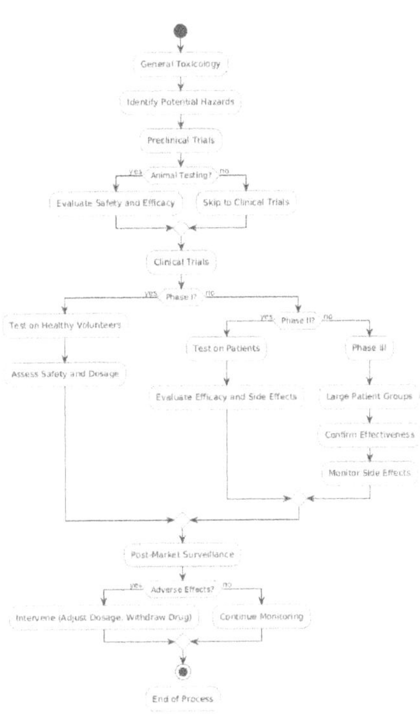

Fig 1: Overview of Drug Safety Assessment in General Toxicology

1.1 Basic Definitions and Types of Toxicology

1.1.1 General Toxicology

Definition and Scope:

Toxicology, often referred to as the science of poisons, is a field that encompasses the study of the adverse effects of chemical substances on living organisms and the environment. This discipline plays a critical role in understanding how various chemicals, whether natural or synthetic, interact with biological systems to cause harm. The **broad applications** of toxicology span several fields, including pharmacology, environmental science, and industrial hygiene. In pharmacology, toxicology helps in identifying the potential hazards of new drugs, ensuring that they are safe for human use. In environmental science, toxicologists study the impact of pollutants on ecosystems, helping to devise strategies for pollution control and remediation. Industrial hygiene relies on toxicology to assess and mitigate the risks associated with chemical exposures in the workplace, protecting workers' health and safety.

Applications in Drug Safety:

Toxicology is indispensable in the field of **drug safety**, where it is used to assess the potential risks of pharmaceuticals. This assessment is carried out through various stages, starting with preclinical trials. During these trials, new drugs are tested on animals to determine their safety and efficacy before they are administered to humans. Toxicologists evaluate parameters such as dosage, exposure duration, and the potential for adverse effects. Following preclinical trials, drugs undergo rigorous testing in clinical trials involving human participants. Post-market surveillance is another crucial aspect, where toxicologists monitor the safety of drugs that have already been approved and are in widespread use. This ongoing assessment helps identify any unforeseen adverse effects, leading to timely interventions such as dosage adjustments or drug withdrawals. There have been notable cases where drugs were withdrawn from the market due to severe toxicity issues. For instance, the anti-inflammatory drug Rofecoxib (Vioxx) was withdrawn after it was found to increase the risk of heart attacks and strokes.

Historical Development:

The field of toxicology has evolved significantly from its ancient origins, where poisons were primarily used for hunting or as weapons. The historical development of toxicology as a scientific discipline can be traced back to notable milestones such as the work of Paracelsus, a Swiss physician and alchemist, in the 16th century. Paracelsus is often credited with the foundational concept of **dose-response**, encapsulated in his famous dictum, "The dose makes the poison." This principle underscores that any substance can be toxic if taken in sufficient quantities, highlighting the importance of dosage in determining the safety of chemicals. Over the centuries, toxicology has expanded its scope to include a wide range of studies, from acute and chronic toxicity to environmental and occupational health, each contributing to a deeper understanding of how chemicals affect living organisms and ecosystems.

Case Studies and Examples:

One of the most impactful real-world incidents in the history of toxicology is the **Thalidomide tragedy**. Thalidomide was a drug marketed in the late 1950s and early 1960s as a treatment for morning sickness in pregnant women. However, it was soon discovered that Thalidomide caused severe birth defects, leading to the birth of thousands of babies with malformed limbs. This tragedy had a profound impact on drug regulation, leading to the establishment of more stringent testing and approval processes for new drugs. The lessons learned from the Thalidomide incident underscored the critical importance of thorough toxicological assessments in ensuring drug safety, ultimately shaping the regulatory landscape and enhancing the protection of public health. Another example is the case of DDT, a pesticide widely used in the mid-20th century. While effective in controlling pests, DDT was found to have devastating environmental and health effects, leading to its ban in many countries and a reevaluation of pesticide use and regulation.

1.1.2 Mechanistic Toxicology

Mechanisms of Toxic Effects:

Mechanistic toxicology delves into the **cellular and molecular mechanisms** that underlie the toxic effects of various substances. Understanding these mechanisms is crucial for predicting how chemicals will interact with biological systems and for developing effective interventions. At the cellular level, toxicants can interfere with critical biological processes, leading to cell damage or death. One primary pathway through which toxic effects manifest is **apoptosis**, a form of programmed cell death. Apoptosis is a controlled process that allows the body to eliminate damaged or unnecessary cells, but when induced by toxicants, it can result in excessive cell loss and tissue damage. Another key pathway is **necrosis**, an uncontrolled form of cell death resulting from acute damage. Unlike apoptosis, necrosis often triggers inflammation and can cause significant harm to surrounding tissues. Additionally, toxicants can induce **oxidative stress**, a state where the production of reactive oxygen species (ROS) overwhelms the body's antioxidant defenses. Oxidative stress can damage cellular components, including lipids, proteins, and DNA, leading to various diseases and conditions.

Examples of Toxicological Mechanisms:

To illustrate the concepts of mechanistic toxicology, consider the action of **cyanide**, a highly toxic compound. Cyanide exerts its lethal effects by inhibiting cytochrome c oxidase, an essential enzyme in the mitochondrial electron transport chain. This inhibition prevents cells from using oxygen to produce ATP, the energy currency of the cell, effectively suffocating the cells. The resulting energy crisis leads to rapid cell death and can cause fatal damage to vital organs, particularly the heart and brain. Another example is the mechanism of action of **lead**, a heavy metal that disrupts several biological processes. Lead can mimic calcium and interfere with neurotransmitter release, leading to neurotoxicity. It also induces oxidative stress and interferes with enzymes involved in heme synthesis, causing anemia and other health issues.

Current Research Trends:

Mechanistic toxicology is a dynamic field, continually evolving with advances in technology and scientific understanding. Two emerging areas of significant interest are **nanotoxicology** and **genetic toxicology**. **Nanotoxicology** focuses on the potential toxic effects of nanoparticles, which are increasingly used in various industries, including medicine, electronics, and cosmetics. Due to their small size, nanoparticles can easily enter cells and interact with cellular structures, potentially causing unique toxicological effects that are not observed with larger particles. Researchers are investigating how the size, shape, and surface properties of nanoparticles influence their toxicity, aiming to develop safer nanomaterials. **Genetic toxicology** explores how chemicals and physical agents can damage genetic material, leading to mutations, cancer, and other genetic disorders. This field employs advanced techniques such as genomic sequencing and CRISPR-Cas9 gene editing to study the mechanisms of DNA damage and repair. Understanding these mechanisms helps in assessing the mutagenic potential of new substances and in developing strategies to mitigate genetic risks.

1.1.3 Regulatory Toxicology

Regulatory Frameworks:
Regulatory toxicology involves the application of toxicological data and principles to establish regulations and guidelines that protect public health and the environment. Several **global regulatory bodies** play pivotal roles in this domain, including the **Food and Drug Administration (FDA)** in the United States, the **European Medicines Agency (EMA)** in Europe, and the **World Health Organization (WHO)** on an international level. These agencies are responsible for setting safety standards, approving new drugs, and ensuring that marketed products do not pose undue risks to consumers. The FDA, for instance, has comprehensive guidelines that cover preclinical and clinical testing of drugs, including detailed requirements for toxicity studies. The EMA similarly provides guidelines that ensure the safety, efficacy, and quality of medicinal products in the European Union. WHO's guidelines often serve as a reference for many countries, especially in regions with developing regulatory infrastructures, helping to harmonize safety standards globally.

Roles in Drug Approval Processes:
The **drug approval process** involves several critical steps, each requiring rigorous toxicological assessments to ensure the safety of new pharmaceutical products. Initially, during the preclinical phase, drugs are tested in laboratory settings and on animals to identify any potential toxic effects. These tests assess acute, sub-chronic, and chronic toxicity, as well as reproductive toxicity, genotoxicity, and carcinogenicity. After successful preclinical testing, the drug moves to clinical trials, which are conducted in three phases. Phase I trials involve a small group of healthy volunteers to evaluate the drug's safety and dosage. Phase II trials expand the testing to a larger group of patients to assess efficacy and side effects. Phase III trials involve even larger patient groups to confirm the drug's effectiveness, monitor side effects, and compare it to commonly used treatments. Toxicological data from these phases are crucial for determining whether

the drug is safe enough for market approval. Regulatory agencies like the FDA and EMA review this data meticulously before granting approval, ensuring that only drugs that meet stringent safety standards reach the market.

Key Regulatory Agencies:

Key **regulatory agencies** like the FDA, EMA, and WHO have distinct but complementary roles in safeguarding public health. The FDA's responsibilities include regulating food, drugs, medical devices, cosmetics, and tobacco products in the United States. It conducts inspections, monitors adverse event reports, and can enforce recalls of unsafe products. The EMA, based in the European Union, coordinates the evaluation and supervision of medicinal products, providing a centralized procedure for drug approval that is recognized across EU member states. The WHO sets international health standards and provides guidance on a wide range of public health issues, including the safety of pharmaceuticals. It plays a crucial role in promoting harmonization of regulations and guidelines globally, facilitating international trade and ensuring that health products are safe and effective.

Case Studies in Regulatory Toxicology:

Numerous **case studies** highlight the importance of regulatory toxicology in protecting public health. One notable example is the case of **thalidomide**, a drug initially marketed in the late 1950s as a treatment for morning sickness. Thalidomide caused severe birth defects in thousands of babies, leading to its withdrawal from the market and prompting significant changes in drug regulatory practices. This tragedy underscored the need for comprehensive teratogenicity testing before approving drugs for use in pregnant women. Another example is the withdrawal of **rofecoxib (Vioxx)**, a nonsteroidal anti-inflammatory drug (NSAID) that was linked to an increased risk of heart attacks and strokes. After post-market surveillance and detailed reviews of clinical trial data, the FDA and other regulatory bodies decided to withdraw the drug from the market to protect patients. These cases demonstrate how regulatory interventions based on toxicological assessments can prevent harm and ensure the safety of pharmaceutical products.

1.1.4 Descriptive Toxicology

Descriptive Studies and Their Purposes:

Descriptive toxicology involves the systematic observation and recording of toxic effects produced by substances. The primary purpose of these studies is to generate data that can be used to identify the potential hazards of chemicals and to understand the conditions under which these hazards might be realized. Methods in descriptive toxicology include acute, sub-chronic, and chronic toxicity studies. Acute toxicity studies are designed to observe the effects of a single dose or short-term exposure to a substance, providing immediate insights into its potential hazards. Sub-chronic and chronic studies extend this observation over weeks, months, or even years, revealing long-term health effects and cumulative toxicity. These studies involve various models, including in vivo (animal studies) and in vitro (cell culture studies), to capture a comprehensive picture of how a substance interacts with biological systems. Observations from these studies are meticulously recorded, noting the dose, duration of exposure, route of administration, and the specific toxic effects observed.

Examples of Descriptive Toxicology:

To understand the applications of descriptive toxicology, consider studies on **common poisons** such as arsenic and lead. **Arsenic** is a naturally occurring element that can be highly toxic, particularly in its inorganic forms. Descriptive toxicology studies on arsenic have shown that it can cause a range of adverse effects, including skin lesions, developmental effects, cardiovascular diseases, and an increased risk of cancer. These studies often involve monitoring populations exposed to arsenic-contaminated water or evaluating the effects in animal models to determine the dose-response relationship and critical toxicity endpoints. **Lead** is another well-known toxin, especially harmful to children. Studies have documented lead's neurotoxic effects, leading to cognitive deficits, behavioral problems, and developmental delays. By observing the effects of various lead concentrations over different exposure durations, researchers have been able to establish critical safety guidelines and intervention strategies.

Methods and Approaches:

Descriptive toxicology employs several **techniques** to assess and quantify the toxic effects of substances. One fundamental method is the **dose-response study**, which examines the relationship between the dose of a substance and the severity of its toxic effects. This approach helps in identifying the threshold dose below which no adverse effects are observed (NOAEL - No Observed Adverse Effect Level) and the lowest dose at which adverse effects are observed (LOAEL - Lowest Observed Adverse Effect Level). Another common technique is **toxicity testing**, which includes a variety of tests such as the LD50 test, which determines the lethal dose for 50% of the test population, and the Ames test, used to assess the mutagenic potential of a substance. These tests provide critical data on the toxicity profiles of substances, informing risk assessments and regulatory decisions.

Importance in Risk Assessment:

The role of descriptive toxicology in **risk assessment** is pivotal. Risk assessment is the process of determining the potential adverse health effects of exposure to chemicals and other hazardous substances. Descriptive toxicology provides the foundational data needed to evaluate the risks associated with chemical exposures. By establishing **safe exposure levels** and identifying the dose-response relationships, toxicologists can determine acceptable limits for human exposure. These regulatory limits, such as Permissible Exposure Limits (PELs) and Reference Doses (RfDs), are essential for protecting public health and ensuring the safety of consumer products, pharmaceuticals, and environmental pollutants. For instance, regulatory agencies like the Environmental Protection Agency (EPA) and the Food and Drug Administration (FDA) rely on descriptive toxicology data to set safety standards and enforce regulations that limit human exposure to harmful substances.

1.2 Regulatory Guidelines for Conducting Toxicity Studies

1.2.1 OECD Guidelines

Overview of Guidelines:

The **Organisation for Economic Co-operation and Development (OECD)** provides a comprehensive set of guidelines for conducting toxicity studies, known as the OECD Guidelines for the Testing of Chemicals. These guidelines are internationally recognized standards designed to ensure the quality and comparability of toxicological data. They cover a wide range of testing methods, including those for acute, sub-chronic, chronic, reproductive, and genetic toxicity. The primary objective of these guidelines is to harmonize testing procedures across member countries, facilitating mutual acceptance of data (MAD) and reducing the need for duplicate testing. This harmonization helps streamline the regulatory process, promotes international trade, and ensures that safety assessments are based on reliable and consistent data.

Key Protocols and Procedures:

The **OECD guidelines** include detailed protocols and procedures for a variety of toxicity tests. For example, the OECD Guideline 420 outlines the **Acute Oral Toxicity – Fixed Dose Procedure**, which determines the acute toxicity of a substance when administered orally. This method involves administering a single dose of the test substance to a group of animals and observing them for signs of toxicity over a specified period. Another important guideline is OECD 451, which describes the **Carcinogenicity Studies**. This guideline provides procedures for long-term studies to evaluate the potential of a substance to cause cancer in laboratory animals. The studies involve exposing animals to the test substance for the majority of their lifespan and monitoring for tumor development. OECD 474, the **Mammalian Erythrocyte Micronucleus Test**, is another key protocol used to assess the genotoxic potential of substances by detecting chromosomal damage in the red blood cells of animals. Each of these guidelines specifies the number of animals to be used, the conditions of exposure, the duration of the study, and the criteria for evaluating results, ensuring that studies are conducted in a scientifically rigorous and ethically responsible manner.

Case Studies and Applications:

The application of **OECD guidelines** in industry practices is crucial for ensuring the safety and efficacy of chemical substances. One notable case study is the assessment of a new pharmaceutical compound intended for human use. The pharmaceutical company followed OECD Guideline 407, which outlines the procedures for a **Repeated Dose 28-Day Oral Toxicity Study in Rodents**. This study involved administering the compound daily to rats for 28 days and observing them for clinical signs of toxicity, changes in body weight, food consumption, and pathological changes in organs. The data obtained from this study were critical for determining the safe starting dose for subsequent human clinical trials. Another example is the evaluation of a pesticide under OECD Guideline 425, the **Acute Oral Toxicity – Up-and-Down Procedure**. This method helped determine the lethal dose of the pesticide, ensuring that it was safe for use in agricultural settings while minimizing the risk to human health and the environment.

In addition, the **cosmetics industry** relies heavily on OECD guidelines to ensure product safety. For instance, OECD Guideline 431 outlines the **In Vitro Skin Corrosion: Reconstructed Human Epidermis (RHE) Test**

Method, which is used to assess the corrosive potential of cosmetic ingredients. By following this guideline, companies can avoid animal testing and still obtain reliable data on skin corrosion, ensuring that their products are safe for consumers. These case studies highlight the importance of adhering to OECD guidelines in various industries to ensure the safety and regulatory compliance of chemical substances.

1.2.2 ICH Guidelines

International Harmonization:
The **International Council for Harmonisation of Technical Requirements for Pharmaceuticals for Human Use (ICH)** plays a pivotal role in establishing global drug safety standards. Formed in 1990, the ICH aims to harmonize the regulatory requirements for drug registration among the United States, Europe, and Japan, thus facilitating the development and approval of new pharmaceuticals worldwide. By creating a unified set of guidelines, the ICH ensures that drug safety, quality, and efficacy are consistently maintained across different regions, reducing discrepancies and simplifying the regulatory process. This international harmonization not only accelerates the availability of new medications but also minimizes the need for duplicate testing, thereby saving time and resources while protecting public health.

Specific Guidelines for Drug Safety:
The **ICH S-series guidelines** are particularly focused on the safety of pharmaceutical products, covering various aspects of non-clinical safety studies. These guidelines include:

- **ICH S1:** This series provides guidance on **carcinogenicity testing** of pharmaceuticals. It outlines the requirements for long-term carcinogenicity studies in rodents and includes protocols for both single and combined studies to assess the potential cancer risk of new drugs. S1 guidelines help ensure that any carcinogenic potential is identified before a drug reaches the market.
- **ICH S2:** These guidelines address **genotoxicity testing** and the evaluation of the mutagenic potential of pharmaceuticals. The S2 series specifies the types of tests required, such as the Ames test, in vitro mammalian cell gene mutation test, and in vivo mammalian erythrocyte micronucleus test. By identifying genotoxic compounds early in drug

development, these guidelines help prevent the approval of substances that could cause genetic damage.

- **ICH S3**: The S3 guidelines provide recommendations for **toxicokinetics and pharmacokinetics**. They focus on the study design, data collection, and analysis methods necessary to understand the absorption, distribution, metabolism, and excretion (ADME) of pharmaceuticals. These studies are crucial for interpreting toxicological data and for designing safe and effective dosage regimens.
- **ICH S4**: This series deals with **toxicology studies for biotechnology-derived pharmaceuticals**, offering guidance on the specific safety studies required for biologics. These guidelines address issues such as immunogenicity, reproductive toxicity, and long-term safety.
- **ICH S5**: The S5 guidelines focus on **reproductive and developmental toxicity** studies, outlining the types of tests required to assess the potential effects of pharmaceuticals on reproduction and development. This includes testing for effects on fertility, embryo-fetal development, and pre- and postnatal development.
- **ICH S6**: These guidelines provide recommendations for **preclinical safety evaluation of biotechnology-derived pharmaceuticals**. They cover unique considerations for biologics, including species selection, immunogenicity, and the need for specialized study designs.
- **ICH S7**: The S7 series addresses **safety pharmacology studies**, which are designed to identify potential adverse effects on physiological functions such as the cardiovascular, respiratory, and central nervous systems. These guidelines ensure that any adverse pharmacological effects are detected early in the drug development process.

Case Studies and Industry Practices:

Several industry examples highlight the practical application of ICH guidelines in ensuring drug safety. One notable case involves the development of a new **anti-cancer drug**. Following the ICH S1 guidelines, the pharmaceutical company conducted long-term carcinogenicity studies in rodents to assess the potential cancer risk associated with the drug. The studies revealed a dose-dependent increase in tumor incidence, leading the company to modify the drug's formulation to reduce its carcinogenic potential before proceeding with clinical trials.

Another example is the application of **ICH S2 guidelines** in the development of a new **antiviral medication**. The genotoxicity testing, including the Ames test and in vivo micronucleus test, indicated that the compound had mutagenic potential. Based on these findings, the company conducted additional studies to understand the mechanism of genotoxicity and adjusted the chemical structure of the drug to eliminate the genotoxic effects, ensuring its safety for human use.

In the case of a **biotechnology-derived drug** aimed at treating autoimmune diseases, the company adhered to the ICH S6 guidelines. They conducted extensive preclinical safety evaluations, including immunogenicity studies and long-term toxicity assessments in relevant animal models. These studies provided critical data on the drug's safety profile, supporting its successful approval by regulatory authorities.

The development of a new **antihypertensive medication** also showcases the importance of the ICH S7 guidelines. Safety pharmacology studies were conducted to evaluate the drug's effects on the cardiovascular and central nervous systems. These studies identified a potential adverse effect on heart rate, prompting further investigation and adjustment of the drug's dosage regimen to ensure patient safety.

1.2.3 EPA Guidelines

Environmental Protection Aspects:
The **Environmental Protection Agency (EPA)** in the United States plays a vital role in safeguarding the environment from the potential hazards posed by various industries, including the pharmaceutical sector. The EPA has established comprehensive guidelines that address the environmental impact of pharmaceuticals and other chemicals. These guidelines are designed to prevent pollution, protect ecosystems, and ensure that chemical substances do not pose undue risks to human health or the environment. The EPA guidelines cover various aspects such as the disposal of pharmaceutical waste, the management of hazardous substances, and the assessment of environmental risks associated with pharmaceutical production and usage. These guidelines are crucial for maintaining environmental integrity and public health, ensuring that pharmaceutical activities do not lead to environmental contamination or degradation.

Guidelines Related to Pharmaceutical Impacts:

The **EPA guidelines** have significant implications for the **pharmaceutical industry**, influencing various stages of drug development, production, and disposal. One key area is the management of **pharmaceutical waste**. The EPA's Resource Conservation and Recovery Act (RCRA) provides detailed regulations on the proper disposal of hazardous waste, including pharmaceuticals. This includes guidelines on the segregation, storage, transportation, and disposal of pharmaceutical waste to prevent environmental contamination. Pharmaceutical companies must adhere to these regulations to minimize the release of harmful substances into the environment.

Another critical aspect is the assessment of **environmental risks** associated with the production and use of pharmaceuticals. The EPA requires environmental risk assessments (ERAs) to evaluate the potential impact of pharmaceutical compounds on ecosystems. These assessments involve studying the persistence, bioaccumulation, and toxicity (PBT) of pharmaceutical substances in the environment. For instance, the EPA's guidelines for conducting ERAs include evaluating the potential effects of active pharmaceutical ingredients (APIs) on aquatic and terrestrial organisms. This helps ensure that pharmaceuticals entering the market do not adversely affect wildlife or disrupt ecological balance.

The EPA also provides guidelines for the **manufacturing processes** of pharmaceuticals, emphasizing the need for sustainable and environmentally friendly practices. This includes reducing emissions of volatile organic compounds (VOCs), controlling wastewater discharges, and minimizing the use of hazardous chemicals. By implementing these guidelines, pharmaceutical companies can reduce their environmental footprint and contribute to sustainable development.

Examples of EPA Guidelines in Practice:

Several case studies highlight the practical application of **EPA guidelines** in the pharmaceutical industry. One notable example involves the **disposal of expired or unused medications**. The EPA's guidelines under the RCRA mandate that pharmaceutical waste, including expired medications, be classified as hazardous waste if it meets certain criteria. A pharmaceutical company implemented a comprehensive waste management program that included training employees on proper waste segregation, establishing secure storage facilities for hazardous waste, and partnering with certified waste disposal companies to ensure compliance with EPA regulations. This program significantly reduced the risk of environmental contamination and improved the company's regulatory compliance.

Another example is the application of **EPA guidelines for wastewater management** in a pharmaceutical manufacturing plant. The company conducted an environmental risk assessment as per EPA guidelines, identifying the presence of APIs in their wastewater. To mitigate the environmental impact, the company invested in advanced wastewater treatment technologies, such as membrane bioreactors and activated carbon filtration, to remove pharmaceutical residues before discharge. This initiative not only ensured compliance with EPA standards but also protected local water bodies from pharmaceutical pollution.

The EPA's guidelines for **environmental risk assessments** have also been instrumental in regulating the impact of veterinary pharmaceuticals. A veterinary pharmaceutical company conducted a comprehensive ERA to evaluate the potential effects of their products on the environment. Following EPA guidelines, the assessment included laboratory tests on the persistence and bioaccumulation of the active ingredients in soil and water, as well as toxicity tests on non-target organisms. The results indicated that certain compounds had a high potential for environmental persistence and bioaccumulation. Based on these findings, the company reformulated their products to reduce environmental impact and implemented measures to limit the use of these compounds in sensitive areas.

1.2.4 Schedule Y Guidelines

Indian Regulatory Framework:

Schedule Y is a crucial part of the Drugs and Cosmetics Rules, 1945, under the Drugs and Cosmetics Act of India, which provides detailed regulations for the clinical trials of pharmaceuticals in India. These guidelines ensure that clinical trials are conducted in a scientifically sound and ethical manner, protecting the rights, safety, and well-being of trial participants. Schedule Y encompasses all phases of clinical trials (Phase I to Phase IV), specifying the requirements for obtaining permission to initiate trials, the ethical considerations, the documentation needed, and the responsibilities of sponsors and investigators. It aligns with international standards, ensuring that the data generated is credible and acceptable globally, which is crucial for the approval and marketing of new drugs both within and outside India.

Specific Requirements and Studies:

Under **Schedule Y**, there are specific requirements and protocols for conducting toxicity studies that form the foundation of preclinical testing before human trials. These studies are vital for understanding the safety profile of a drug. Key requirements include:

- **Acute Toxicity Studies:** These are short-term studies designed to determine the toxic effects of a substance following a single dose or multiple doses administered within 24 hours. The results help in identifying the lethal dose (LD50) and in establishing initial dose levels for human trials.
- **Sub-acute and Sub-chronic Toxicity Studies:** Conducted over a period of 28 to 90 days, these studies assess the effects of repeated exposure to a substance. They provide information on potential target organs and the reversibility of toxic effects, helping to determine the No Observed Adverse Effect Level (NOAEL).
- **Chronic Toxicity Studies:** These long-term studies, extending over months to years, evaluate the effects of prolonged exposure to a substance. They are crucial for identifying any cumulative toxic effects and for assessing the risk of long-term use in humans.
- **Reproductive and Developmental Toxicity Studies:** These studies assess the potential impact of a substance on reproductive capability and development, including effects on fertility, embryonic development, and postnatal development.
- **Genotoxicity Studies:** These tests evaluate the potential of a substance to cause genetic mutations or chromosomal damage. Standard tests include the Ames test, in vitro mammalian cell gene mutation test, and in vivo micronucleus test.
- **Carcinogenicity Studies:** Conducted over a significant portion of the lifespan of test animals, these studies assess the potential of a substance to induce cancer. They are essential for identifying any carcinogenic risk associated with long-term exposure.

These detailed requirements ensure that any potential risks associated with a new pharmaceutical are thoroughly investigated before human exposure, safeguarding the health and safety of clinical trial participants.

1.3 OECD Principles of Good Laboratory Practice (GLP)

1.3.1 History of GLP

Origin and Evolution:

The concept of **Good Laboratory Practice (GLP)** originated in the 1970s in response to concerns about the quality and integrity of non-clinical safety data submitted to regulatory authorities. Before GLP, there were numerous instances of fraud, poor documentation, and inconsistent practices in laboratories, leading to unreliable data and compromised public safety. The first GLP regulations were established by the U.S. Food and Drug Administration (FDA) in 1978 to address these issues. These initial guidelines aimed to ensure that laboratory studies related to safety assessment were conducted with high standards of quality and integrity. The OECD subsequently developed its own set of GLP principles in 1981, which have since been adopted by many countries worldwide. These principles provide a comprehensive framework for ensuring the quality, reliability, and integrity of non-clinical laboratory studies, harmonizing practices across international borders.

Milestones in GLP Development:

Several **key historical events** have marked the development and adoption of GLP standards globally. In the late 1970s, the FDA's investigation into toxicological laboratories revealed significant issues with data integrity and laboratory practices, prompting the creation of the first GLP regulations. The OECD's adoption of GLP principles in 1981 was another significant milestone, providing a harmonized set of standards that facilitated international cooperation and mutual acceptance of data. Over the years, these principles have been updated to reflect advances in technology and changes in regulatory requirements. For instance, in 1997, the OECD revised its GLP principles to include electronic data management systems, ensuring that digital records met the same standards of integrity as paper records.

Historical Case Studies:

Historical **case studies** highlight the importance of GLP in laboratory practices. One notable example is the **Industrial Bio-Test Laboratories (IBT) scandal** in the 1970s. IBT was found to have falsified data in numerous safety studies, leading to widespread regulatory scrutiny and the eventual closure of the laboratory. This scandal underscored the need for stringent GLP standards to prevent such fraudulent practices and ensure the reliability of safety data. Another case is the **1987 OECD evaluation of non-clinical safety data**, which found significant variability in the quality of data submitted by different countries. This led to the reinforcement of GLP principles globally, ensuring that all data submitted to regulatory authorities met high standards of quality and integrity.

1.3.2 Concept of GLP

Core Principles:
The core principles of **GLP** revolve around ensuring the quality, integrity, and reliability of non-clinical laboratory studies. These principles include:

- **Quality Assurance:** Establishing a quality assurance unit (QAU) to oversee all aspects of the study, ensuring compliance with GLP standards.
- **Standard Operating Procedures (SOPs):** Developing and adhering to detailed SOPs for all laboratory activities to ensure consistency and reproducibility.
- **Documentation:** Maintaining comprehensive and accurate records of all aspects of the study, including raw data, test methods, and results.
- **Study Personnel:** Ensuring that all personnel involved in the study are adequately trained and qualified.
- **Facilities and Equipment:** Maintaining suitable facilities and equipment that are regularly inspected and calibrated.

Implementation in Laboratories:
Implementing GLP in research laboratories involves several **practical steps**:

- **Establishing a Quality Assurance Unit (QAU):** The QAU monitors all phases of the study, ensuring compliance with GLP principles.
- **Developing SOPs:** Detailed SOPs are created for all laboratory procedures, from sample handling to data analysis.
- **Training Personnel:** Regular training programs are conducted to ensure that all staff are familiar with GLP requirements and procedures.
- **Maintaining Documentation:** Comprehensive records are kept for all study-related activities, including raw data, test protocols, and quality control measures.

- **Regular Audits and Inspections:** Internal audits and external inspections are conducted to verify compliance with GLP standards.

1.3.3 Importance of GLP in Drug Development

Ensuring Data Integrity:

GLP plays a critical role in ensuring the **integrity and reliability** of data generated during non-clinical laboratory studies. By adhering to GLP principles, laboratories can produce high-quality data that accurately reflects the safety and efficacy of new drug candidates. This is essential for regulatory submissions, as agencies such as the FDA and EMA rely on this data to make informed decisions about the approval of new pharmaceuticals. GLP ensures that all data is collected, recorded, and reported in a consistent and transparent manner, minimizing the risk of errors or fraudulent practices.

Enhancing Reproducibility and Reliability:

The adoption of GLP enhances the **reproducibility and reliability** of scientific research. Standardized procedures and rigorous quality control measures ensure that studies can be reliably reproduced, which is crucial for validating results and confirming the safety and efficacy of new drugs. This reproducibility builds trust in the data generated and facilitates collaboration between different laboratories and regulatory agencies.

Examples of GLP in Drug Development:

Several **case studies** illustrate the impact of GLP on drug development processes. One example is the development of a new **antiviral drug**. The pharmaceutical company conducted comprehensive toxicology studies under GLP conditions, ensuring that the data generated was reliable and met regulatory standards. This rigorous adherence to GLP facilitated the approval process, allowing the drug to reach the market more quickly. Another example involves a **biotechnology company** developing a novel therapeutic protein. By conducting all preclinical safety studies in compliance with GLP, the company was able to provide high-quality data to regulatory authorities, supporting the safe and effective use of the product in clinical trials and eventual market approval.

Aspect	Preclinical Trials	Clinical Trials
Objective	Evaluate safety and efficacy in animal models	Assess safety and efficacy in humans
Subjects	Animals	Human volunteers (healthy and patients)
Phases	Single phase involving various tests	Phase I, II, III, and IV
Focus	Toxicity, pharmacokinetics, pharmacodynamics	Dosage, side effects, effectiveness, comparison
Regulatory Approval	Not required for start but data needed for human trials	Strict regulatory oversight required for all phases
Duration	Short to medium term (weeks to months)	Longer term (months to years)

Table 1: Comparison of Preclinical and Clinical Trials

Aspect	Acute Toxicity Studies	Chronic Toxicity Studies
Duration	Short-term exposure (single dose or 24 hours)	Long-term exposure (months to years)
Objective	Identify immediate toxic effects	Assess cumulative and long-term effects
Outcome	LD50 (lethal dose for 50% of subjects)	NOAEL (No Observed Adverse Effect Level), LOAEL
Subjects	Usually animals	Animals, sometimes followed by human observations
Use	Initial safety screening	Risk assessment for chronic exposure

Table 2:Differences between Acute and Chronic Toxicity Studies

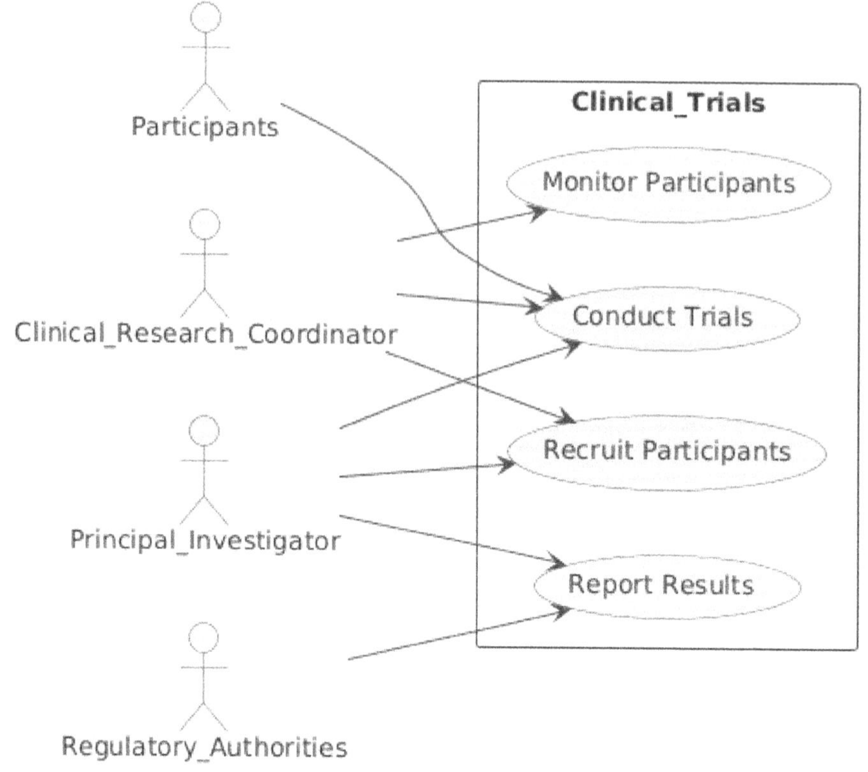

Fig 2 : "Clinical Trials Workflow"

Fig 3: Key Activities in General Toxicology for Drug Safety

II

Acute, Sub-acute, and Chronic Toxicity Studies

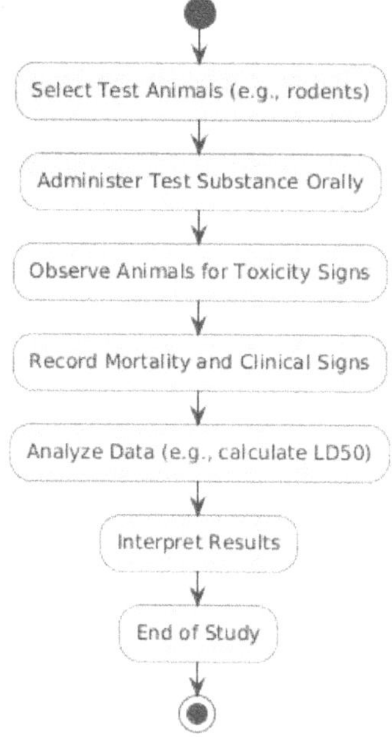

INTRODUCTION

Acute Toxicity Studies

Acute toxicity studies are conducted to evaluate the harmful effects of a substance following a single dose or multiple doses within a short period, typically 24 hours. The primary objective is to determine the **lethal dose (LD50)**, which is the dose that causes death in 50% of the test population. These studies provide initial information on the substance's toxicity and help identify potential risks associated with short-term exposure.
Key Features:

- **Duration**: Single dose or multiple doses within 24 hours.
- **Observation Period**: Usually up to 14 days.
- **Endpoints**: Mortality, clinical signs of toxicity, body weight changes, and gross pathology.
- **Purpose**: To establish the immediate toxic effects and LD50, guide dosage for further studies, and identify target organs affected by the substance.

Sub-acute Toxicity Studies

Sub-acute toxicity studies, also known as repeat-dose toxicity studies, assess the effects of repeated exposure to a substance over a longer period, typically ranging from 14 to 28 days. These studies provide information on the cumulative toxic effects and help identify potential target organs and toxic mechanisms.
Key Features:

- **Duration**: 14 to 28 days.
- **Observation Period**: Throughout the study and usually includes a recovery phase.
- **Endpoints**: Clinical signs, body weight, food consumption, hematology, clinical chemistry, organ weights, and histopathology.
- **Purpose**: To evaluate cumulative toxicity, establish NOAEL (No-Observed-Adverse-Effect Level), and identify target organs and potential

mechanisms of toxicity.

Chronic Toxicity Studies

Chronic toxicity studies are designed to investigate the long-term effects of a substance over an extended period, typically six months to two years. These studies provide comprehensive data on the potential chronic health effects, including carcinogenicity, reproductive toxicity, and other long-term adverse effects.

Key Features:

- **Duration**: Six months to two years.
- **Observation Period**: Throughout the study and often includes a recovery phase.
- **Endpoints**: Clinical signs, body weight, food consumption, hematology, clinical chemistry, organ weights, histopathology, and specific tests for chronic effects such as carcinogenicity and reproductive toxicity.
- **Purpose**: To evaluate long-term toxicity, establish chronic NOAEL, identify potential carcinogenic and reproductive effects, and provide data for regulatory risk assessment.

Understanding the different types of toxicity studies—acute, sub-acute, and chronic—is crucial for assessing the safety of substances and protecting public health. These studies provide a comprehensive evaluation of the toxicological profile of substances, guiding regulatory decisions and risk management strategies to ensure safe use and minimize adverse health effects.

2.1 Acute Toxicity Studies

2.1.1 Oral Acute Toxicity

Methods and Protocols:

Oral acute toxicity studies are essential for determining the harmful effects of a substance following a single dose or multiple doses administered within a short period, typically 24 hours. One of the most common methods used in these studies is the determination of the **LD50 (Lethal Dose 50)**, which is the dose required to kill 50% of the test population. The LD50 test provides a quantitative measure of a substance's acute toxicity.

The **protocol for LD50 determination** involves several critical steps:

1. **Selection of Test Animals:** Commonly used animals include rodents such as rats and mice due to their well-characterized biology and manageable size.
2. **Dose Administration:** The test substance is administered orally, usually via gavage (a tube directly into the stomach), to ensure precise dosing. Multiple groups of animals receive different doses of the substance to establish a dose-response relationship.
3. **Observation Period:** Animals are observed closely for signs of toxicity, such as changes in behavior, appearance, body weight, and mortality, over a specified period (usually up to 14 days).
4. **Data Collection:** Detailed records of the dose levels, number of deaths, and any clinical signs of toxicity are maintained.
5. **Data Analysis:** The LD50 value is calculated using statistical methods, typically involving probit analysis or other regression techniques.

Other protocols for acute oral toxicity studies include the **Fixed Dose Procedure (FDP)**, the **Up-and-Down Procedure (UDP)**, and the **Acute Toxic Class Method (ATCM)**. These methods aim to reduce the number of animals used and refine testing procedures to minimize animal suffering while still obtaining reliable toxicity data.

Interpretation of Results:

Interpreting acute toxicity data involves analyzing the observed effects and determining the dose-response relationship. Key considerations include:

- **Mortality Rate:** The number of deaths at each dose level is recorded, and the LD50 is calculated to provide a measure of the substance's acute toxicity.
- **Clinical Signs:** Observations of clinical signs such as lethargy, convulsions, diarrhea, or changes in body weight help identify the specific toxic effects and potential target organs.
- **Behavioral Changes:** Changes in behavior, such as reduced activity or altered feeding patterns, can indicate neurotoxicity or general distress.
- **Pathological Findings:** Post-mortem examinations may reveal organ damage, hemorrhage, or other pathological changes that contribute to understanding the toxic effects.

The data collected is used to classify the substance's toxicity according to globally recognized standards, such as the Globally Harmonized System of Classification and Labelling of Chemicals (GHS). This classification helps in risk assessment and regulatory decision-making, guiding safe handling, usage, and disposal practices.

Examples:

Several **case studies** illustrate the application of oral acute toxicity studies in assessing various compounds. For instance, the acute toxicity of **acetaminophen** (paracetamol) was evaluated using the LD50 test in rodents. The study revealed that high doses of acetaminophen caused significant liver damage, evidenced by elevated liver enzyme levels and histopathological changes in the liver tissue. These findings highlighted the importance of dose regulation and informed guidelines for safe therapeutic use.

Another example involves the acute toxicity assessment of **glyphosate**, a widely used herbicide. The LD50 determination in rats indicated moderate toxicity, with clinical signs such as diarrhea, lethargy, and convulsions observed at higher doses. Pathological examination showed gastrointestinal and renal damage, leading to regulatory recommendations for safe exposure levels and protective measures for users.

In a study on the acute toxicity of **essential oils**, such as peppermint oil, the LD50 test in mice revealed relatively low toxicity, with no significant adverse effects observed at doses commonly used in therapeutic applications. However, at very high doses, signs of neurotoxicity and respiratory distress were noted, emphasizing the need for proper dosing and caution in usage.

2.1.2 Dermal Acute Toxicity

Testing Procedures:

Dermal acute toxicity tests are conducted to evaluate the potential harmful effects of a substance when it is applied to the skin. These tests are essential for assessing the safety of chemicals, cosmetics, and pharmaceuticals that may come into direct contact with the skin. The procedure involves several steps:

1. **Selection of Test Animals:** Commonly used animals include rabbits and rodents, chosen for their sensitive skin and ease of handling.

2. **Preparation of Test Animals:** The test animals are usually shaved or clipped to expose a clean, intact area of skin. Care is taken to avoid causing any undue stress or injury to the animals.

3. **Application of Test Substance:** A precise amount of the test substance is applied to the prepared skin area. The application can be either occlusive (covered with a patch) or semi-occlusive (partially covered) to maintain the substance on the skin for the required exposure period.

4. **Exposure Duration:** The test substance remains on the skin for a specified duration, typically 24 hours. After this period, the substance is gently removed, and the skin is cleaned.

5. **Observation Period:** Animals are observed for signs of dermal toxicity over a specified period, usually up to 14 days. Observations include changes in skin appearance, such as erythema (redness), edema (swelling), and other dermal reactions.

6. **Data Collection:** Detailed records of any adverse effects, including mortality, changes in body weight, and clinical signs of toxicity, are maintained.

7. **Post-mortem Examination:** If necessary, a post-mortem examination is conducted to identify any internal damage or pathological changes that may have resulted from dermal exposure.

Safety Evaluations:

Evaluating the safety of a substance in dermal toxicity tests involves several criteria:

- **Dermal Reactions:** The primary focus is on local skin reactions, including erythema, edema, ulceration, and necrosis. These reactions are scored based on their severity and duration.

- **Systemic Toxicity:** Although the substance is applied to the skin, it can still be absorbed and cause systemic effects. Observations for systemic toxicity include changes in behavior, body weight, and overall health.

- **Dose-Response Relationship:** Determining the dose-response relationship is crucial for assessing the toxicity level. This involves identifying the Lowest Observed Adverse Effect Level (LOAEL) and the No Observed Adverse Effect Level (NOAEL).

- **Histopathological Examination:** In some cases, histopathological examination of the skin and other organs may be conducted to identify microscopic changes that are not visible during the observation period.

These evaluations help in classifying the dermal toxicity of substances according to international standards, such as those provided by the OECD and the Globally Harmonized System (GHS). This classification informs regulatory decisions and safety guidelines for the use of these substances.

2.1.3 Inhalational Acute Toxicity

Inhalation Exposure Studies:
Inhalation exposure studies are designed to evaluate the toxic effects of substances when inhaled. These studies are crucial for assessing the safety of chemicals, gases, aerosols, and other airborne substances. The methodologies for assessing inhalational toxicity involve several key steps:

1. **Selection of Test Animals:** Commonly used animals include rodents such as rats and mice, chosen for their well-understood respiratory physiology and ease of handling.
2. **Exposure Chambers:** Animals are placed in specialized inhalation exposure chambers that ensure controlled delivery of the test substance. These chambers can vary in size and design but must maintain consistent airflow and concentration of the substance.
3. **Generation and Delivery of Test Substance:** The test substance is generated in a form suitable for inhalation, such as vapor, aerosol, or particulate matter. The concentration of the substance is precisely controlled and monitored to ensure accurate dosing.
4. **Exposure Duration:** Animals are exposed to the test substance for a specified duration, typically ranging from a few minutes to several hours, depending on the study objectives.
5. **Observation Period:** After exposure, animals are observed for signs of toxicity over a defined period, usually up to 14 days. Observations include respiratory distress, changes in behavior, body weight, and other clinical signs of toxicity.
6. **Data Collection:** Detailed records of the concentration of the substance, exposure duration, and any adverse effects observed are maintained.
7. **Post-mortem Examination:** If necessary, a post-mortem examination is conducted to identify any internal damage or pathological changes resulting from inhalational exposure.

Health Impact Assessments:

Evaluating health risks from inhalational exposure involves several criteria:

- **Respiratory Effects:** The primary focus is on respiratory effects, including difficulty breathing, coughing, and changes in respiratory rate. Acute inhalation toxicity can lead to conditions such as bronchitis, pneumonitis, or pulmonary edema.
- **Systemic Effects:** Inhaled substances can be absorbed into the bloodstream and cause systemic toxicity. Observations for systemic effects include changes in behavior, body weight, and overall health.
- **Dose-Response Relationship:** Establishing the dose-response relationship is crucial for assessing toxicity levels. This involves identifying the Lowest Observed Adverse Effect Level (LOAEL) and the No Observed Adverse Effect Level (NOAEL).
- **Histopathological Examination:** Histopathological examination of the respiratory tract and other organs may be conducted to identify microscopic changes not visible during the observation period.

These assessments help in classifying the inhalational toxicity of substances according to international standards, such as those provided by the OECD and the Globally Harmonized System (GHS). This classification informs regulatory decisions and safety guidelines for the use of these substances.

Examples: One notable example involves the testing of **chlorine gas**, a common industrial chemical. An inhalational toxicity study on rats revealed severe respiratory distress, pulmonary edema, and high mortality rates at higher concentrations. These findings underscored the importance of stringent safety measures and emergency response protocols in industries using chlorine gas.

Another example is the evaluation of **household cleaning products** that produce aerosols during use. A study on a new disinfectant spray involved inhalational toxicity testing on mice. The results showed mild respiratory irritation at lower concentrations and severe effects, including lung inflammation and systemic toxicity, at higher concentrations. Based on these findings, the product label included warnings and usage instructions to minimize inhalational exposure.

A significant case involves the assessment of **nanoparticles** used in various consumer products. An inhalational toxicity study on titanium dioxide nanoparticles in rats revealed dose-dependent respiratory and systemic effects, including inflammation, oxidative stress, and potential carcinogenicity. These findings informed regulatory guidelines for safe exposure levels and the use of personal protective equipment (PPE) in manufacturing settings.

2.2 Sub-acute Toxicity Studies

2.2.1 Oral Sub-acute Toxicity
Study Designs:

Sub-acute oral toxicity studies are conducted to evaluate the toxic effects of a substance following repeated oral exposure over a period of 28 to 90 days. These studies help in understanding the cumulative toxicity and potential target organ effects of the substance. The design considerations for sub-acute oral toxicity studies include:

- **Selection of Test Animals:** Commonly used species include rodents such as rats and mice. The choice of species depends on factors such as the similarity of metabolism to humans, ease of handling, and availability of background data.
- **Dosing Regimen:** Animals are divided into different groups, including a control group and several treatment groups receiving varying doses of the test substance. The dosing is typically done daily, and the doses are chosen based on the results of acute toxicity studies.
- **Route of Administration:** The test substance is administered orally, usually via gavage, to ensure accurate dosing. This method is preferred to mimic human oral exposure.
- **Observation Period:** Animals are observed daily for clinical signs of toxicity, changes in behavior, body weight, and food consumption. The duration of the study is generally 28 to 90 days.
- **Sampling and Testing:** Blood and urine samples are collected at regular intervals to evaluate biochemical and hematological parameters. Organ weights are recorded, and histopathological examinations are conducted on major organs to identify any microscopic changes.
- **Environmental Conditions:** The study is conducted under controlled environmental conditions, including temperature, humidity, and light/ dark cycles, to minimize variability.

Data Analysis Techniques:
Analyzing data from sub-acute toxicity studies involves several methods to ensure accurate interpretation of results:

- **Descriptive Statistics:** Initial data analysis includes calculating means, standard deviations, and ranges for various parameters such as body weight, food consumption, and organ weights.
- **Biochemical and Hematological Analysis:** Data from blood and urine samples are analyzed to identify any significant changes in biochemical and hematological parameters, such as liver enzymes, kidney function markers, and blood cell counts.
- **Histopathological Examination:** Tissue samples from major organs are examined microscopically to identify any pathological changes. Findings are compared between control and treated groups to determine the substance's impact.
- **Dose-Response Analysis:** The relationship between dose and observed effects is analyzed to establish the Lowest Observed Adverse Effect Level (LOAEL) and the No Observed Adverse Effect Level (NOAEL).
- **Statistical Analysis:** Advanced statistical methods, such as analysis of variance (ANOVA) and regression analysis, are used to determine the significance of observed differences between control and treated groups.

These analysis techniques help in identifying potential target organs, understanding the toxicological profile of the substance, and establishing safe exposure levels.

2.2.2 Dermal Sub-acute Toxicity

Exposure Assessments:
Dermal sub-acute toxicity studies are designed to evaluate the effects of repeated dermal exposure to a substance over a period of 28 to 90 days. These studies help in understanding the potential cumulative effects and identifying target organs affected by dermal exposure. The techniques for assessing dermal sub-acute exposure include:

- **Selection of Test Animals:** Commonly used animals include rabbits and rodents, particularly rats. These animals are selected for their well-characterized skin structure and sensitivity to dermal applications.

- **Preparation of Test Site:** The test area on the animal's skin is shaved or clipped to ensure even application of the test substance. Care is taken to avoid causing any undue stress or injury to the animals during this process.
- **Application of Test Substance:** The test substance is applied to the prepared skin area daily for the duration of the study. The application can be either occlusive (covered with a patch) or semi-occlusive (partially covered) to maintain the substance on the skin and prevent evaporation or removal.
- **Dose Levels:** Multiple groups of animals are exposed to different doses of the test substance to establish a dose-response relationship. A control group with no exposure is also included for comparison.
- **Observation and Monitoring:** Animals are observed daily for signs of dermal and systemic toxicity. This includes monitoring for changes in skin appearance (e.g., erythema, edema, and lesions), behavior, body weight, and food consumption.
- **Data Collection:** Detailed records of dermal reactions, clinical signs of toxicity, and any mortality are maintained. Blood samples may be collected periodically for biochemical and hematological analysis.
- **Histopathological Examination:** At the end of the study, skin samples from the test site and major organs are collected for histopathological examination to identify any microscopic changes.

Regulatory Requirements:

Regulatory guidelines for dermal sub-acute toxicity studies ensure that these studies are conducted in a scientifically rigorous and ethically responsible manner. Key regulatory requirements include:

- **OECD Guidelines:** The Organisation for Economic Co-operation and Development (OECD) provides standardized guidelines for conducting dermal toxicity studies, such as OECD Test Guideline 410. This guideline outlines the procedures for assessing sub-acute dermal toxicity, including animal selection, dosing regimen, and data analysis.
- **Good Laboratory Practice (GLP):** Compliance with GLP principles is essential for ensuring the quality and integrity of the study data. GLP guidelines cover all aspects of the study, from study planning and conduct to data recording and reporting.

- **Regulatory Agencies:** Various regulatory agencies, such as the U.S. Environmental Protection Agency (EPA) and the European Medicines Agency (EMA), require sub-acute dermal toxicity studies as part of the safety assessment for new chemicals, pharmaceuticals, and cosmetics. These agencies provide specific requirements and protocols that must be followed to ensure the safety and efficacy of the products.
- **Ethical Considerations:** Ethical guidelines ensure the humane treatment of animals used in toxicity studies. This includes minimizing pain and distress, providing appropriate housing and care, and using the minimum number of animals necessary to achieve reliable results.

2.2.3 Inhalational Sub-acute Toxicity

Methodologies:

Inhalational sub-acute toxicity studies are designed to evaluate the effects of repeated inhalation exposure to a substance over a period of 28 to 90 days. These studies are crucial for understanding the potential health risks associated with prolonged exposure to airborne substances. The detailed methodologies for conducting these studies include:

- **Selection of Test Animals:** Commonly used species are rodents, such as rats and mice, due to their well-characterized respiratory physiology and relevance to human inhalation exposure.
- **Exposure Chambers:** Animals are placed in specialized inhalation exposure chambers that ensure controlled delivery of the test substance. These chambers maintain consistent airflow and concentration of the substance, with continuous monitoring to ensure accuracy.
- **Generation and Delivery of Test Substance:** The test substance is generated in an appropriate form for inhalation, such as aerosol, vapor, or particulate matter. The concentration of the substance is precisely controlled and monitored throughout the exposure period.
- **Exposure Duration and Frequency:** Animals are exposed to the test substance for a specified duration each day, typically 6 to 8 hours, over a period of 28 to 90 days. The frequency and duration of exposure are designed to mimic potential human exposure scenarios.
- **Observation and Monitoring:** Animals are observed daily for signs of respiratory and systemic toxicity. This includes monitoring for changes

in breathing patterns, behavior, body weight, and food consumption.
- **Data Collection:** Detailed records of the concentration of the substance, exposure duration, and any adverse effects observed are maintained. Blood samples are collected periodically for biochemical and hematological analysis.
- **Post-mortem Examination:** At the end of the study, a comprehensive post-mortem examination is conducted. This includes histopathological examination of the respiratory tract and other major organs to identify any microscopic changes.

Health Impact Assessments:

Assessing the long-term health impacts from sub-acute inhalation exposure involves several key criteria:

- **Respiratory Effects:** The primary focus is on respiratory effects, including changes in respiratory rate, patterns, and signs of respiratory distress. Chronic inflammation, fibrosis, and other pathological changes in the lungs are critically evaluated.
- **Systemic Effects:** Inhaled substances can be absorbed into the bloodstream and cause systemic toxicity. Observations for systemic effects include changes in behavior, body weight, and biochemical markers of organ function.
- **Dose-Response Relationship:** Establishing the dose-response relationship is crucial for understanding the toxicity levels. This involves identifying the Lowest Observed Adverse Effect Level (LOAEL) and the No Observed Adverse Effect Level (NOAEL).
- **Histopathological Examination:** Detailed microscopic examination of the respiratory tract and other organs helps identify any cellular and tissue-level changes that result from prolonged inhalation exposure.

2.3 Chronic Toxicity Studies

2.3.1 Oral Chronic Toxicity

Long-term Exposure Studies:

Chronic toxicity studies are designed to evaluate the effects of prolonged exposure to a substance over a significant portion of an animal's lifespan, typically lasting from six months to two years. These studies are critical for identifying potential cumulative and delayed toxic effects and for understanding the long-term safety profile of a substance. The design and conduct of long-term chronic toxicity studies involve several key considerations:

- **Selection of Test Animals:** Commonly used species include rodents such as rats and mice due to their well-characterized biology and lifespan. Non-rodent species such as dogs or primates may also be used for certain substances.
- **Dosing Regimen:** Animals are divided into different groups, including a control group and several treatment groups receiving varying doses of the test substance. The dosing is usually done daily, and the doses are chosen based on the results of sub-acute and sub-chronic toxicity studies.
- **Route of Administration:** The test substance is administered orally, typically via gavage or mixed with food or drinking water, to mimic human exposure scenarios.
- **Observation Period:** Animals are observed daily for clinical signs of toxicity, changes in behavior, body weight, and food consumption. The study duration ranges from several months to two years, depending on regulatory requirements and the nature of the substance.
- **Sampling and Testing:** Blood and urine samples are collected at regular intervals to evaluate biochemical and hematological parameters. At the end of the study, organ weights are recorded, and histopathological examinations are conducted on major organs to identify any microscopic changes.
- **Environmental Conditions:** The study is conducted under controlled environmental conditions, including temperature, humidity, and light/dark cycles, to minimize variability.

Impact on Organ Systems:
Chronic toxicity studies assess the impact of long-term exposure on various organ systems. Key observations include:

- **Hepatic System:** Liver function tests, histopathological examination of liver tissues, and monitoring of liver enzyme levels to detect hepatotoxicity.
- **Renal System:** Evaluation of kidney function markers, histopathological examination of kidney tissues, and observation of any changes in urine

composition to identify nephrotoxicity.

- **Cardiovascular System:** Monitoring of blood pressure, heart rate, and histopathological examination of heart tissues to detect cardiotoxicity.
- **Respiratory System:** Observations of respiratory rate, lung function tests, and histopathological examination of lung tissues to detect pulmonary toxicity.
- **Nervous System:** Behavioral assessments, neurological examinations, and histopathological examination of brain and nerve tissues to identify neurotoxicity.
- **Reproductive System:** Evaluation of reproductive organ weights, fertility tests, and histopathological examination of reproductive tissues to detect reproductive toxicity.
- **Immune System:** Monitoring of immune function markers and histopathological examination of lymphoid tissues to detect immunotoxicity.

2.3.2 Dermal Chronic Toxicity

Prolonged Dermal Exposure:
Chronic dermal toxicity studies are designed to evaluate the effects of long-term exposure to a substance applied to the skin over a significant portion of an animal's lifespan, typically lasting from six months to two years. These studies help in understanding the potential cumulative and delayed toxic effects of substances that come into contact with the skin. The methodologies for studying prolonged dermal exposure include:

- **Selection of Test Animals:** Commonly used species include rabbits and rodents, particularly rats and mice, due to their well-characterized skin structure and sensitivity.
- **Preparation of Test Site:** The test area on the animal's skin is shaved or clipped to ensure even application of the test substance. Care is taken to avoid causing any undue stress or injury to the animals during this process.
- **Application of Test Substance:** The test substance is applied to the prepared skin area daily for the duration of the study. The application can be occlusive (covered with a patch) or semi-occlusive (partially covered) to maintain the substance on the skin and prevent evaporation

or removal.

- **Dosing Regimen:** Multiple groups of animals are exposed to different doses of the test substance to establish a dose-response relationship. A control group with no exposure is also included for comparison.
- **Observation Period:** Animals are observed daily for clinical signs of dermal and systemic toxicity. Observations include changes in skin appearance (e.g., erythema, edema, lesions), behavior, body weight, and food consumption.
- **Sampling and Testing:** Blood and urine samples are collected at regular intervals to evaluate biochemical and hematological parameters. At the end of the study, organ weights are recorded, and histopathological examinations are conducted on major organs and the skin.
- **Environmental Conditions:** The study is conducted under controlled environmental conditions, including temperature, humidity, and light/dark cycles, to minimize variability.

Risk Assessment Strategies:

Assessing risks from chronic dermal exposure involves several strategies:

- **Dermal Reactions:** The primary focus is on local skin reactions, including erythema, edema, ulceration, and necrosis. These reactions are scored based on their severity and duration.
- **Systemic Effects:** Substances applied to the skin can be absorbed and cause systemic toxicity. Observations for systemic effects include changes in behavior, body weight, and biochemical markers of organ function.
- **Dose-Response Relationship:** Establishing the dose-response relationship is crucial for assessing toxicity levels. This involves identifying the Lowest Observed Adverse Effect Level (LOAEL) and the No Observed Adverse Effect Level (NOAEL).
- **Histopathological Examination:** Detailed microscopic examination of the skin and other organs helps identify any cellular and tissue-level changes that result from prolonged dermal exposure.
- **Cumulative Toxicity:** Evaluating the cumulative effects of prolonged exposure, including the potential for delayed onset of toxic effects and chronic conditions such as dermatitis, skin cancer, and systemic organ damage.

- **Regulatory Compliance:** Ensuring that the study design and data collection comply with regulatory guidelines such as those provided by the OECD and other regulatory agencies. This includes adhering to Good Laboratory Practice (GLP) standards.

Examples:

- **Example 1: Testing of a Topical Steroid:** A chronic dermal toxicity study was conducted on rabbits over a period of 12 months to evaluate the long-term safety of a new topical steroid. The study included daily application of the steroid at various doses. Results showed dose-dependent skin thinning (atrophy) and changes in skin texture, but no significant systemic toxicity was observed. Histopathological examination confirmed localized skin effects without major organ damage. These findings supported the safe use of the steroid at recommended doses, leading to its approval for clinical use.
- **Example 2: Evaluation of a Cosmetic Ingredient:** A chronic dermal toxicity study was conducted on rats to assess the safety of a new cosmetic ingredient intended for use in skin care products. The study lasted for one year, with daily application of the ingredient at different concentrations. The results indicated no significant adverse effects at low to moderate doses, but higher doses resulted in mild skin irritation and systemic toxicity, including changes in liver enzyme levels. These findings informed regulatory guidelines and established safe usage levels for the ingredient.
- **Example 3: Assessment of an Industrial Chemical:** A chronic dermal toxicity study on a new industrial chemical was conducted on mice over 18 months. The study involved daily dermal exposure to the chemical at various doses. Observations included changes in skin appearance, behavior, and body weight, as well as comprehensive biochemical and histopathological analyses. The study revealed moderate skin irritation at higher doses, along with systemic effects such as liver and kidney damage. Based on these findings, regulatory agencies implemented safety guidelines and usage restrictions to protect workers handling the chemical.

2.3.3 Inhalational Chronic Toxicity

Chronic Inhalation Studies:

Chronic inhalation toxicity studies are conducted to evaluate the effects of long-term exposure to airborne substances over a significant portion of an animal's lifespan, typically lasting from six months to two years. These studies are essential for identifying potential chronic and cumulative toxic effects of substances that are inhaled regularly. The methodologies for conducting chronic inhalation studies include:

- **Selection of Test Animals:** Commonly used species include rodents such as rats and mice, chosen for their well-understood respiratory systems and relevance to human exposure.
- **Exposure Chambers:** Animals are placed in specialized inhalation exposure chambers that ensure controlled delivery of the test substance. These chambers maintain consistent airflow and concentration of the substance, with continuous monitoring to ensure accuracy.
- **Generation and Delivery of Test Substance:** The test substance is generated in an appropriate form for inhalation, such as aerosol, vapor, or particulate matter. The concentration of the substance is precisely controlled and monitored throughout the exposure period.
- **Exposure Duration and Frequency:** Animals are exposed to the test substance for a specified duration each day, typically 6 to 8 hours, over a period of 6 months to 2 years. The frequency and duration of exposure are designed to mimic potential human exposure scenarios.
- **Observation and Monitoring:** Animals are observed daily for signs of respiratory and systemic toxicity. This includes monitoring for changes in breathing patterns, behavior, body weight, and food consumption.
- **Data Collection:** Detailed records of the concentration of the substance, exposure duration, and any adverse effects observed are maintained. Blood samples are collected periodically for biochemical and hematological analysis.
- **Post-mortem Examination:** At the end of the study, a comprehensive post-mortem examination is conducted. This includes histopathological examination of the respiratory tract and other major organs to identify any microscopic changes.

Implications for Respiratory Health:

Chronic inhalation exposure can have significant long-term impacts on respiratory health. Key observations include:

- **Respiratory Function:** Monitoring changes in respiratory rate, patterns, and signs of respiratory distress, such as coughing, wheezing, or labored breathing.
- **Pulmonary Inflammation:** Chronic exposure to inhaled substances can lead to persistent inflammation in the lungs, which can be detected through histopathological examination showing inflammatory cell infiltration and tissue changes.
- **Fibrosis:** Long-term exposure may cause pulmonary fibrosis, characterized by the thickening and scarring of lung tissue, leading to reduced lung function and difficulty breathing.
- **Carcinogenicity:** Certain inhaled substances, such as asbestos and tobacco smoke, are known to be carcinogenic, leading to the development of lung cancer and other respiratory tumors over prolonged exposure periods.
- **Systemic Effects:** Inhaled substances can be absorbed into the bloodstream and cause systemic toxicity, affecting organs such as the liver, kidneys, and cardiovascular system.

Examples:

- **Example 1: Testing of Industrial Solvents:** A chronic inhalation study was conducted on rats exposed to **benzene vapors** for 6 hours daily over a period of 12 months. The study revealed dose-dependent respiratory and systemic effects, including increased incidence of leukemia, liver damage, and bone marrow toxicity. Histopathological examination showed significant inflammation and fibrosis in lung tissues. These findings were critical for establishing occupational exposure limits and protective measures for workers handling benzene.
- **Example 2: Evaluation of Air Pollutants:** A chronic inhalation study on mice exposed to **particulate matter (PM2.5)** from urban air pollution over 18 months showed persistent pulmonary inflammation, oxidative stress, and early signs of lung cancer. The study highlighted the need for stringent air quality regulations and measures to reduce particulate emissions from industrial and vehicular sources to protect public health.

- **Example 3: Assessment of Nanomaterials:** A chronic inhalation toxicity study on rats exposed to **carbon nanotubes** for 6 hours daily over two years revealed significant respiratory and systemic effects, including lung inflammation, fibrosis, and cardiovascular toxicity. The study provided valuable data on the potential long-term health risks of nanomaterials, informing safety guidelines and regulatory standards for their use in consumer and industrial products.
- **Example 4: Inhalation of Tobacco Smoke:** A well-known example is the chronic inhalation study on rats exposed to **tobacco smoke** for several hours daily over two years. The study demonstrated a clear dose-response relationship between tobacco smoke exposure and the development of lung cancer, emphysema, and chronic bronchitis. These findings have been instrumental in establishing the health risks associated with smoking and in the development of public health campaigns and regulations to reduce tobacco use.

2.4 Additional Toxicity Studies

2.4.1 Acute Eye Irritation

Testing Methods:

Acute eye irritation tests are conducted to evaluate the potential irritant effects of substances on the eyes. These tests are essential for assessing the safety of chemicals, pharmaceuticals, and consumer products that may come into contact with the eyes. The methods for assessing acute eye irritation include:

- **Draize Eye Test:** This is the traditional method used for assessing eye irritation. It involves the application of a test substance directly into the conjunctival sac of one eye of an animal, usually a rabbit, while the other eye serves as a control. The eyes are observed at various intervals over 72 hours to assess the degree of irritation, including redness, swelling, discharge, and corneal opacity. The severity of the irritation is scored using a standardized scale.
- **In Vitro Tests:** Due to ethical concerns and regulatory push towards reducing animal testing, various in vitro methods have been developed. These include:

- **Bovine Corneal Opacity and Permeability (BCOP) Assay:** This test uses bovine corneas obtained from slaughterhouses to assess the potential of a substance to cause corneal damage. The changes in corneal opacity and permeability are measured after exposure to the test substance.
- **Hen's Egg Test on Chorioallantoic Membrane (HET-CAM):** This test uses fertilized chicken eggs to evaluate the potential irritation caused by a substance to the chorioallantoic membrane. The test assesses the vascular changes, such as hemorrhage, lysis, and coagulation, which are indicative of irritation.
- **EpiOcular Test:** This test uses a reconstructed human corneal epithelial model to evaluate the irritation potential of a substance. The test measures the viability of the cells after exposure to the test substance.

Regulatory Guidelines:

Regulatory guidelines for eye irritation studies ensure that these studies are conducted in a scientifically rigorous and ethically responsible manner. Key regulatory guidelines include:

- **OECD Guidelines:** The Organisation for Economic Co-operation and Development (OECD) provides standardized guidelines for conducting eye irritation studies. OECD Test Guideline 405 outlines the procedure for in vivo eye irritation testing using rabbits, while OECD Test Guidelines 437, 438, and 492 outline procedures for in vitro tests such as BCOP, HET-CAM, and EpiOcular tests, respectively.
- **Good Laboratory Practice (GLP):** Compliance with GLP principles is essential for ensuring the quality and integrity of the study data. GLP guidelines cover all aspects of the study, from study planning and conduct to data recording and reporting.
- **Regulatory Agencies:** Various regulatory agencies, such as the U.S. Environmental Protection Agency (EPA) and the European Medicines Agency (EMA), require eye irritation studies as part of the safety assessment for new chemicals, pharmaceuticals, and cosmetics. These agencies provide specific requirements and protocols that must be followed to ensure the safety and efficacy of the products.
- **Ethical Considerations:** Ethical guidelines ensure the humane treatment of animals used in eye irritation studies. This includes minimizing pain

and distress, providing appropriate housing and care, and using in vitro methods whenever possible to reduce the reliance on animal testing.

Examples:

- **Example 1: Testing of Household Cleaners:** A study was conducted to evaluate the eye irritation potential of a new household cleaning product. The Draize Eye Test was initially used, which showed moderate to severe irritation in rabbits, including redness, swelling, and corneal opacity. Based on these findings, the formulation was modified to reduce the irritant ingredients, and the revised product was re-tested using the BCOP assay, which confirmed reduced irritation potential. This study ensured that the final product was safe for consumer use and complied with regulatory guidelines.
- **Example 2: Evaluation of Cosmetic Ingredients:** A series of in vitro tests, including the EpiOcular test and HET-CAM, were used to assess the eye irritation potential of a new cosmetic preservative. The results indicated mild irritation potential, which was within acceptable limits for cosmetic use. These findings were validated by a limited in vivo study using rabbits, which showed similar mild irritation effects. The preservative was approved for use in cosmetic products, highlighting the effectiveness of using in vitro methods to screen for irritation potential before in vivo testing.
- **Example 3: Assessment of Pharmaceutical Formulations:** A pharmaceutical company conducted an eye irritation study to evaluate the safety of a new eye drop formulation. The Draize Eye Test revealed minimal irritation, with slight redness and no corneal damage. The formulation was further tested using the BCOP assay, which confirmed the absence of significant corneal irritation. These results supported the safety of the eye drop formulation, leading to its approval for clinical use.

2.4.2 Skin Sensitization

Evaluation Techniques:

Skin sensitization refers to the allergic reaction that occurs when the skin becomes hypersensitive to a particular substance following initial exposure. Evaluating skin sensitization is crucial for ensuring the safety of chemicals, cosmetics, pharmaceuticals, and other consumer products. The techniques for evaluating skin sensitization include:

- **Local Lymph Node Assay (LLNA):** This is a widely used in vivo test that measures the proliferative response of lymph node cells following topical application of the test substance. Mice are treated with the substance on their ears, and after a few days, the lymph nodes are excised and examined for cellular proliferation.
- **Guinea Pig Maximization Test (GPMT):** In this in vivo test, guinea pigs are exposed to the test substance both intradermally and topically. Following a period of sensitization, the animals are challenged with the substance, and any hypersensitivity reactions (such as redness or swelling) are recorded.
- **Buehler Test:** Another in vivo test using guinea pigs, the Buehler test involves repeated topical applications of the test substance to induce sensitization. After a rest period, the substance is applied again, and the skin reactions are observed and scored.
- **In Vitro and In Chemico Methods:** To reduce animal testing, several in vitro and in chemico methods have been developed, including:

  - **Direct Peptide Reactivity Assay (DPRA):** This in chemico test measures the reactivity of a substance with synthetic peptides, which mimic skin proteins. The degree of peptide binding is indicative of the sensitizing potential.
  - **KeratinoSens Assay:** This in vitro assay uses a reporter gene in a human keratinocyte cell line to detect the activation of the antioxidant response element (ARE), which is involved in the sensitization pathway.
  - **Human Cell Line Activation Test (h-CLAT):** This in vitro test uses human dendritic-like cells to measure the expression of cell surface markers associated with sensitization.

Interpretation of Data:
Interpreting data from skin sensitization studies involves several steps:

- **LLNA:** The results of the Local Lymph Node Assay are interpreted based on the stimulation index (SI), which compares the proliferation of lymph node cells in treated animals to that in control animals. An SI of 3 or more indicates a positive sensitization response.

- **GPMT and Buehler Test:** The results are interpreted based on the incidence and severity of skin reactions, such as erythema and edema, observed after the challenge exposure. These reactions are scored and compared to control animals to determine sensitization potential.
- **In Vitro and In Chemico Methods:** For tests like DPRA, KeratinoSens, and h-CLAT, results are interpreted based on the degree of peptide reactivity, gene activation, or cell surface marker expression, respectively. Thresholds and criteria provided by regulatory guidelines are used to classify the sensitization potential as low, moderate, or high.
- **Integration of Data:** Often, a weight-of-evidence approach is used, integrating results from multiple tests (in vivo, in vitro, and in chemico) to arrive at a comprehensive assessment of the sensitization potential of a substance.

Real-world Applications:

Skin sensitization studies have critical applications in product safety across various industries:

- **Cosmetics and Personal Care Products:** Skin sensitization testing is essential for ensuring that ingredients in cosmetics and personal care products do not cause allergic reactions. For example, a new fragrance compound might be evaluated using the LLNA and in vitro methods to confirm its safety before being included in a perfume.
- **Pharmaceuticals:** Topical medications and transdermal patches must be tested for skin sensitization potential to ensure they are safe for long-term use. For instance, a new topical antibiotic might undergo GPMT testing to assess its potential to cause allergic dermatitis.
- **Chemical Industry:** Industrial chemicals, especially those that come into contact with the skin during manufacturing processes, must be evaluated for sensitization risks. A new cleaning agent might be tested using the Buehler test and in chemico methods to ensure it does not pose a risk to workers.
- **Regulatory Compliance:** Regulatory agencies such as the U.S. Environmental Protection Agency (EPA) and the European Chemicals Agency (ECHA) require skin sensitization data as part of the safety assessment for new chemicals. Compliance with guidelines such as the OECD Test Guidelines ensures that products meet safety standards and

can be marketed globally.

2.4.3 Dermal Irritation and Toxicity

Assessment Protocols:

Dermal irritation and toxicity studies are designed to evaluate the adverse effects of substances when applied to the skin. These studies are essential for assessing the safety of chemicals, cosmetics, pharmaceuticals, and other consumer products. The protocols for assessing dermal irritation and toxicity include:

- **Primary Dermal Irritation Test:** This test evaluates the irritant potential of a substance by applying it to the shaved skin of test animals, usually rabbits. The substance is applied to a small area, covered with a gauze patch, and left in place for 4 hours. The patch is then removed, and the skin is observed at various intervals (e.g., 24, 48, and 72 hours) for signs of erythema (redness) and edema (swelling). The reactions are scored using a standardized scale.
- **Cumulative Irritation Test:** This test assesses the potential for cumulative irritation from repeated applications of a substance. The substance is applied daily to the same skin site for a specified period, typically 21 days. The skin is observed daily for signs of irritation, and the reactions are scored to determine the cumulative effect.
- **Human Repeat Insult Patch Test (HRIPT):** For cosmetics and personal care products, the HRIPT is often used to assess dermal irritation in human volunteers. Small patches containing the test substance are applied to the skin of volunteers, usually on the back, and left in place for 24 to 48 hours. The patches are reapplied at regular intervals over several weeks. The skin is observed for signs of irritation and allergic reactions.
- **In Vitro Tests:** To reduce animal testing, in vitro methods such as the reconstructed human epidermis (RHE) model are used. These models simulate human skin and allow for the assessment of dermal irritation by measuring cell viability and release of inflammatory markers after exposure to the test substance.

Safety Measures:

Conducting dermal irritation and toxicity studies involves several safety measures to ensure the well-being of test animals and human volunteers, as well as the integrity of the study data:

- **Ethical Considerations**: Animal studies must comply with ethical guidelines to minimize pain and distress. This includes using the minimum number of animals necessary to achieve reliable results and providing appropriate housing, care, and humane handling.
- **Good Laboratory Practice (GLP)**: Compliance with GLP principles ensures the quality and integrity of the study data. GLP guidelines cover all aspects of the study, from planning and conduct to data recording and reporting.
- **Regulatory Compliance**: Studies must adhere to regulatory guidelines provided by organizations such as the Organisation for Economic Co-operation and Development (OECD). For example, OECD Test Guideline 404 outlines the procedure for acute dermal irritation/corrosion testing, while OECD Test Guideline 439 covers in vitro skin irritation testing using reconstructed human epidermis models.
- **Volunteer Safety**: For human studies, informed consent is obtained from all participants. The study protocols are reviewed and approved by an ethics committee to ensure that the risks to volunteers are minimized and managed appropriately.

Examples:

- **Example 1: Testing of Household Cleaners**: A new household cleaner was evaluated for dermal irritation potential using the primary dermal irritation test. The cleaner was applied to the shaved skin of rabbits, and the reactions were observed and scored. The study revealed moderate irritation, including erythema and edema. Based on these findings, the formulation was modified to reduce the irritant ingredients, and the revised product was re-tested, showing significantly reduced irritation potential. This ensured that the final product was safe for consumer use and complied with regulatory guidelines.
- **Example 2: Evaluation of Cosmetic Ingredients**: A new cosmetic ingredient intended for use in skin care products was evaluated for dermal irritation potential using the HRIPT. The ingredient was applied to patches and placed on the skin of human volunteers over several

weeks. The results indicated no significant irritation or allergic reactions, confirming the ingredient's safety for use in cosmetics. These findings supported the approval of the ingredient for inclusion in various cosmetic formulations.

- **Example 3: Assessment of Industrial Chemicals**: An industrial chemical used in manufacturing processes was evaluated for dermal irritation and toxicity using the cumulative irritation test. The chemical was applied daily to the skin of rabbits for 21 days. Observations included monitoring for signs of irritation, such as redness, swelling, and ulceration. The study revealed severe irritation and skin damage at higher concentrations, leading to the implementation of safety measures, including the use of protective clothing and equipment for workers handling the chemical.

2.5 Test Item Characterization

2.5.1 Importance in Regulatory Toxicology
Role in Safety Assessments:

The **characterization of test items** is a critical aspect of regulatory toxicology, ensuring that the substances being tested are well-defined and understood. This process involves determining the chemical composition, physical properties, and purity of the test item. Proper characterization is essential for several reasons:

- **Safety Evaluations:** Accurate test item characterization is crucial for evaluating the safety of a substance. It ensures that the substance being tested is consistent and comparable across different studies, allowing for reliable and reproducible results. Without proper characterization, it is challenging to determine the true cause of observed toxic effects, which may be due to impurities or variations in the test item.
- **Regulatory Compliance:** Regulatory agencies such as the FDA, EMA, and OECD require detailed characterization of test items as part of the submission process for new chemicals, drugs, and other products. This information is necessary to assess the safety and efficacy of the product and to ensure compliance with regulatory standards.
- **Risk Assessment:** Proper characterization provides the foundation for accurate risk assessment. It allows toxicologists to identify potential

hazards associated with the test item and to determine safe exposure levels for humans and the environment.

Impact on Study Outcomes:

Test item characterization has a significant impact on the outcomes of toxicity studies. Key impacts include:

- **Data Reliability:** Well-characterized test items lead to more reliable and reproducible data. This reliability is crucial for drawing accurate conclusions about the safety and toxicity of a substance.
- **Inter-study Comparisons:** Proper characterization allows for meaningful comparisons between studies conducted by different researchers or organizations. It ensures that variations in study outcomes are due to differences in experimental conditions rather than inconsistencies in the test item.
- **Identification of Impurities:** Characterization helps identify impurities or contaminants that may influence the results of toxicity studies. By understanding the composition of the test item, researchers can attribute observed effects to the correct component, whether it is the main substance or an impurity.

2.5.2 Methods for Test Item Characterization

Analytical Techniques:

Several **analytical techniques** are used for characterizing test items, ensuring that their chemical and physical properties are well-defined:

- **Chromatography:** Techniques such as High-Performance Liquid Chromatography (HPLC) and Gas Chromatography (GC) are used to separate, identify, and quantify the components of a test item. These techniques are essential for determining the purity and identifying impurities in the test item.
- **Mass Spectrometry (MS):** MS is used to determine the molecular weight and structure of the components in a test item. It provides detailed information about the chemical composition and can identify trace impurities that may affect toxicity.

- **Nuclear Magnetic Resonance (NMR) Spectroscopy:** NMR is used to determine the molecular structure and dynamics of the test item. It provides detailed information about the chemical environment of atoms within the molecule, helping to identify and quantify impurities.
- **Infrared (IR) Spectroscopy:** IR spectroscopy is used to identify functional groups and characterize the chemical bonds in a test item. It provides information about the molecular structure and can be used to identify impurities.
- **X-ray Diffraction (XRD):** XRD is used to determine the crystalline structure of solid test items. It provides information about the arrangement of atoms in the crystal lattice, which can influence the physical properties and stability of the substance.
- **Thermal Analysis:** Techniques such as Differential Scanning Calorimetry (DSC) and Thermogravimetric Analysis (TGA) are used to study the thermal properties of test items. These techniques provide information about the melting point, decomposition temperature, and thermal stability of the substance.

III

Reproductive and Genotoxicity Studies

Reproductive and Genotoxicity Studies

Reproductive and genotoxicity studies are essential components of preclinical safety evaluation for new pharmaceutical compounds. These studies aim to assess the potential effects of a substance on the reproductive system and its ability to cause genetic damage.

Reproductive toxicity studies evaluate the impact of a substance on the reproductive organs, fertility, pregnancy, and development of the offspring. These studies are crucial to ensure that a drug does not adversely affect the reproductive capabilities of males and females, nor harm the developing embryo or fetus. They include tests on animal models to observe any potential abnormalities or adverse effects on reproductive organs and functions.

Genotoxicity studies, on the other hand, are designed to detect compounds that can cause genetic mutations or chromosomal damage. These studies are important because genetic mutations can lead to cancer and hereditary defects. Genotoxicity testing includes a variety of assays, such as the Ames test, chromosomal aberration test, and micronucleus test, which help identify any genetic risks posed by the substance.

Together, reproductive and genotoxicity studies provide a comprehensive understanding of the potential risks a new drug might pose to human health, particularly in terms of reproduction and genetic stability. These studies are mandatory for regulatory approval and play a critical role in the safe development of pharmaceuticals.

3.1 Reproductive Toxicology Studies

3.1.1 Male Reproductive Toxicity

Methods of Assessment:

Male reproductive toxicity studies are essential for evaluating the potential adverse effects of chemicals, pharmaceuticals, and other substances on male reproductive health. These studies focus on identifying toxic effects on male reproductive organs, sperm quality, hormonal function, and overall fertility. Various methods are employed to assess male reproductive toxicity, including:

- **Histopathological Examination:**

  - **Testis and Epididymis Analysis:** Microscopic examination of the testes and epididymis to identify structural changes, such as atrophy, degeneration, and disruption of spermatogenesis.
  - **Seminiferous Tubule Analysis:** Assessment of the integrity and function of seminiferous tubules, where sperm production occurs. This includes evaluating the stages of spermatogenesis and the presence of mature spermatozoa.

- **Sperm Analysis:**

  - **Sperm Count:** Measurement of the number of sperm produced, typically from the epididymis or ejaculate, to identify reductions in sperm production.
  - **Sperm Motility:** Assessment of the movement and swimming capability of sperm, which is critical for fertilization. This includes analyzing parameters such as motility percentage, velocity, and trajectory.
  - **Sperm Morphology:** Evaluation of the shape and structure of sperm to identify abnormalities that could affect fertility. This involves assessing head, midpiece, and tail morphology.
  - **Sperm Viability:** Determination of the percentage of live versus dead sperm using dye exclusion tests, such as eosin-nigrosin staining.

- **Hormonal Analysis:**

  - **Serum Testosterone Levels:** Measurement of testosterone levels in the blood to assess endocrine function and its role in spermatogenesis and male reproductive health.
  - **Luteinizing Hormone (LH) and Follicle-Stimulating Hormone (FSH) Levels:** Evaluation of these pituitary hormones, which regulate testicular function and spermatogenesis.

- **Mating Studies:**

  - **Fertility Assessment:** Mating treated males with untreated females to evaluate fertility outcomes, including the number of successful pregnancies, litter size, and offspring viability.

- **Copulatory Behavior:** Observation of mating behavior, such as mounting frequency, intromission frequency, and ejaculation, to identify any disruptions in sexual behavior.

- **Genetic and Molecular Analysis:**

  - **DNA Integrity:** Assessment of sperm DNA integrity using techniques such as the Comet assay and sperm chromatin structure assay (SCSA) to detect DNA fragmentation and damage.
  - **Gene Expression Analysis:** Evaluation of gene expression in reproductive tissues to identify molecular changes associated with toxicity. This includes examining genes involved in spermatogenesis, hormonal regulation, and oxidative stress response.

- **Additional Tests:**

  - **Oxidative Stress Markers:** Measurement of oxidative stress markers, such as malondialdehyde (MDA) and glutathione (GSH), in reproductive tissues to assess oxidative damage and antioxidant capacity.
  - **Apoptosis Markers:** Evaluation of apoptotic cell death in testicular tissue using markers such as caspase-3 and TUNEL assay to identify increased cell death contributing to reproductive toxicity.

Examples:

- **Example 1: Pesticide Exposure:** A study on the effects of a commonly used pesticide on male reproductive health involved administering the pesticide to male rats for 90 days. Histopathological examination revealed testicular atrophy and disruption of spermatogenesis. Sperm analysis showed decreased sperm count, motility, and increased abnormalities. Hormonal analysis indicated reduced serum testosterone levels. These findings suggested significant male reproductive toxicity, leading to regulatory restrictions on the pesticide's use.
- **Example 2: Pharmaceutical Testing:** During the development of a new drug, male reproductive toxicity studies were conducted to evaluate its safety. The drug was administered to male mice for 12 weeks. Sperm

analysis showed reduced motility and increased DNA fragmentation. Mating studies revealed decreased fertility rates. Hormonal analysis indicated altered levels of LH and FSH. These results prompted further investigation and modification of the drug formulation to mitigate reproductive risks.

- **Example 3: Industrial Chemical Exposure**: Workers in an industrial setting were exposed to a chemical suspected of causing reproductive toxicity. An epidemiological study was conducted, including semen analysis and hormonal profiling of exposed workers. The results showed reduced sperm count and motility, along with decreased serum testosterone levels. These findings led to the implementation of safety measures and exposure limits to protect workers' reproductive health.

Impact on Fertility:

Male reproductive toxicity studies are essential for assessing how exposure to toxicants can adversely affect male fertility. The impact of toxicants on male fertility can manifest through various mechanisms, including alterations in sperm production, quality, and function, as well as hormonal imbalances and structural damage to reproductive organs. Key impacts on fertility include:

- **Reduced Sperm Count (Oligospermia)**: Exposure to toxicants can lead to a decrease in the number of sperm produced. This reduction can significantly impair fertility since fewer sperm are available to fertilize an egg.
- **Decreased Sperm Motility (Asthenospermia)**: Toxicants can affect the ability of sperm to swim effectively. Reduced motility can hinder sperm from reaching and fertilizing the egg, leading to decreased chances of successful conception.
- **Abnormal Sperm Morphology (Teratospermia)**: Toxicants can cause structural abnormalities in sperm, affecting their head, midpiece, or tail. Abnormal sperm are less likely to fertilize an egg successfully.
- **Sperm DNA Damage**: Exposure to certain chemicals can lead to DNA fragmentation and other genetic damage in sperm. Sperm with damaged DNA may lead to failed fertilization, early pregnancy loss, or developmental defects in offspring.
- **Hormonal Imbalances**: Toxicants can disrupt the endocrine system, leading to imbalances in hormones such as testosterone, LH, and FSH.

These hormones are critical for regulating spermatogenesis and overall reproductive function.

- **Testicular Damage:** Direct damage to the testes, where sperm are produced, can result from toxicant exposure. This damage can impair spermatogenesis and lead to decreased sperm production and quality.
- **Impaired Spermatogenesis:** Toxicants can interfere with the process of spermatogenesis, the development of sperm cells, leading to a decrease in the production of healthy, mature sperm.
- **Oxidative Stress:** Many toxicants induce oxidative stress, which can damage sperm cells and reproductive tissues. Oxidative stress is associated with decreased sperm motility, viability, and increased DNA damage.

Examples::

- **Example 1: Bisphenol A (BPA) Exposure:** Bisphenol A (BPA) is a chemical commonly used in plastics. A study investigated the effects of BPA on male fertility by administering various doses to male rats for 90 days. Results showed a significant reduction in sperm count and motility, along with increased sperm abnormalities and DNA fragmentation. Histopathological examination revealed testicular degeneration and decreased seminiferous tubule integrity. Hormonal analysis indicated reduced serum testosterone levels. These findings highlighted the adverse effects of BPA on male fertility and supported regulatory measures to limit BPA exposure.
- **Example 2: Phthalate Exposure:** Phthalates are chemicals used as plasticizers in many consumer products. A study on the effects of di(2-ethylhexyl) phthalate (DEHP) on male fertility involved administering DEHP to male mice for 10 weeks. Sperm analysis showed a dose-dependent decrease in sperm count, motility, and increased abnormal morphology. Mating studies revealed decreased fertility rates, with fewer successful pregnancies and smaller litter sizes. Hormonal analysis indicated disruptions in testosterone levels. These results underscored the reproductive toxicity of DEHP and informed regulatory actions to reduce phthalate exposure in consumer products.
- **Example 3: Cadmium Toxicity:** Cadmium is a heavy metal found in industrial environments. A study evaluated the effects of cadmium on male reproductive health by exposing male rats to cadmium chloride

for 8 weeks. Sperm analysis demonstrated reduced sperm count and motility, along with increased sperm abnormalities and oxidative stress markers. Histopathological examination showed significant testicular damage, including necrosis and disruption of spermatogenesis. These findings illustrated the severe impact of cadmium exposure on male fertility and led to increased safety regulations for cadmium exposure in occupational settings.

- **Example 4: Cyclophosphamide (Chemotherapy Drug):** Cyclophosphamide is a chemotherapeutic agent known to cause reproductive toxicity. A study on male rats administered cyclophosphamide for 12 weeks showed substantial reductions in sperm count, motility, and increased DNA fragmentation. Histopathological analysis revealed testicular atrophy and impaired spermatogenesis. Mating studies indicated reduced fertility, with lower pregnancy rates and litter sizes. These findings highlighted the need for fertility preservation strategies in male patients undergoing chemotherapy.

3.1.2 Female Reproductive Toxicity (Segment I and Segment III)

Evaluation Protocols:

Female reproductive toxicity studies are conducted to assess the potential adverse effects of chemicals, pharmaceuticals, and other substances on female reproductive health. These studies focus on identifying toxic effects on female reproductive organs, hormonal function, fertility, and fetal development. The evaluation protocols for female reproductive toxicity are divided into two main segments: Segment I (Pre-mating to Fertilization) and Segment III (Perinatal and Postnatal Development).

Segment I: Pre-mating to Fertilization

Segment I studies assess the effects of substances on female fertility and early pregnancy stages. The protocols include:

- **Animal Selection and Dosing:** Typically, rodents such as rats or mice are used. Female animals are dosed with the test substance for a specified period before mating, throughout the mating period, and up to confirmation of pregnancy.

- **Estrous Cycle Monitoring:** The estrous cycle is monitored to detect any disruptions caused by the test substance. This includes recording the length and regularity of the estrous cycle stages (proestrus, estrus, metestrus, and diestrus).
- **Mating and Fertility Assessment:** Females are paired with untreated males to assess fertility. The number of successful matings, time to mating, and the number of pregnant females are recorded.
- **Ovarian and Uterine Examination:** Post-mating, females are sacrificed, and their reproductive organs are examined. The ovaries are assessed for the number of corpora lutea, indicating ovulation, and the uterus is examined for implantation sites.
- **Histopathological Analysis:** Ovaries, uterus, and other reproductive tissues are subjected to microscopic examination to identify structural changes or lesions caused by the test substance.

Segment III: Perinatal and Postnatal Development

Segment III studies evaluate the effects of substances on fetal development, birth outcomes, and postnatal development. The protocols include:

- **Animal Selection and Dosing:** Pregnant female rodents are dosed with the test substance from implantation through lactation. The dosing period typically spans gestation days (GD) 6-20 and lactation days (LD) 1-21.
- **Gestation and Parturition Monitoring:** The females are monitored throughout gestation for signs of toxicity, abnormal behavior, and complications during parturition (birth).
- **Fetal and Neonatal Assessment:** At birth, the number of live and dead pups, litter size, pup weight, and physical abnormalities are recorded. Observations continue through the lactation period to monitor pup growth, development, and survival.
- **Postnatal Development:** The development of offspring is monitored postnatally for parameters such as body weight gain, physical development milestones (e.g., eye opening, fur development), and behavioral assessments (e.g., reflexes, motor activity).
- **Reproductive Organ Examination:** After weaning, the reproductive organs of the female offspring are examined for any abnormalities or

structural changes.

- **Histopathological Analysis:** Reproductive tissues of the dams and offspring are examined microscopically to identify any lesions or developmental anomalies caused by the test substance.

Examples:

- **Example 1: Pharmaceutical Development:** A pharmaceutical company conducted Segment I and III studies to evaluate the reproductive toxicity of a new drug. In Segment I, female rats were dosed for two weeks before mating and throughout the mating period. Results showed disrupted estrous cycles and decreased pregnancy rates. Ovarian histopathology revealed follicular atresia. In Segment III, the drug was administered during gestation and lactation, resulting in increased neonatal mortality and developmental delays. These findings led to modifications in the drug formulation and additional safety testing.
- **Example 2: Chemical Safety Assessment:** A study evaluated the reproductive toxicity of a pesticide in female mice. Segment I studies revealed decreased ovulation rates and increased resorption of embryos. Segment III studies showed low birth weights and delayed physical development in pups. Histopathological examination indicated uterine and ovarian lesions. These results informed regulatory decisions and established safe exposure limits for the pesticide.
- **Example 3: Food Additive Testing:** A new food additive was tested for reproductive toxicity in Segment I and III studies. Female rats showed no significant changes in fertility or pregnancy outcomes in Segment I. However, Segment III studies revealed slight reductions in pup weight gain and minor developmental delays. The additive was deemed safe for use within established limits, and further monitoring was recommended.

Pregnancy and Development Effects:

Effects of toxicants on pregnancy and fetal development are critical aspects of female reproductive toxicity studies. These studies assess how exposure to various substances during pregnancy impacts maternal health, fetal development, birth outcomes, and postnatal growth. The effects of toxicants on pregnancy and fetal development include:

- **Maternal Toxicity:** Toxicants can cause adverse effects on the pregnant female, such as weight loss, decreased food consumption, lethargy, and altered behavior. Severe maternal toxicity can lead to pregnancy complications or loss.
- **Embryotoxicity and Fetotoxicity:** Exposure to toxicants can result in embryotoxicity (damage to the embryo) or fetotoxicity (damage to the fetus). This can lead to increased resorptions (loss of the embryo), stillbirths, or malformations.
- **Teratogenicity:** Teratogenic effects refer to structural abnormalities or congenital malformations in the developing fetus caused by exposure to toxicants. Common teratogenic effects include skeletal deformities, craniofacial abnormalities, and organ malformations.
- **Growth Retardation:** Toxicants can impair fetal growth, leading to low birth weight and small-for-gestational-age (SGA) infants. Growth retardation can result from placental insufficiency, nutrient deprivation, or direct effects on fetal tissues.
- **Developmental Delays:** Exposure to toxicants during pregnancy can cause delays in developmental milestones. This includes delayed physical development (e.g., eye opening, fur growth), neurodevelopmental delays, and impaired motor skills.
- **Preterm Birth:** Some toxicants can induce preterm labor, resulting in early delivery and associated complications such as respiratory distress syndrome and underdeveloped organs in the newborn.
- **Neurotoxicity:** Certain substances can cross the placental barrier and affect fetal brain development, leading to neurodevelopmental disorders, cognitive impairments, and behavioral abnormalities.
- **Placental Effects:** Toxicants can adversely affect the placenta, leading to placental insufficiency, reduced nutrient and oxygen transfer to the fetus, and placental inflammation or lesions.
- **Postnatal Effects:** The impact of toxicants can extend beyond birth, affecting postnatal growth and development. This includes ongoing growth retardation, developmental delays, and increased susceptibility to diseases.

Examples:

- **Example 1: Thalidomide:** Thalidomide is a well-known teratogen that caused severe birth defects when taken by pregnant women in the 1950s and 1960s. Studies revealed that exposure to thalidomide during early pregnancy led to limb malformations, such as phocomelia (shortened or absent limbs), as well as other congenital anomalies like cardiac defects and ear malformations. This case led to stricter regulations on drug testing during pregnancy and the establishment of pregnancy safety categories for medications.
- **Example 2: Alcohol (Fetal Alcohol Syndrome):** Chronic alcohol consumption during pregnancy can result in fetal alcohol syndrome (FAS), characterized by growth retardation, craniofacial abnormalities, and neurodevelopmental deficits. Studies in animal models and epidemiological studies in humans have shown that alcohol exposure during pregnancy affects brain development, leading to cognitive impairments, behavioral problems, and learning disabilities. This has led to public health campaigns advocating for complete abstinence from alcohol during pregnancy.
- **Example 3: Diethylstilbestrol (DES):** Diethylstilbestrol (DES) is a synthetic estrogen previously prescribed to prevent miscarriages and other pregnancy complications. Studies revealed that in utero exposure to DES resulted in an increased risk of clear cell adenocarcinoma of the vagina and cervix in female offspring, as well as reproductive tract abnormalities and infertility. This case highlighted the long-term effects of prenatal exposure to endocrine-disrupting chemicals and influenced regulatory policies on drug use during pregnancy.
- **Example 4: Methylmercury:** Methylmercury exposure during pregnancy, primarily through the consumption of contaminated fish, has been linked to neurodevelopmental deficits in children. Studies showed that prenatal exposure to methylmercury leads to cognitive impairments, motor dysfunction, and sensory deficits. These findings have informed dietary recommendations for pregnant women to limit fish consumption and avoid species with high mercury levels.
- **Example 5: Phthalates:** Phthalates, commonly used as plasticizers, have been associated with adverse reproductive outcomes. Studies in animals have shown that prenatal exposure to certain phthalates can lead to reduced anogenital distance, a marker of reproductive toxicity, and malformations in the male reproductive system. Human epidemiological studies have also linked prenatal phthalate exposure to developmental

delays and behavioral problems in children. These findings have prompted regulatory agencies to limit the use of phthalates in consumer products, especially those used by pregnant women and children.

3.1.3 Teratogenicity Studies (Segment II)

Testing Procedures:

Teratogenicity studies (Segment II) are designed to assess the potential of a substance to cause developmental abnormalities or congenital malformations in the offspring when exposed during pregnancy. These studies are critical for identifying teratogenic risks and ensuring the safety of pharmaceuticals, chemicals, and other substances during pregnancy. The procedures for conducting teratogenicity studies include several key steps:

1. **Selection of Test Animals:**

   - Commonly used species include rodents (rats and mice) and rabbits due to their well-characterized reproductive cycles and development stages.
   - Pregnant females are selected for testing to assess the effects of the test substance on fetal development.

2. **Dosing Regimen:**

   - The test substance is administered to pregnant females during the organogenesis period (the critical window of fetal development when organs are forming). For rodents, this period typically spans gestation days (GD) 6-15, and for rabbits, GD 6-18.
   - Doses are selected based on preliminary studies to cover a range of exposures, including a high dose that induces maternal toxicity but does not cause excessive mortality, and at least two lower doses.

3. **Route of Administration:**

   - The test substance can be administered via various routes, including oral (gavage or mixed with food/water), inhalation, dermal, or intravenous, depending on the intended human exposure route.

4. **Observation and Monitoring:**

- Pregnant females are observed daily for clinical signs of toxicity, changes in behavior, body weight, and food consumption.
- Specific attention is given to signs of maternal toxicity, as this can influence fetal outcomes.

5. **Necropsy and Examination:**

- On or near the expected day of delivery (e.g., GD 20 for rats, GD 29 for rabbits), the pregnant females are humanely euthanized.
- The uterus is examined for the number of implantation sites, resorptions (early and late), live and dead fetuses.
- Fetal weights and sex are recorded.

6. **Fetal Examination:**

- External Examination: Each fetus is examined for external abnormalities, including limb and craniofacial malformations.
- Visceral Examination: Fetuses are dissected to examine internal organs for structural abnormalities.
- Skeletal Examination: Fetuses are stained with a skeletal dye (e.g., Alizarin Red S) to visualize bones and assess skeletal malformations.

7. **Data Analysis:**

- The incidence of malformations and variations is compared between control and treated groups.
- Statistical analysis is performed to determine the significance of any observed differences.
- Maternal toxicity data are correlated with fetal outcomes to differentiate between direct teratogenic effects and secondary effects due to maternal toxicity.

Example of Teratogenicity Study Protocol:

- **Objective:** To evaluate the potential teratogenic effects of a new pharmaceutical compound.

- **Species:** Pregnant Sprague-Dawley rats.
- **Dosing Period:** GD 6-15.
- **Doses:** Control (vehicle only), Low Dose, Mid Dose, High Dose.
- **Route of Administration:** Oral gavage.
- **Observations:** Daily monitoring of clinical signs, body weight, and food consumption.
- **Necropsy:** GD 20, examination of uterine contents, recording of implantation sites, resorptions, live/dead fetuses.
- **Fetal Examination:** External, visceral, and skeletal examinations of fetuses.
- **Data Analysis:** Statistical comparison of malformations and variations between groups, correlation with maternal toxicity.

Examples:

Example 1: Thalidomide: Thalidomide was prescribed as a sedative and anti-nausea medication for pregnant women in the late 1950s and early 1960s. Teratogenicity studies conducted after the discovery of its adverse effects showed severe limb malformations (phocomelia) and other congenital defects when administered to pregnant animals during organogenesis. These findings led to the withdrawal of thalidomide from the market and highlighted the need for rigorous teratogenicity testing of drugs intended for use during pregnancy.

- **Example 2: Isotretinoin (Accutane):** Isotretinoin, used for severe acne treatment, was found to be a potent teratogen. Teratogenicity studies in rodents and rabbits showed a high incidence of craniofacial, cardiovascular, and central nervous system malformations when administered during pregnancy. These studies informed strict regulatory controls and pregnancy prevention programs to prevent fetal exposure to isotretinoin.
- **Example 3: Valproic Acid:** Valproic acid, an anticonvulsant and mood-stabilizing drug, was tested for teratogenic effects. Studies revealed neural tube defects, such as spina bifida, in offspring of treated pregnant animals. This led to warnings and recommendations for folic acid supplementation and alternative therapies for women of childbearing age.

Analysis of Teratogenic Effects:

Teratogenicity studies are conducted to assess the potential of a substance to cause developmental abnormalities or congenital malformations in the offspring when exposed during pregnancy. Analyzing the effects of toxicants on fetal development involves several critical steps, each aimed at identifying and characterizing the nature and extent of teratogenic effects. The analysis includes:

1. **Data Collection and Recording:**

    ○ **Maternal Observations:** Recording daily observations of the pregnant females for signs of toxicity, including changes in behavior, body weight, and food consumption. Specific attention is given to any signs of stress or toxicity that could influence fetal outcomes.

    ○ **Uterine Examination:** At necropsy, the uterus is examined for the number of implantation sites, resorptions (both early and late), live and dead fetuses. This data provides an initial indication of embryonic or fetal loss.

2. **Fetal Observations and Measurements:**

    ○ **External Examination:** Each fetus is examined for external malformations, such as limb deformities, craniofacial abnormalities, and body wall defects. These observations are recorded systematically.

    ○ **Visceral Examination:** Internal organs of the fetuses are dissected and examined for visceral malformations. This includes checking for heart defects, kidney malformations, and other internal abnormalities.

    ○ **Skeletal Examination:** Fetuses are stained with a skeletal dye (e.g., Alizarin Red S) to visualize bones and assess skeletal malformations. This includes counting ossification centers, examining the shape and structure of bones, and identifying any skeletal deformities.

3. **Quantitative Analysis:**

- ○ **Incidence of Malformations:** The frequency of each type of malformation is calculated and compared between control and treated groups. This includes both external and internal malformations.
- ○ **Fetal Body Weights:** Recording and comparing the body weights of fetuses between groups to assess the impact on growth and development.
- ○ **Litter-Based Analysis:** Since multiple fetuses come from the same mother, the data is analyzed on a per-litter basis to account for the potential clustering of effects within litters.

4. **Statistical Analysis:**

- ○ **Comparative Statistics:** Statistical tests (e.g., t-tests, ANOVA, chi-square tests) are used to compare the incidence of malformations and variations between control and treated groups. Significance levels are determined to identify statistically significant differences.
- ○ **Dose-Response Relationship:** Analysis of the relationship between the dose of the test substance and the observed effects. This helps in determining the lowest observed adverse effect level (LOAEL) and the no observed adverse effect level (NOAEL).

5. **Correlation with Maternal Toxicity:**

- ○ **Maternal-Fetal Correlation:** Correlating the observed fetal effects with maternal toxicity data to differentiate direct teratogenic effects from secondary effects due to maternal toxicity. For instance, if maternal toxicity is severe, some fetal effects might be secondary to the maternal condition.

6. **Mechanistic Insights:**

- ○ **Mechanism of Action:** Investigating the potential mechanisms through which the test substance induces teratogenic effects. This may involve additional studies on the absorption, distribution, metabolism, and excretion (ADME) of the substance, as well as its interaction with specific biological pathways.

3.2 Genotoxicity Studies

3.2.1 Ames Test

Procedure and Applications:

The **Ames test** is a widely used assay to evaluate the mutagenic potential of chemical compounds. Named after its developer, Bruce Ames, the test uses strains of the bacterium *Salmonella typhimurium* that carry mutations in genes involved in histidine synthesis. These bacteria are unable to grow on a medium lacking histidine unless a mutation restores their ability to synthesize it. The test assesses whether the test compound induces such mutations, suggesting its potential to cause genetic damage in living organisms.

Steps Involved in Conducting the Ames Test:

1. **Preparation of Test Strains:**

   - **Selection of Strains:** Multiple *Salmonella typhimurium* strains are used, each with a specific mutation in the histidine operon. Common strains include TA98, TA100, TA1535, TA1537, and TA102, which differ in their sensitivity to different types of mutagens (e.g., base-pair substitutions or frameshift mutations).

2. **Preparation of Test Plates:**

   - **Agar Plates:** Prepare minimal glucose agar plates that lack histidine. The plates provide a limited amount of histidine to allow the bacteria to undergo a few cell divisions, which is crucial for detecting mutations.

3. **Addition of Test Substance:**

   - **Test Compound Preparation:** The test compound is dissolved in an appropriate solvent. Serial dilutions are prepared to test different concentrations.

- **Control Substances:** Include both positive controls (known mutagens) and negative controls (solvent only) to validate the test.

4. **Plate Incorporation Method:**

- **Mixing with Bacteria:** In the plate incorporation method, a mixture of the test compound, bacterial culture, and molten top agar (containing a trace amount of histidine) is prepared. The mixture is then poured onto the surface of minimal agar plates.
- **Overlay Method:** Alternatively, the pre-incubation method can be used, where the bacteria and test compound are incubated together before being added to the top agar and plated.

5. **Metabolic Activation:**

- **S9 Mix:** To mimic metabolic activation in mammals, a rat liver S9 fraction (containing metabolic enzymes) is often included in the test. This allows detection of mutagens that require metabolic activation to exert their effects.

6. **Incubation:**

- **Incubation Period:** The plates are incubated at 37°C for 48-72 hours to allow bacterial growth and mutation expression.

7. **Counting Colonies:**

- **Revertant Colonies:** After incubation, the plates are examined, and the number of revertant colonies (bacteria that have regained the ability to synthesize histidine) is counted. The presence of more revertant colonies on the test plates compared to the control plates indicates a mutagenic effect.

8. **Data Analysis:**

- **Comparison with Controls:** The number of revertants in the treated samples is compared to the number in the negative control. An increase in revertant colonies suggests that the test compound is mutagenic.

- **Dose-Response Relationship:** Analyze the data to determine if there is a dose-response relationship, which strengthens the evidence for mutagenicity.

Applications of the Ames Test:

- **Screening Chemicals for Mutagenicity:** The Ames test is widely used in the initial screening of chemicals, pharmaceuticals, and environmental samples for their potential to cause genetic mutations.
- **Regulatory Requirements:** Regulatory agencies such as the FDA, EPA, and ECHA require genotoxicity testing, including the Ames test, as part of the safety assessment for new drugs, chemicals, and pesticides.
- **Investigating Mechanisms of Mutagenesis:** The test helps in understanding the mechanisms by which certain chemicals induce mutations, contributing to broader toxicological research.
- **Environmental Monitoring:** The Ames test is used to monitor environmental samples, such as water and soil, for the presence of mutagenic pollutants, ensuring public health safety.

Interpretation of Results:

The **interpretation of results** from the Ames test involves several steps to determine whether a test substance is mutagenic. Understanding the outcomes helps in making informed decisions about the safety and potential risks associated with the substance.

1. Revertant Colony Count:

- **Counting Revertants:** After the incubation period, the plates are examined for revertant colonies—bacterial colonies that have regained the ability to grow in the absence of histidine due to mutations induced by the test substance.
- **Control Plates:** Compare the number of revertant colonies on the test plates to the negative control plates (solvent only). The negative control provides a baseline for spontaneous mutation rates.

2. Positive and Negative Controls:

- **Negative Control:** The solvent-only plates should show a consistent, low number of revertant colonies, representing the spontaneous mutation rate.
- **Positive Control:** Plates treated with a known mutagen should show a significant increase in revertant colonies, validating the test's ability to detect mutagenicity.

3. Dose-Response Relationship:

- **Different Concentrations:** Analyze the results across various concentrations of the test substance. A mutagenic substance typically shows a dose-response relationship, where higher concentrations lead to more revertant colonies.
- **Threshold Effects:** Determine if there is a threshold below which no increase in revertants is observed. Some substances may exhibit mutagenicity only at higher doses.

4. Statistical Analysis:

- **Comparison to Controls:** Use statistical tests (e.g., t-tests, chi-square tests) to compare the number of revertant colonies in the test samples to the negative control. Significant differences suggest mutagenicity.
- **Significance Levels:** A statistically significant increase in revertant colonies at any dose level compared to the negative control indicates a mutagenic response.

5. Strain Sensitivity:

- **Multiple Strains:** Since different strains of *Salmonella typhimurium* are sensitive to different types of mutations, observe the results across all tested strains. A substance that induces mutations in multiple strains has a broader mutagenic potential.
- **Specific Mutations:** Note which strains show increased revertants to understand the type of genetic damage (e.g., base-pair substitutions or frameshift mutations).

6. S9 Metabolic Activation:

- **With and Without S9 Mix:** Compare the results with and without the addition of the S9 metabolic activation mix. Some compounds may only be mutagenic after metabolic activation, indicating the importance of metabolic processes in their mutagenicity.
- **Differentiating Effects:** The presence of revertant colonies in the plates with S9 but not in those without suggests that the substance requires metabolic activation to become mutagenic.

7. Interpretation Summary:

- **Positive Result:** A substance is considered mutagenic if there is a statistically significant increase in the number of revertant colonies compared to the negative control, with or without a dose-response relationship, across one or more strains.
- **Negative Result:** A substance is considered non-mutagenic if there is no significant increase in revertant colonies compared to the negative control across all tested strains, even at the highest concentration tested.
- **Equivocal Result:** If the results are inconsistent or only marginally significant, further testing may be required to clarify the substance's mutagenic potential.

Case Study Example:
Example: Testing a New Chemical Compound

1. **Setup:** The compound was tested at five different concentrations, along with negative (solvent) and positive controls (known mutagen).
2. **Results Without S9:**

   - **Control Plates:** Negative control showed an average of 20 revertants.
   - **Positive Control:** Known mutagen showed an average of 500 revertants.
   - **Test Plates:** The number of revertants at increasing concentrations were 22, 25, 28, 30, and 33.

3. **Results With S9:**

   - **Control Plates:** Negative control showed an average of 18 revertants.

- **Positive Control:** Known mutagen showed an average of 480 revertants.
- **Test Plates:** The number of revertants at increasing concentrations were 21, 50, 120, 200, and 400.

Interpretation:

- **Without S9 Mix:** No significant increase in revertant colonies compared to the negative control, suggesting no direct mutagenicity.
- **With S9 Mix:** Significant, dose-dependent increase in revertant colonies compared to the negative control, indicating mutagenicity after metabolic activation.
- **Conclusion:** The compound is considered mutagenic in the presence of metabolic activation, as it significantly increased the number of revertant colonies in a dose-dependent manner when S9 was included.

3.2.2 In Vitro Micronucleus Test

Methods and Protocols:

The **in vitro micronucleus test** is a widely used assay for detecting the genotoxic potential of chemical substances. It measures the formation of micronuclei in the cytoplasm of interphase cells. Micronuclei are small, extranuclear bodies that contain chromosomal fragments or whole chromosomes that were not incorporated into the daughter nuclei during cell division. This test is significant for identifying clastogenic (chromosome-breaking) and aneugenic (chromosome number-altering) agents.

Protocols for Conducting In Vitro Micronucleus Tests:

1. **Cell Culture Preparation:**

   - **Selection of Cell Lines:** Commonly used cell lines include human lymphocytes, Chinese hamster ovary (CHO) cells, and V79 cells. Human lymphocytes are often preferred for their relevance to human health.
   - **Cell Growth:** Cells are cultured in appropriate media with necessary supplements (e.g., fetal bovine serum) and incubated at 37°C with 5%

CO_2 until they reach the desired confluency.

2. **Exposure to Test Substance:**

   - **Dosing:** Cells are exposed to different concentrations of the test substance. Typically, a range of doses is used to observe any dose-dependent effects.
   - **Controls:** Include both negative controls (untreated or solvent-treated cells) and positive controls (known genotoxic agents such as mitomycin C or colchicine) to validate the test.
   - **Metabolic Activation:** Some tests include the use of an S9 mix (rat liver extract) to simulate metabolic activation, assessing the potential genotoxicity of metabolites.

3. **Treatment Duration:**

   - **Short-Term Treatment:** Cells are exposed to the test substance for 3-6 hours, followed by washing and incubation in fresh medium for an additional period to allow cell division.
   - **Continuous Treatment:** Cells are exposed continuously for 20-24 hours, depending on the cell cycle duration of the chosen cell line.

4. **Cytokinesis-Block Protocol (Optional):**

   - **Cytochalasin B:** To facilitate the identification of binucleated cells, cytochalasin B is added post-exposure to inhibit cytokinesis. This results in the formation of binucleated cells, which are easier to score for micronuclei.

5. **Harvesting and Slide Preparation:**

   - **Cell Harvesting:** Cells are harvested by centrifugation and fixed using a methanol-acetic acid mixture.
   - **Slide Preparation:** Fixed cells are dropped onto clean microscope slides and air-dried. The slides are then stained with a DNA-specific stain such as Giemsa or acridine orange.

6. **Microscopic Examination:**

- **Scoring Micronuclei:** Micronuclei are scored in a set number of binucleated cells (usually 1000 binucleated cells per concentration) under a microscope. The presence of one or more micronuclei per binucleated cell is recorded.
- **Criteria for Scoring:** Micronuclei should be less than one-third the size of the main nucleus, non-refractive, and not connected to the main nucleus. They should also be similar in staining properties to the main nucleus.

7. **Data Analysis:**

- **Frequency Calculation:** The frequency of micronucleated cells is calculated for each treatment group and compared to the control groups.
- **Statistical Analysis:** Statistical tests (e.g., chi-square test, Fisher's exact test) are used to determine the significance of the increase in micronucleated cells compared to the control.

8. **Interpretation of Results:**

- **Positive Result:** A statistically significant increase in the number of micronucleated cells compared to the negative control indicates genotoxic potential.
- **Negative Result:** No significant increase in micronucleated cells compared to the negative control suggests the substance is not genotoxic.
- **Equivocal Result:** If the results are inconsistent or marginally significant, further testing may be required.

Applications:

- **Screening Chemicals for Genotoxicity:** The in vitro micronucleus test is widely used in the initial screening of chemicals, pharmaceuticals, and environmental samples for genotoxic potential.
- **Regulatory Requirements:** Regulatory agencies such as the FDA, EMA, and OECD require genotoxicity testing, including the in vitro micronucleus test, as part of the safety assessment for new drugs, chemicals, and pesticides.

- **Mechanistic Studies:** The test helps in understanding the mechanisms of genotoxicity, contributing to broader toxicological research.
- **Environmental Monitoring:** The test is used to monitor environmental samples, such as water and soil, for the presence of genotoxic pollutants, ensuring public health safety.

Case Studies and Examples:

- **Example 1: Pharmaceutical Testing:** A new drug candidate was tested using the in vitro micronucleus assay. Human lymphocytes were exposed to various concentrations of the drug. A significant increase in micronucleated cells was observed at higher concentrations, indicating potential genotoxicity. This result led to further investigation and modifications to reduce the genotoxic risk before clinical development.
- **Example 2: Chemical Safety Assessment:** An industrial chemical was evaluated for genotoxicity. CHO cells were treated with the chemical, both with and without metabolic activation. The test showed a dose-dependent increase in micronucleated cells, especially with metabolic activation, indicating that the chemical or its metabolites are genotoxic. These findings prompted additional safety measures and exposure limits for workers.
- **Example 3: Environmental Monitoring:** Water samples from a river near an industrial site were tested for genotoxic pollutants. Human lymphocytes exposed to the water samples showed a significant increase in micronucleated cells, suggesting the presence of genotoxic contaminants. This led to further investigation and regulatory action to address the pollution source.

Data Analysis:

Analyzing data from in vitro micronucleus tests involves several techniques to ensure accurate interpretation of results and to determine the genotoxic potential of the test substance. The key steps in data analysis include:

    1. Data Collection:

- **Scoring Micronuclei:** The number of micronuclei in binucleated cells is counted. Typically, at least 1000 binucleated cells per treatment group are scored to ensure statistical robustness.

- **Binucleated Cell Count:** The total number of binucleated cells examined is recorded to calculate the frequency of micronucleated cells.

2. Calculation of Micronucleus Frequency:

- **Micronucleus Frequency:** The frequency of micronucleated cells is calculated as the number of micronucleated cells per 1000 binucleated cells. This is expressed as a percentage or per mille (‰). Micronucleus Frequency=(Number of Micronucleated Cells / Total Number of Binucleated Cells)×1000

- **Comparison to Controls:** The frequency of micronucleated cells in the treated groups is compared to that in the negative control group. This helps determine if there is a significant increase in micronuclei formation due to the test substance.
- **Statistical Tests:** Common statistical tests used include:

  - **Chi-Square Test:** Used to compare the frequencies of micronucleated cells between groups.
  - **Fisher's Exact Test:** Used when sample sizes are small, providing an exact p-value for comparison.
  - **Analysis of Variance (ANOVA):** Used to compare mean micronucleus frequencies among multiple groups, followed by post hoc tests (e.g., Dunnett's test) to identify specific group differences.

- **Dose-Response Analysis:** Statistical methods such as regression analysis can be used to assess the relationship between the dose of the test substance and the frequency of micronuclei. This helps establish a dose-response relationship.

4. Interpretation Criteria:

- **Positive Result:** A statistically significant increase in micronucleus frequency in one or more treatment groups compared to the negative control, indicating genotoxic potential.
- **Negative Result:** No significant increase in micronucleus frequency compared to the negative control, suggesting the substance is not

genotoxic.

- **Equivocal Result:** Marginal or inconsistent results may require additional testing or repeat experiments to clarify the genotoxic potential.

5. Correlation with Cytotoxicity:

- **Cytotoxicity Assessment:** The level of cytotoxicity in the treated cells is assessed, typically by measuring the relative cell counts, mitotic index, or nuclear division index. High cytotoxicity can confound the interpretation of micronucleus data.
- **Adjustment for Cytotoxicity:** Data may be adjusted to account for cytotoxicity, ensuring that the observed increase in micronuclei is not simply due to a reduction in cell viability.

Case Studies and Examples:
Example 1: Pharmaceutical Testing
Objective: Evaluate the genotoxic potential of a new drug candidate.
Methods:

- Human lymphocytes were exposed to the drug at various concentrations (0.1, 1, 10, and 100 µM) for 24 hours.
- Both with and without S9 metabolic activation.
- Cytochalasin B was added post-exposure to block cytokinesis.

Results:

- **Negative Control:** 5 micronucleated cells per 1000 binucleated cells.
- **Positive Control:** 150 micronucleated cells per 1000 binucleated cells.
- **Drug Treatment:** 10, 15, 30, and 80 micronucleated cells per 1000 binucleated cells for increasing concentrations.

Analysis:

- Statistically significant increase in micronucleated cells at 10 µM and higher concentrations compared to the negative control ($p < 0.05$).
- Dose-response relationship observed.

- Conclusion: The drug candidate exhibits genotoxic potential at higher concentrations.

Example 2: Chemical Safety Assessment
Objective: Assess the genotoxicity of an industrial solvent.
Methods:

- CHO cells were exposed to the solvent at 0.5, 1, 2, and 5% concentrations for 24 hours.
- S9 metabolic activation included.

Results:

- **Negative Control:** 8 micronucleated cells per 1000 binucleated cells.
- **Positive Control:** 120 micronucleated cells per 1000 binucleated cells.
- **Solvent Treatment:** 10, 12, 18, and 50 micronucleated cells per 1000 binucleated cells.

Analysis:

- Statistically significant increase in micronucleated cells at 2% and higher concentrations compared to the negative control ($p < 0.01$).
- High cytotoxicity observed at 5% concentration, requiring adjustment in data interpretation.
- Conclusion: The solvent has genotoxic effects, particularly after metabolic activation.

Example 3: Environmental Monitoring
Objective: Monitor river water for genotoxic pollutants.
Methods:

- Human lymphocytes were exposed to water samples from different sites along the river.
- Exposure for 24 hours, no metabolic activation.

Results:

- **Upstream (Control):** 6 micronucleated cells per 1000 binucleated cells.

- **Midstream:** 20 micronucleated cells per 1000 binucleated cells.
- **Downstream:** 40 micronucleated cells per 1000 binucleated cells.

Analysis:

- Statistically significant increase in micronucleated cells midstream and downstream compared to upstream ($p < 0.05$ and $p < 0.01$, respectively).
- Indicates the presence of genotoxic pollutants in the river.
- Conclusion: Further investigation and regulatory action needed to address pollution sources.

Testing Strategies:

The **in vivo micronucleus test** is used to evaluate the genotoxic potential of substances by detecting the formation of micronuclei in the bone marrow or peripheral blood erythrocytes of treated animals. Micronuclei contain chromosome fragments or whole chromosomes that were not incorporated into the daughter nuclei during cell division. This test is essential for confirming genotoxicity findings from in vitro tests and assessing the genotoxic potential of substances in a living organism.

Strategies for Conducting In Vivo Micronucleus Tests:

1. **Selection of Test Animals:**

   - **Common Species:** Mice and rats are the most commonly used species due to their well-characterized genetics and ease of handling.
   - **Age and Sex:** Young adult animals, typically 6-10 weeks old, of both sexes are used to ensure robust data and to identify any sex-specific effects.

2. **Dosing Regimen:**

   - **Route of Administration:** The test substance can be administered via various routes, including oral (gavage), intraperitoneal, intravenous, or inhalation, depending on the intended human exposure route.
   - **Dose Levels:** At least three dose levels are used, including a high dose that induces observable signs of toxicity but not excessive mortality,

and two lower doses. A negative control (vehicle only) and a positive control (known genotoxic agent) are also included.

- **Treatment Duration:** Single-dose administration or repeated doses (typically over 2-3 days) can be used depending on the study design and the expected mode of action of the test substance.

3. **Sample Collection:**

- **Bone Marrow Sampling:** Bone marrow cells are collected from the femurs or tibiae of sacrificed animals 24-48 hours after the final treatment. Bone marrow is the preferred tissue due to its high mitotic activity and sensitivity to genotoxic agents.
- **Peripheral Blood Sampling:** Alternatively, peripheral blood samples can be collected via tail vein or cardiac puncture, particularly in species where repeated sampling is feasible without euthanizing the animals.

4. **Slide Preparation and Staining:**

- **Slide Preparation:** Bone marrow or peripheral blood cells are spread onto microscope slides and air-dried. Slides are fixed in methanol or another suitable fixative.
- **Staining:** Slides are stained with a DNA-specific stain such as Giemsa or acridine orange to differentiate micronuclei from other cellular components.

5. **Microscopic Examination:**

- **Scoring Micronuclei:** At least 2000 polychromatic erythrocytes (PCEs) per animal are scored for the presence of micronuclei. Micronucleated PCEs (MnPCEs) are identified by their small, extranuclear bodies stained similarly to the main nucleus.
- **Ratio of PCEs to Normochromatic Erythrocytes (NCEs):** The ratio of PCEs to NCEs is also recorded to assess bone marrow toxicity and the impact of the test substance on erythropoiesis.

6. **Data Analysis:**

- ◦ **Micronucleus Frequency:** The frequency of MnPCEs is calculated for each treatment group and compared to the control groups.
- ◦ **Statistical Analysis:** Statistical tests (e.g., chi-square test, Fisher's exact test) are used to determine the significance of the increase in micronucleated cells compared to the control.
- ◦ **Dose-Response Relationship:** Analyzing the dose-response relationship helps in determining the genotoxic potential and the lowest observed adverse effect level (LOAEL).

7. **Interpretation of Results:**

- ◦ **Positive Result:** A statistically significant increase in the frequency of MnPCEs compared to the negative control indicates genotoxic potential.
- ◦ **Negative Result:** No significant increase in MnPCEs compared to the negative control suggests the substance is not genotoxic.
- ◦ **Equivocal Result:** Marginal or inconsistent results may require additional testing or repeat experiments to clarify the genotoxic potential.

Case Studies and Examples:
Example 1: Pharmaceutical Testing
Objective: Evaluate the genotoxic potential of a new drug candidate.
Methods:

- **Species:** Mice (both sexes).
- **Doses:** 0 (control), 50, 100, and 200 mg/kg.
- **Route:** Oral gavage.
- **Sampling:** Bone marrow cells collected 24 hours after the final dose.
- **Positive Control:** Cyclophosphamide (known genotoxic agent).

Results:

- **Negative Control:** 2 MnPCEs per 2000 PCEs.
- **Positive Control:** 40 MnPCEs per 2000 PCEs.
- **Drug Treatment:** 3, 5, 15, and 30 MnPCEs per 2000 PCEs for increasing doses.

Analysis:

- Statistically significant increase in MnPCEs at 100 mg/kg and higher doses compared to the negative control (p < 0.05).
- Conclusion: The drug candidate exhibits genotoxic potential at higher doses.

Example 2: Chemical Safety Assessment
Objective: Assess the genotoxicity of an industrial chemical.
Methods:

- **Species:** Rats (both sexes).
- **Doses:** 0 (control), 10, 50, and 100 mg/kg.
- **Route:** Intraperitoneal injection.
- **Sampling:** Peripheral blood samples collected 48 hours after the final dose.
- **Positive Control:** Mitomycin C (known genotoxic agent).

Results:

- **Negative Control:** 1 MnPCE per 2000 PCEs.
- **Positive Control:** 35 MnPCEs per 2000 PCEs.
- **Chemical Treatment:** 2, 4, 10, and 20 MnPCEs per 2000 PCEs for increasing doses.

Analysis:

- Statistically significant increase in MnPCEs at 50 mg/kg and higher doses compared to the negative control (p < 0.01).
- Conclusion: The industrial chemical has genotoxic effects, particularly at higher doses.

Example 3: Environmental Monitoring
Objective: Monitor the genotoxic potential of water samples from a contaminated site.
Methods:

- **Species:** Mice (both sexes).

- **Doses:** 0 (control), 1, 10, and 100 μL/L of water sample.
- **Route:** Oral gavage.
- **Sampling:** Bone marrow cells collected 24 hours after the final dose.
- **Positive Control:** Ethyl methanesulfonate (EMS, known genotoxic agent).

Results:

- **Negative Control:** 1 MnPCE per 2000 PCEs.
- **Positive Control:** 45 MnPCEs per 2000 PCEs.
- **Water Sample Treatment:** 2, 5, 25, and 50 MnPCEs per 2000 PCEs for increasing concentrations.

Analysis:

- Statistically significant increase in MnPCEs at 10 μL/L and higher concentrations compared to the negative control ($p < 0.01$).
- Conclusion: The water samples contain genotoxic pollutants.

Evaluation of Genotoxic Potential:

Evaluating the **genotoxic potential** of substances using the in vivo micronucleus test involves several key steps to ensure that the findings are accurate, reliable, and meaningful. This evaluation helps determine if a substance can cause genetic damage, which is critical for risk assessment and regulatory decision-making.

1. Selection of Appropriate Test System:

- **Animal Model:** Choose a suitable animal model, typically mice or rats, known for their relevance to human biology and established use in genotoxicity testing.
- **Test Substance Doses:** Select at least three dose levels of the test substance, including a high dose that causes observable signs of toxicity but not excessive mortality, and two lower doses to assess dose-response relationships.

2. Administration of Test Substance:

- **Route of Exposure:** Administer the test substance via a route relevant to human exposure (oral, intraperitoneal, intravenous, or inhalation).
- **Dosing Schedule:** Determine the appropriate dosing schedule (single dose or repeated doses) based on the substance's expected mode of action and metabolism.

3. Sample Collection and Preparation:

- **Timing:** Collect bone marrow or peripheral blood samples at optimal time points post-exposure, typically 24-48 hours after the final dose, to capture cells in the mitotic cycle.
- **Slide Preparation:** Prepare microscope slides with fixed and stained cells, ensuring proper handling to maintain sample integrity.

4. Microscopic Examination:

- **Scoring Micronuclei:** Count the number of micronuclei in a sufficient number of polychromatic erythrocytes (PCEs), typically at least 2000 PCEs per animal, to ensure statistical robustness.
- **PCE/NCE Ratio:** Record the ratio of PCEs to normochromatic erythrocytes (NCEs) to assess cytotoxicity and bone marrow suppression.

5. Data Analysis:

- **Micronucleus Frequency Calculation:** Calculate the frequency of micronucleated PCEs (MnPCEs) for each treatment group. Micronucleus Frequency=(Number of MnPCEs / Total Number of PCEs)×1000
- **Statistical Comparison:** Use statistical tests such as chi-square, Fisher's exact test, or ANOVA to compare the frequency of MnPCEs between the treatment groups and the control group. Determine the significance level (e.g., $p < 0.05$) for detecting significant differences.

6. Interpretation of Results:

- **Positive Result:** A statistically significant increase in MnPCE frequency in one or more treatment groups compared to the negative control indicates genotoxic potential.

- **Negative Result:** No significant increase in MnPCE frequency compared to the negative control suggests the substance is not genotoxic.
- **Equivocal Result:** Marginal or inconsistent results may require further testing or repeat experiments to clarify the genotoxic potential.
- **Dose-Response Relationship:** A clear dose-response relationship strengthens the evidence for genotoxicity, while the absence of such a relationship requires careful interpretation.

Case Studies and Examples:
Case Study 1: Pharmaceutical Testing
Objective: Evaluate the genotoxic potential of a new drug candidate.
Methods:

- **Species:** Mice (both sexes).
- **Doses:** 0 (control), 50, 100, and 200 mg/kg.
- **Route:** Oral gavage.
- **Sampling:** Bone marrow cells collected 24 hours after the final dose.
- **Positive Control:** Cyclophosphamide (known genotoxic agent).

Results:

- **Negative Control:** 2 MnPCEs per 2000 PCEs.
- **Positive Control:** 40 MnPCEs per 2000 PCEs.
- **Drug Treatment:** 3, 5, 15, and 30 MnPCEs per 2000 PCEs for increasing doses.

Analysis:

- Statistically significant increase in MnPCEs at 100 mg/kg and higher doses compared to the negative control ($p < 0.05$).
- **Conclusion:** The drug candidate exhibits genotoxic potential at higher doses.

Case Study 2: Chemical Safety Assessment
Objective: Assess the genotoxicity of an industrial chemical.
Methods:

- **Species:** Rats (both sexes).

- **Doses:** 0 (control), 10, 50, and 100 mg/kg.
- **Route:** Intraperitoneal injection.
- **Sampling:** Peripheral blood samples collected 48 hours after the final dose.
- **Positive Control:** Mitomycin C (known genotoxic agent).

Results:

- **Negative Control:** 1 MnPCE per 2000 PCEs.
- **Positive Control:** 35 MnPCEs per 2000 PCEs.
- **Chemical Treatment:** 2, 4, 10, and 20 MnPCEs per 2000 PCEs for increasing doses.

Analysis:

- Statistically significant increase in MnPCEs at 50 mg/kg and higher doses compared to the negative control ($p < 0.01$).
- **Conclusion:** The industrial chemical has genotoxic effects, particularly at higher doses.

Case Study 3: Environmental Monitoring
Objective: Monitor the genotoxic potential of water samples from a contaminated site.
Methods:

- **Species:** Mice (both sexes).
- **Doses:** 0 (control), 1, 10, and 100 µL/L of water sample.
- **Route:** Oral gavage.
- **Sampling:** Bone marrow cells collected 24 hours after the final dose.
- **Positive Control:** Ethyl methanesulfonate (EMS, known genotoxic agent).

Results:

- **Negative Control:** 1 MnPCE per 2000 PCEs.
- **Positive Control:** 45 MnPCEs per 2000 PCEs.
- **Water Sample Treatment:** 2, 5, 25, and 50 MnPCEs per 2000 PCEs for increasing concentrations.

Analysis:

- Statistically significant increase in MnPCEs at 10 µL/L and higher concentrations compared to the negative control ($p < 0.01$).
- **Conclusion:** The water samples contain genotoxic pollutants.

3.2.4 Chromosomal Aberrations Studies

Techniques and Methodologies:
Chromosomal aberrations studies are essential for identifying substances that can cause structural changes in chromosomes, which may lead to genetic mutations and cancer. These studies typically involve both in vitro and in vivo methodologies to detect chromosomal damage, such as breaks, deletions, translocations, and other structural alterations.
Techniques Used in Chromosomal Aberrations Studies:

1. **In Vitro Chromosomal Aberration Test:**

   - **Cell Culture:** Commonly used cell lines include Chinese hamster ovary (CHO) cells, human lymphocytes, and V79 cells. Cells are cultured in appropriate media and incubated until they reach the desired confluency.
   - **Exposure to Test Substance:** Cells are exposed to various concentrations of the test substance, with and without metabolic activation (using an S9 mix), for a specified duration (typically 3-6 hours for short-term exposure or 20-24 hours for continuous exposure).
   - **Mitotic Arrest:** Colcemid or colchicine is added to the culture 1-2 hours before harvesting to arrest cells in metaphase, facilitating the observation of chromosomes.
   - **Cell Harvesting:** Cells are harvested, subjected to hypotonic treatment to swell the cells, and then fixed using a methanol-acetic acid mixture.
   - **Slide Preparation:** Fixed cells are dropped onto clean microscope slides and air-dried. The slides are stained using Giemsa or another suitable chromosomal stain.

- ○ **Microscopic Examination:** Metaphase cells are examined under a microscope, and chromosomal aberrations are scored. Types of aberrations include chromatid and chromosome breaks, gaps, exchanges, and rings.

2. **In Vivo Chromosomal Aberration Test:**

- ○ **Animal Selection:** Rodents (mice or rats) are commonly used. Animals are selected based on age and sex, typically young adults.
- ○ **Dosing Regimen:** The test substance is administered via a relevant route (oral, intraperitoneal, intravenous, etc.). Dosing can be single or repeated, depending on the study design.
- ○ **Sample Collection:** Bone marrow cells are typically collected from the femurs of sacrificed animals 24-48 hours after the final dose.
- ○ **Slide Preparation:** Bone marrow cells are prepared similarly to in vitro studies, with hypotonic treatment, fixation, and staining.
- ○ **Microscopic Examination:** Metaphase spreads are examined, and chromosomal aberrations are scored.

Case Studies and Implications:
Several **case studies** illustrate the implications of chromosomal aberrations detected through these studies:
Case Study 1: Pharmaceutical Development
Objective: Evaluate the genotoxic potential of a new anticancer drug.
Methods:

- **In Vitro Study:** Human lymphocytes were exposed to the drug at concentrations of 0.1, 1, and 10 µM, both with and without S9 metabolic activation, for 4 hours. Colcemid was added before harvesting, and cells were fixed and stained.
- **In Vivo Study:** Mice were administered the drug at doses of 10, 50, and 100 mg/kg via intraperitoneal injection. Bone marrow cells were collected 24 hours after dosing.

Results:

- **In Vitro:** Significant increase in chromosomal aberrations (chromatid breaks, dicentric chromosomes) at 1 and 10 µM, particularly with S9 activation.

- **In Vivo:** Dose-dependent increase in chromosomal aberrations in bone marrow cells, with the highest dose showing the most significant effects.

Implications:

- The drug candidate was found to have genotoxic potential, necessitating further modification and testing to mitigate these effects before proceeding with clinical trials.

Case Study 2: Industrial Chemical Assessment

Objective: Assess the genotoxicity of a new industrial solvent.

Methods:

- **In Vitro Study:** CHO cells were exposed to the solvent at concentrations of 0.01, 0.1, and 1% for 24 hours. Cells were harvested, fixed, and stained.
- **In Vivo Study:** Rats were dosed with the solvent at 50, 100, and 200 mg/kg orally for 3 consecutive days. Bone marrow cells were collected 48 hours after the last dose.

Results:

- **In Vitro:** Significant increase in chromosomal aberrations (chromosome breaks, translocations) at 0.1% and 1%.
- **In Vivo:** Significant increase in chromosomal aberrations in bone marrow cells at 100 and 200 mg/kg.

Implications:

- The solvent was found to be genotoxic, prompting the implementation of safety measures and exposure limits to protect workers.

Case Study 3: Environmental Monitoring

Objective: Monitor the genotoxic potential of water samples from an industrial area.

Methods:

- **In Vitro Study:** Human lymphocytes were exposed to water samples at different concentrations (1, 10, and 100 μL/L) for 24 hours. Colcemid was added before harvesting, and cells were fixed and stained.
- **In Vivo Study:** Mice were given water samples at concentrations of 10, 50, and 100 μL/L via oral gavage for 7 days. Bone marrow cells were collected 24 hours after the last dose.

Results:

- **In Vitro:** Significant increase in chromosomal aberrations (gaps, breaks, and rings) at 10 and 100 μL/L.
- **In Vivo:** Dose-dependent increase in chromosomal aberrations in bone marrow cells at all tested concentrations.

Implications:

- The presence of genotoxic pollutants in the water samples was confirmed, necessitating regulatory action to clean up the contaminated site and prevent further environmental and public health risks.

3.3 Carcinogenicity Studies

3.3.1 In Vivo Carcinogenicity Studies

Long-term Testing Methods:

In vivo carcinogenicity studies are designed to evaluate the potential of substances to induce cancer in animals over a long period, typically the majority of the animal's lifespan. These studies are critical for understanding the carcinogenic risk of pharmaceuticals, chemicals, and environmental pollutants. The methods for conducting long-term in vivo carcinogenicity studies include several key steps to ensure the reliability and relevance of the results.

Methods for Conducting Long-term In Vivo Carcinogenicity Studies:

1. **Selection of Test Animals:**

   - **Species:** Commonly used species include rats and mice due to their well-characterized genetics, lifespan, and susceptibility to tumor formation.
   - **Age and Sex:** Young adult animals, typically 6-8 weeks old, of both sexes are used to ensure a broad understanding of the carcinogenic potential.

2. **Dosing Regimen:**

   - **Route of Administration:** The test substance is administered via a relevant route based on expected human exposure (oral, inhalation, dermal, etc.).
   - **Dose Levels:** At least three dose levels are used, including a high dose that induces observable toxicity but not excessive mortality, and two lower doses to assess dose-response relationships. A control group receiving only the vehicle is also included.
   - **Duration:** The study typically lasts for 18-24 months in rats and 24-30 months in mice, covering the majority of the animals' lifespan.

3. **Study Design:**

   - **Randomization:** Animals are randomly assigned to control and treatment groups to minimize bias.
   - **Environmental Conditions:** Animals are housed under controlled environmental conditions (temperature, humidity, light/dark cycle) to reduce variability.
   - **Health Monitoring:** Animals are observed daily for clinical signs of toxicity, changes in behavior, and overall health. Body weight and food consumption are recorded regularly.

4. **Necropsy and Histopathological Examination:**

   - **Necropsy:** At the end of the study, or when animals exhibit signs of severe illness, they are humanely euthanized. A comprehensive necropsy is conducted to examine all major organs and tissues for signs of tumors or other pathological changes.

- ◦ **Histopathology:** Tissues are fixed, processed, and stained for microscopic examination. All suspected tumors and a representative sample of non-tumorous tissues are examined histologically to identify the type, frequency, and malignancy of tumors.

5. **Data Analysis:**

- ◦ **Tumor Incidence:** The number and types of tumors are recorded for each group. Tumor incidence rates are calculated and compared between control and treated groups.
- ◦ **Statistical Analysis:** Statistical tests such as Fisher's exact test, chi-square test, and survival-adjusted analyses (e.g., Kaplan-Meier analysis) are used to determine the significance of differences in tumor incidence.
- ◦ **Dose-Response Relationship:** Analysis of the dose-response relationship helps establish the carcinogenic potential and the lowest observed effect level (LOEL).

Case Studies and Examples:
Example 1: Pharmaceutical Carcinogenicity Study
Objective: Evaluate the long-term carcinogenic potential of a new drug.
Methods:

- **Species:** Rats (both sexes).
- **Doses:** 0 (control), 10, 50, and 100 mg/kg/day.
- **Route:** Oral gavage.
- **Duration:** 24 months.
- **Health Monitoring:** Regular monitoring of clinical signs, body weight, and food consumption.
- **Necropsy:** Comprehensive necropsy and histopathological examination of all major organs and tissues.

Results:

- **Control Group:** No significant tumors observed.
- **Low Dose:** No significant increase in tumor incidence.
- **Mid Dose:** Slight increase in liver adenomas.

- **High Dose:** Significant increase in liver adenomas and carcinomas (p < 0.01).

Implications:

- The drug showed a dose-dependent increase in liver tumors, indicating potential carcinogenicity at high doses. Further investigations were conducted to understand the mechanism and to establish safe exposure levels for humans.

Example 2: Industrial Chemical Carcinogenicity Study
Objective: Assess the carcinogenicity of a widely used industrial solvent.
Methods:

- **Species:** Mice (both sexes).
- **Doses:** 0 (control), 50, 100, and 200 mg/kg/day.
- **Route:** Inhalation exposure.
- **Duration:** 24 months.
- **Health Monitoring:** Daily observations and regular recording of body weight and food consumption.
- **Necropsy:** Full necropsy and histopathological examination of respiratory tissues and other major organs.

Results:

- **Control Group:** Few sporadic tumors typical of the species.
- **Low Dose:** No significant increase in tumor incidence.
- **Mid Dose:** Increase in benign lung tumors.
- **High Dose:** Significant increase in malignant lung tumors and nasal cavity carcinomas (p < 0.05).

Implications:

- The solvent was found to induce respiratory tract tumors, necessitating stricter occupational exposure limits and safety measures to protect workers.

Example 3: Environmental Carcinogenicity Study

Objective: Evaluate the long-term carcinogenic effects of a pesticide used in agriculture.

Methods:

- **Species:** Rats (both sexes).
- **Doses:** 0 (control), 5, 25, and 100 ppm in feed.
- **Route:** Oral ingestion through diet.
- **Duration:** 24 months.
- **Health Monitoring:** Daily observations, body weight, and food consumption monitoring.
- **Necropsy:** Comprehensive necropsy and histopathological examination of all major organs and tissues.

Results:

- **Control Group:** Baseline tumor incidence typical of the species.
- **Low Dose:** No significant increase in tumor incidence.
- **Mid Dose:** Increased incidence of kidney adenomas.
- **High Dose:** Significant increase in kidney adenomas and carcinomas ($p < 0.05$).

Implications:

- The pesticide showed a dose-dependent increase in kidney tumors, indicating a carcinogenic risk. Regulatory agencies reviewed and adjusted the acceptable daily intake levels for the pesticide to ensure consumer safety.

IV

Investigational New Drug (IND) Enabling Studies

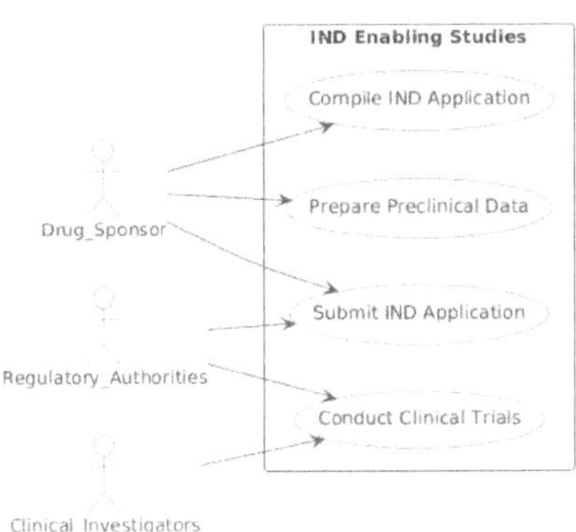

4.1 Definition of IND

4.1.1 Importance of IND
Role in Drug Development:

The **Investigational New Drug (IND)** application is a critical component in the drug development process. It serves as a request for authorization from regulatory agencies to administer an investigational drug to humans. The primary regulatory agency overseeing IND applications in the United States is the Food and Drug Administration (FDA). Understanding the importance of IND in the drug development process is essential for ensuring the safe and effective development of new pharmaceuticals.

Importance of IND in the Drug Development Process:

1. **Regulatory Oversight:**

   ○ The IND application ensures that regulatory agencies have oversight over the initial stages of clinical testing in humans. This oversight is crucial for protecting the safety and rights of participants in clinical trials.
   ○ Regulatory agencies review the IND to ensure that the proposed clinical trials are scientifically sound and that the potential benefits justify the risks.

2. **Safety and Ethical Considerations:**

   ○ The IND process involves a thorough evaluation of preclinical data, including toxicology, pharmacology, and safety studies conducted in animal models. This data is reviewed to ensure that the investigational drug is reasonably safe for initial testing in humans.
   ○ Ethical considerations, such as informed consent and the protection of vulnerable populations, are also addressed in the IND application. This ensures that clinical trials are conducted in compliance with ethical standards and guidelines.

3. **Clinical Trial Design:**

   ○ The IND application outlines the proposed clinical trial protocols, including study design, patient population, dosing regimens, and endpoints. This detailed information allows regulatory agencies to assess the scientific validity and feasibility of the clinical trials.
   ○ The application also includes information on the qualifications of the investigators and the facilities where the trials will be conducted, ensuring that the trials are carried out by competent professionals in suitable environments.

4. **Data Collection and Analysis:**

   - The IND process establishes a framework for systematic data collection and analysis during clinical trials. This framework includes protocols for monitoring patient safety, managing adverse events, and ensuring data integrity.
   - Regulatory agencies review the proposed methods for data collection and analysis to ensure that they are robust and capable of generating reliable and interpretable results.

5. **Risk Management:**

   - The IND application requires the submission of a risk management plan, which outlines strategies for identifying, assessing, and mitigating potential risks associated with the investigational drug.
   - This plan includes measures for monitoring and managing adverse events, as well as protocols for stopping the trial if safety concerns arise.

6. **Facilitating Communication:**

   - The IND process facilitates communication between the drug sponsor and regulatory agencies. This communication ensures that any concerns or questions raised by the regulatory agencies are addressed promptly and thoroughly.
   - Regular updates and amendments to the IND application may be required as new data becomes available or as the clinical trials progress.

7. **Pathway to Market Approval:**

   - Obtaining an IND is the first step in the pathway to market approval for a new drug. Successful completion of the clinical trials outlined in the IND application can lead to the submission of a New Drug Application (NDA) or Biologics License Application (BLA).
   - The data collected during the IND phase forms the basis for the NDA or BLA, which regulatory agencies review to determine whether the drug is safe, effective, and of high quality for commercial distribution.

Example 1: Oncology Drug Development
Objective: Development of a new targeted therapy for cancer.
Process:

- **Preclinical Studies:** Conducted extensive in vitro and in vivo studies to evaluate the drug's mechanism of action, efficacy, and safety in animal models.
- **IND Submission:** Compiled preclinical data and submitted an IND application to the FDA, outlining the proposed phase I clinical trial in patients with advanced cancers.
- **FDA Review:** The FDA reviewed the IND application, focusing on the safety data, trial design, and risk management plan.
- **Approval and Clinical Trials:** The IND was approved, allowing the sponsor to initiate the clinical trial. Data from the trial provided valuable insights into the drug's pharmacokinetics, safety profile, and preliminary efficacy.

Outcome:

- The successful completion of phase I trials led to subsequent phase II and III trials, ultimately resulting in the drug's approval for the treatment of specific cancer types.

Example 2: Rare Disease Therapy
Objective: Development of a gene therapy for a rare genetic disorder.
Process:

- **Preclinical Studies:** Conducted preclinical studies to demonstrate the safety and efficacy of the gene therapy vector in animal models.
- **IND Submission:** Submitted an IND application, including detailed information on the manufacturing process, quality control, and clinical trial design.
- **FDA Review:** The FDA evaluated the IND, paying particular attention to the innovative nature of the therapy and the ethical considerations for testing in a small patient population.
- **Approval and Clinical Trials:** The IND was approved, allowing the sponsor to begin clinical trials in patients with the rare genetic disorder. The trials were designed to assess the safety, tolerability, and preliminary

efficacy of the gene therapy.

Outcome:

- Positive results from the clinical trials supported the submission of a Biologics License Application (BLA), leading to the approval of the gene therapy for treating the rare genetic disorder.

4.1 Definition of IND
4.1.1 Importance of IND
Regulatory Significance:

The **Investigational New Drug (IND)** application holds significant regulatory importance as it is the key mechanism through which new drugs are authorized for clinical testing in humans. The submission of an IND is a critical regulatory milestone that ensures the safety, efficacy, and ethical standards of clinical trials. The regulatory significance of IND submissions includes:

1. Ensuring Safety and Ethical Standards:

- **Regulatory Oversight:** Regulatory agencies such as the FDA in the United States ensure that clinical trials are conducted safely and ethically. The IND submission includes detailed information on preclinical studies, ensuring that the investigational drug is reasonably safe for initial human testing.
- **Ethical Compliance:** The IND process mandates adherence to ethical standards, including informed consent, protection of vulnerable populations, and Institutional Review Board (IRB) approval. This ensures that participants' rights and well-being are safeguarded.

2. Scientific Rigor:

- **Review of Scientific Data:** The IND submission includes comprehensive preclinical data, including pharmacology, toxicology, and pharmacokinetics studies. Regulatory agencies review this data to ensure that the investigational drug has a sound scientific basis for proceeding to human trials.
- **Study Design and Methodology:** The IND outlines the clinical trial protocols, including study design, endpoints, and statistical analysis

plans. This ensures that the trials are scientifically rigorous and capable of generating reliable data.

3. Facilitating Drug Development:

- **Early Interaction with Regulators:** Submitting an IND allows sponsors to engage with regulatory agencies early in the drug development process. This interaction can provide valuable guidance on study design, regulatory requirements, and potential challenges, facilitating a smoother development pathway.
- **Pathway to Market Approval:** Successful completion of IND-authorized clinical trials is a prerequisite for submitting a New Drug Application (NDA) or Biologics License Application (BLA). The data collected during the IND phase forms the foundation for these submissions, which are necessary for market approval.

4. Risk Management:

- **Safety Monitoring:** The IND process includes a framework for monitoring patient safety, managing adverse events, and ensuring data integrity. This is crucial for identifying and mitigating risks associated with the investigational drug.
- **Risk-Benefit Assessment:** Regulatory agencies assess the potential benefits of the investigational drug against its risks. This ensures that only those drugs with a favorable risk-benefit profile proceed to further clinical development.

5. Regulatory Compliance:

- **Legal Authorization:** An IND provides legal authorization to administer an investigational drug to humans. This is essential for compliance with regulatory requirements and for protecting public health.
- **Documentation and Transparency:** The IND submission includes detailed documentation of the drug's development, manufacturing, and proposed clinical trials. This transparency is crucial for regulatory oversight and accountability.

4.1 Definition of IND

4.1.2 Industry Perspective on IND

Key Considerations for Submissions:

Preparing an **Investigational New Drug (IND)** submission is a complex and critical task in the drug development process. It requires meticulous planning, detailed documentation, and strategic considerations to ensure a successful regulatory review. From the industry perspective, key considerations for preparing IND submissions include:

1. Comprehensive Preclinical Data:

- **Safety and Toxicology Studies:**

  - Conduct thorough preclinical safety and toxicology studies to demonstrate that the investigational drug is reasonably safe for initial human testing. This includes acute, sub-chronic, and chronic toxicity studies in relevant animal models.
  - Include data on the potential for genotoxicity, carcinogenicity, reproductive and developmental toxicity.

- **Pharmacokinetics and Pharmacodynamics:**

  - Provide detailed information on the drug's pharmacokinetics (absorption, distribution, metabolism, and excretion) and pharmacodynamics (mechanism of action, dose-response relationships).
  - Use in vitro and in vivo studies to characterize the drug's behavior in biological systems.

2. Detailed Chemistry, Manufacturing, and Controls (CMC):

- **Drug Substance and Drug Product:**

  - Include comprehensive information on the chemical composition, structure, and properties of the drug substance and drug product.
  - Describe the formulation, stability, and purity of the drug product, including methods used to ensure consistency and quality.

- **Manufacturing Process:**

- ○ Provide a detailed description of the manufacturing process, including raw materials, equipment, and controls used to produce the drug substance and drug product.
- ○ Outline the quality control measures and specifications to ensure product consistency and safety.

3. Clinical Trial Protocols:

- **Study Design and Objectives:**

  - ○ Develop robust clinical trial protocols that clearly outline the study design, objectives, endpoints, and statistical analysis plan.
  - ○ Ensure the study design is scientifically sound and capable of generating meaningful data on safety and efficacy.

- **Patient Population and Inclusion/Exclusion Criteria:**

  - ○ Define the target patient population and establish clear inclusion and exclusion criteria to ensure the selection of appropriate study participants.
  - ○ Consider the potential impact of demographic factors such as age, sex, race, and comorbidities on the study outcomes.

- **Dosing and Administration:**

  - ○ Determine the initial dosing regimen based on preclinical data and pharmacokinetic modeling.
  - ○ Include provisions for dose escalation, de-escalation, and stopping rules to manage potential safety concerns.

4. Safety Monitoring and Risk Management:

- **Adverse Event Reporting:**

  - ○ Establish a comprehensive plan for monitoring, documenting, and reporting adverse events during the clinical trial.
  - ○ Include procedures for assessing the severity, causality, and frequency of adverse events.

- **Risk Mitigation Strategies:**

  - Develop risk mitigation strategies to address potential safety concerns identified in preclinical studies.
  - Implement measures such as patient monitoring, safety check-ins, and predefined criteria for halting the study if necessary.

5. Regulatory Compliance and Ethical Considerations:

- **Good Clinical Practice (GCP):**

  - Ensure that the clinical trial design and conduct comply with Good Clinical Practice (GCP) guidelines and ethical standards.
  - Obtain Institutional Review Board (IRB) or Ethics Committee approval for the study protocol.

- **Informed Consent:**

  - Develop a clear and comprehensive informed consent document that explains the study's purpose, procedures, risks, and benefits to potential participants.
  - Ensure that participants provide voluntary and informed consent before enrollment in the study.

6. Clear and Organized Documentation:

- **Module Structure:**

  - Organize the IND submission according to the Common Technical Document (CTD) format, which includes modules for administrative information, summary documents, quality information, nonclinical study reports, and clinical study reports.
  - Ensure that each section is clearly labeled and contains all required information.

- **Writing Quality:**

- ○ Prepare high-quality, clear, and concise documents that are easy for regulatory reviewers to understand.
- ○ Include well-organized tables, figures, and appendices to support the data presented in the submission.

4.1 Definition of IND
4.1.2 Industry Perspective on IND
Case Studies from Industry:

Case studies from the industry provide valuable insights into the practical considerations and strategic planning involved in preparing successful IND submissions. These examples illustrate how companies navigate regulatory requirements, address scientific and safety concerns, and ensure the ethical conduct of clinical trials.

Case Study 1: Expedited IND for a Breakthrough Therapy

Objective: Expedite the development of a novel gene therapy for a rare and life-threatening genetic disorder.

Company: Spark Therapeutics

Key Considerations:

- **Comprehensive Preclinical Data:** The company conducted extensive preclinical studies in animal models to demonstrate the safety and efficacy of the gene therapy. The studies included toxicology, biodistribution, and long-term follow-up to assess the therapeutic potential and safety profile.
- **Detailed CMC Information:** Spark Therapeutics provided detailed descriptions of the manufacturing process, including vector production, purification, and quality control measures. The company ensured that the gene therapy product was consistent and met high-quality standards.
- **Streamlined Clinical Protocols:** The clinical trial protocol was designed with clear objectives, endpoints, and an adaptive design to allow for modifications based on interim results. This approach aimed to accelerate the collection of safety and efficacy data.
- **Risk Management:** A robust safety monitoring plan was implemented, including regular assessments, adverse event reporting, and predefined stopping rules to manage potential safety concerns. The company prioritized patient safety throughout the trial.
- **Regulatory Interactions:** Early and frequent interactions with the FDA facilitated the identification and resolution of regulatory concerns.

Spark Therapeutics engaged in pre-IND meetings and maintained open communication with regulatory authorities to expedite the review process.

Outcome:

- The IND was approved rapidly, allowing Spark Therapeutics to initiate clinical trials quickly. The expedited development process ultimately led to the successful approval of Luxturna, a groundbreaking gene therapy for patients with biallelic RPE65 mutation-associated retinal dystrophy. This case highlights the importance of strategic planning, comprehensive data, and regulatory engagement in achieving IND approval for breakthrough therapies.

Case Study 2: Oncology Drug Development
Objective: Obtain IND approval for a targeted therapy for non-small cell lung cancer (NSCLC).
Company: AstraZeneca
Key Considerations:

- **Preclinical Safety and Efficacy:** AstraZeneca conducted extensive preclinical studies, including in vitro and in vivo models, to demonstrate the drug's ability to selectively target cancer cells harboring specific genetic mutations. The studies showed promising efficacy and manageable safety profiles.
- **CMC Documentation:** Detailed information on the drug's formulation, stability, and manufacturing process was provided to ensure high-quality production. The company included data on the characterization of the active pharmaceutical ingredient (API) and the final drug product.
- **Clinical Trial Design:** The phase I clinical trial protocol was designed to evaluate the safety, tolerability, and preliminary efficacy of the drug in patients with advanced NSCLC. The trial included multiple dose levels and incorporated biomarker analysis to identify responsive patient populations.
- **Patient Safety:** AstraZeneca established a comprehensive safety monitoring plan, including regular assessments, adverse event reporting, and predefined criteria for dose modifications or discontinuation. The company prioritized patient safety and ethical conduct throughout the

trial.

- **Regulatory Compliance:** The clinical trial was designed to comply with Good Clinical Practice (GCP) guidelines and ethical standards. AstraZeneca obtained IRB approval and developed a clear informed consent process to ensure that participants were fully informed about the study's purpose, procedures, risks, and benefits.

Outcome:

- The IND was approved, allowing AstraZeneca to proceed with the phase I clinical trial. Positive results from this trial, including evidence of clinical benefit in a subset of patients, supported further clinical development. The drug, osimertinib (Tagrisso), was eventually approved for the treatment of NSCLC patients with specific EGFR mutations, demonstrating the critical role of IND submissions in advancing oncology drug development.

Case Study 3: Development of a Novel Antiviral Drug
Objective: Develop a novel antiviral drug for the treatment of chronic hepatitis C infection.
Company: Gilead Sciences
Key Considerations:

- **Preclinical Data:** Gilead Sciences conducted comprehensive preclinical studies, including antiviral efficacy assays, pharmacokinetics, and toxicology studies in relevant animal models. The data demonstrated potent antiviral activity and a favorable safety profile.
- **CMC Information:** Detailed CMC documentation was provided, including information on the synthesis, purification, and characterization of the drug substance and drug product. Stability studies were conducted to ensure the drug's integrity over time.
- **Clinical Trial Protocols:** The phase I clinical trial protocol was designed to assess the safety, tolerability, and pharmacokinetics of the drug in healthy volunteers. The protocol included dose-escalation cohorts to determine the optimal dosing regimen.
- **Risk Management:** A robust safety monitoring plan was implemented, including regular safety assessments, adverse event monitoring, and predefined criteria for dose adjustments. The company ensured that

potential risks were identified and mitigated throughout the trial.

- **Regulatory Interactions:** Gilead Sciences engaged in pre-IND meetings with the FDA to discuss the preclinical data, proposed clinical trial design, and regulatory requirements. This proactive approach facilitated a smooth IND submission and review process.

Outcome:

- The IND was approved, allowing Gilead Sciences to initiate phase I clinical trials. Positive safety and pharmacokinetic data from these trials supported the progression to phase II and III studies. The drug, sofosbuvir (Sovaldi), was eventually approved for the treatment of chronic hepatitis C infection, revolutionizing the treatment landscape and achieving high cure rates. This case underscores the importance of thorough preparation and strategic planning in successful IND submissions for antiviral drugs.

4.2 Studies Needed for IND Submission

4.2.1 List of Required Studies

Essential Studies and Protocols:

Preparing an **Investigational New Drug (IND)** submission involves a series of essential studies and protocols to demonstrate the safety, efficacy, and quality of the investigational drug. These studies provide the foundational data necessary for regulatory agencies to evaluate the potential risks and benefits of the drug for initial human testing. The essential studies required for IND submissions include:

1. Preclinical Safety Studies:

a. Acute Toxicity Studies:

- **Objective:** Assess the immediate toxic effects of a single dose of the drug.
- **Protocols:** Typically conducted in two animal species (one rodent and one non-rodent). Animals are observed for signs of toxicity and mortality for at least 14 days post-administration. The study helps determine the maximum tolerated dose (MTD).

b. Sub-chronic and Chronic Toxicity Studies:

- **Objective:** Evaluate the effects of repeated dosing over a specified period.
- **Protocols:** Sub-chronic studies usually last for 28-90 days, while chronic studies extend beyond 90 days. These studies assess multiple dose levels and include detailed clinical observations, body weight measurements, food consumption, and comprehensive pathological examinations.

c. Genotoxicity Studies:

- **Objective:** Assess the potential of the drug to cause genetic mutations and chromosomal damage.
- **Protocols:** Key tests include the Ames test (bacterial reverse mutation test), in vitro micronucleus test, and in vivo micronucleus test. These studies evaluate mutagenicity and clastogenicity to identify potential genotoxic risks.

d. Carcinogenicity Studies:

- **Objective:** Determine the potential of the drug to cause cancer over long-term exposure.
- **Protocols:** Long-term studies conducted in rodents (typically mice and rats) over their lifespan. These studies assess tumor incidence, type, and location, providing data on the carcinogenic potential of the drug.

e. Reproductive and Developmental Toxicity Studies:

- **Objective:** Assess the effects of the drug on fertility, embryonic development, and postnatal development.
- **Protocols:** Key studies include Segment I (fertility and early embryonic development), Segment II (embryo-fetal development), and Segment III (pre- and postnatal development). These studies are conducted in rodents and non-rodents to evaluate reproductive health and developmental outcomes.

2. Pharmacokinetics and Pharmacodynamics Studies:

a. Absorption, Distribution, Metabolism, and Excretion (ADME) Studies:

- **Objective:** Characterize the pharmacokinetic profile of the drug.
- **Protocols:** Conducted in multiple animal species to understand the drug's absorption, distribution, metabolism, and excretion. These studies provide critical information on bioavailability, half-life, and metabolic pathways.

b. Pharmacodynamics (PD) Studies:

- **Objective:** Evaluate the drug's biological effects and mechanism of action.
- **Protocols:** Conducted in vitro and in vivo to assess the drug's interaction with its target, dose-response relationships, and therapeutic effects. These studies help establish the pharmacological basis for the drug's efficacy.

3. Chemistry, Manufacturing, and Controls (CMC) Studies:
a. Drug Substance Characterization:

- **Objective:** Provide detailed information on the chemical composition and properties of the drug substance.
- **Protocols:** Include structural characterization, purity analysis, stability studies, and specification setting. These data ensure the drug substance is well-defined and consistent.

b. Drug Product Formulation:

- **Objective:** Develop and characterize the final drug product formulation.
- **Protocols:** Include studies on the formulation's stability, excipient compatibility, and manufacturing process. These studies ensure the drug product maintains its quality and efficacy over time.

c. Stability Studies:

- **Objective:** Determine the shelf-life and storage conditions of the drug product.
- **Protocols:** Conducted under various environmental conditions (temperature, humidity, light) to assess the drug's stability and establish expiration dates.

4. Clinical Trial Protocols:
a. Phase I Clinical Trial Protocol:

- **Objective:** Assess the safety, tolerability, pharmacokinetics, and pharmacodynamics of the drug in healthy volunteers or patients.
- **Protocols:** Include detailed study design, inclusion/exclusion criteria, dosing regimen, safety monitoring, and data analysis plans. These protocols ensure the trial is conducted ethically and scientifically.

b. Safety Monitoring and Risk Management Plan:

- **Objective:** Outline strategies for monitoring and managing adverse events during clinical trials.
- **Protocols:** Include procedures for adverse event reporting, risk mitigation measures, and predefined stopping rules. This plan ensures participant safety and regulatory compliance.

Case Studies and Examples:
Example 1: Development of an Antidiabetic Drug
Objective: Prepare an IND submission for a novel antidiabetic drug.
Preclinical Studies:

- **Acute Toxicity:** Conducted in rats and dogs, determined the MTD.
- **Sub-chronic Toxicity:** 90-day studies in rats and dogs, evaluated multiple dose levels.
- **Genotoxicity:** Ames test, in vitro micronucleus test, and in vivo micronucleus test, all showed no genotoxic effects.
- **Pharmacokinetics:** ADME studies in rats and monkeys, characterized the drug's pharmacokinetic profile.
- **CMC:** Detailed characterization of the drug substance and drug product, including stability studies.

Clinical Trial Protocol:

- **Phase I:** Designed to assess safety, tolerability, and pharmacokinetics in healthy volunteers, included dose-escalation cohorts.

Outcome:

- The comprehensive data package led to the successful submission and approval of the IND, allowing the initiation of clinical trials.

Example 2: Oncology Drug Development
Objective: IND submission for a targeted cancer therapy.
Preclinical Studies:

- **Acute Toxicity:** Conducted in mice and rats, identified the MTD.
- **Chronic Toxicity:** 6-month studies in rats and dogs, detailed clinical observations and histopathological examinations.
- **Genotoxicity:** Ames test and in vivo micronucleus test, no genotoxic effects observed.
- **Carcinogenicity:** Long-term studies in mice and rats, assessed tumor incidence.
- **Pharmacodynamics:** In vitro and in vivo studies demonstrated the drug's mechanism of action and efficacy against cancer cells.

CMC:

- Comprehensive characterization of the drug substance and product, including formulation and stability studies.

Clinical Trial Protocol:

- **Phase I:** Included patients with advanced cancers, assessed safety, tolerability, and preliminary efficacy.

Outcome:

- The IND was approved, enabling the start of clinical trials. Positive results from these trials led to further development and eventual market approval.

4.2 Studies Needed for IND Submission
4.2.1 List of Required Studies

Examples and Case Studies:

The following case studies illustrate the comprehensive set of studies required for IND submissions, showcasing the detailed planning and execution necessary to meet regulatory requirements and ensure the safety and efficacy of investigational drugs.

Case Study 1: Development of an Antidiabetic Drug

Objective: Prepare an IND submission for a novel antidiabetic drug.

Company: PharmaInnovations Inc.

Essential Studies Conducted:

1. **Preclinical Safety Studies:**

   - **Acute Toxicity:**

     - **Objective:** Determine the maximum tolerated dose (MTD).
     - **Protocol:** Conducted in rats and dogs. Single doses administered, followed by a 14-day observation period.
     - **Results:** Identified the MTD and observed dose-dependent toxicity at higher doses.

   - **Sub-chronic Toxicity:**

     - **Objective:** Evaluate the effects of repeated dosing over 90 days.
     - **Protocol:** Conducted in rats and dogs at multiple dose levels. Included daily clinical observations, body weight measurements, and food consumption monitoring.
     - **Results:** Established no observed adverse effect level (NOAEL) and identified target organs for toxicity.

   - **Genotoxicity:**

     - **Objective:** Assess the potential for genetic mutations.
     - **Protocol:** Conducted Ames test, in vitro micronucleus test, and in vivo micronucleus test.
     - **Results:** No genotoxic effects observed in any of the tests.

2. **Pharmacokinetics and Pharmacodynamics Studies:**

   - **ADME Studies:**

- **Objective:** Characterize the pharmacokinetic profile.
- **Protocol:** Conducted in rats and monkeys to assess absorption, distribution, metabolism, and excretion.
- **Results:** Detailed pharmacokinetic parameters, including bioavailability and half-life, were established.

○ **Pharmacodynamics (PD) Studies:**

- **Objective:** Evaluate the drug's mechanism of action and dose-response relationship.
- **Protocol:** In vitro and in vivo studies to assess the drug's effect on glucose levels and insulin sensitivity.
- **Results:** Demonstrated significant antidiabetic activity and identified the optimal therapeutic dose.

3. **Chemistry, Manufacturing, and Controls (CMC) Studies:**

○ **Drug Substance Characterization:**

- **Objective:** Ensure the drug substance is well-defined and consistent.
- **Protocol:** Included structural characterization, purity analysis, and stability studies.
- **Results:** Provided comprehensive data on the drug substance's chemical composition and stability.

○ **Drug Product Formulation:**

- **Objective:** Develop a stable and effective formulation.
- **Protocol:** Included studies on formulation stability, excipient compatibility, and manufacturing process.
- **Results:** Established a stable formulation with consistent quality.

4. **Clinical Trial Protocols:**

○ **Phase I Clinical Trial Protocol:**

- **Objective:** Assess the safety, tolerability, pharmacokinetics, and pharmacodynamics in healthy volunteers.
- **Protocol:** Included dose-escalation cohorts, detailed study design, inclusion/exclusion criteria, safety monitoring, and data analysis plans.
- **Results:** Designed a robust protocol to ensure ethical and scientific conduct of the trial.

Outcome:

- The comprehensive data package led to the successful submission and approval of the IND, allowing the initiation of phase I clinical trials. Positive results from these trials supported further clinical development.

Case Study 2: Oncology Drug Development
Objective: Obtain IND approval for a targeted therapy for non-small cell lung cancer (NSCLC).
Company: OncoPharma Inc.
Essential Studies Conducted:

1. **Preclinical Safety Studies:**

   - **Acute Toxicity:**

     - **Objective:** Identify the maximum tolerated dose (MTD).
     - **Protocol:** Conducted in mice and rats with single doses, followed by a 14-day observation period.
     - **Results:** Established the MTD and observed dose-dependent toxicity at higher doses.

   - **Chronic Toxicity:**

     - **Objective:** Evaluate long-term effects of repeated dosing.
     - **Protocol:** Conducted 6-month studies in rats and dogs, including daily clinical observations, body weight measurements, food consumption, and comprehensive pathological examinations.
     - **Results:** Identified target organs for toxicity and established a NOAEL.

- **Genotoxicity:**

  - **Objective:** Assess the potential for genetic mutations.
  - **Protocol:** Conducted Ames test, in vitro micronucleus test, and in vivo micronucleus test.
  - **Results:** No genotoxic effects observed.

- **Carcinogenicity:**

  - **Objective:** Determine the potential to cause cancer.
  - **Protocol:** Conducted long-term studies in mice and rats over their lifespan to assess tumor incidence and type.
  - **Results:** No significant increase in tumor incidence observed.

2. **Pharmacokinetics and Pharmacodynamics Studies:**

- **ADME Studies:**

  - **Objective:** Characterize the pharmacokinetic profile.
  - **Protocol:** Conducted in rats and monkeys to assess absorption, distribution, metabolism, and excretion.
  - **Results:** Provided detailed pharmacokinetic parameters.

- **Pharmacodynamics (PD) Studies:**

  - **Objective:** Evaluate the drug's mechanism of action and efficacy against cancer cells.
  - **Protocol:** In vitro and in vivo studies demonstrated the drug's ability to selectively target and kill cancer cells.
  - **Results:** Identified the optimal therapeutic dose and demonstrated significant anti-cancer activity.

3. **Chemistry, Manufacturing, and Controls (CMC) Studies:**

- **Drug Substance Characterization:**

  - **Objective:** Ensure the drug substance is well-defined and consistent.

- **Protocol:** Included structural characterization, purity analysis, and stability studies.
- **Results:** Provided comprehensive data on the drug substance's chemical composition and stability.

  - **Drug Product Formulation:**

    - **Objective:** Develop a stable and effective formulation.
    - **Protocol:** Included studies on formulation stability, excipient compatibility, and manufacturing process.
    - **Results:** Established a stable formulation with consistent quality.

4. **Clinical Trial Protocols:**

   - **Phase I Clinical Trial Protocol:**

     - **Objective:** Assess safety, tolerability, and preliminary efficacy in patients with advanced NSCLC.
     - **Protocol:** Included multiple dose levels and biomarker analysis to identify responsive patient populations.
     - **Results:** Designed a robust protocol to ensure ethical and scientific conduct of the trial.

Outcome:

- The IND was approved, enabling the start of phase I clinical trials. Positive results from these trials, including evidence of clinical benefit in a subset of patients, supported further clinical development. The drug, osimertinib (Tagrisso), was eventually approved for the treatment of NSCLC patients with specific EGFR mutations.

Case Study 3: Development of a Novel Antiviral Drug
Objective: Develop a novel antiviral drug for the treatment of chronic hepatitis C infection.
Company: HepaCure Pharmaceuticals
Essential Studies Conducted:

1. **Preclinical Safety Studies:**

- **Acute Toxicity:**

  - **Objective:** Determine the maximum tolerated dose (MTD).
  - **Protocol:** Conducted in rats and dogs with single doses, followed by a 14-day observation period.
  - **Results:** Identified the MTD and observed dose-dependent toxicity at higher doses.

- **Sub-chronic Toxicity:**

  - **Objective:** Evaluate the effects of repeated dosing over 90 days.
  - **Protocol:** Conducted in rats and dogs at multiple dose levels. Included daily clinical observations, body weight measurements, and food consumption monitoring.
  - **Results:** Established no observed adverse effect level (NOAEL) and identified target organs for toxicity.

- **Genotoxicity:**

  - **Objective:** Assess the potential for genetic mutations.
  - **Protocol:** Conducted Ames test, in vitro micronucleus test, and in vivo micronucleus test.
  - **Results:** No genotoxic effects observed in any of the tests.

2. **Pharmacokinetics and Pharmacodynamics Studies:**

- **ADME Studies:**

  - **Objective:** Characterize the pharmacokinetic profile.
  - **Protocol:** Conducted in rats and monkeys to assess absorption, distribution, metabolism, and excretion.
  - **Results:** Detailed pharmacokinetic parameters, including bioavailability and half-life, were established.

- **Pharmacodynamics (PD) Studies:**

  - **Objective:** Evaluate the drug's antiviral efficacy and mechanism of action.

- **Protocol:** In vitro and in vivo studies to assess the drug's effect on viral replication and immune response.
- **Results:** Demonstrated significant antiviral activity and identified the optimal therapeutic dose.

3. **Chemistry, Manufacturing, and Controls (CMC) Studies:**

   ○ **Drug Substance Characterization:**

   - **Objective:** Ensure the drug substance is well-defined and consistent.
   - **Protocol:** Included structural characterization, purity analysis, and stability studies.
   - **Results:** Provided comprehensive data on the drug substance's chemical composition and stability.

   ○ **Drug Product Formulation:**

   - **Objective:** Develop a stable and effective formulation.
   - **Protocol:** Included studies on formulation stability, excipient compatibility, and manufacturing process.
   - **Results:** Established a stable formulation with consistent quality.

4. **Clinical Trial Protocols:**

   ○ **Phase I Clinical Trial Protocol:**

   - **Objective:** Assess the safety, tolerability, pharmacokinetics, and pharmacodynamics in healthy volunteers.
   - **Protocol:** Included dose-escalation cohorts, detailed study design, inclusion/exclusion criteria, safety monitoring, and data analysis plans.
   - **Results:** Designed a robust protocol to ensure ethical and scientific conduct of the trial.

Outcome:

- The comprehensive data package led to the successful submission and approval of the IND, allowing the initiation of phase I clinical trials. Positive results from these trials supported further clinical development and eventual approval of sofosbuvir (Sovaldi), revolutionizing the treatment of chronic hepatitis C infection.

V
Safety Pharmacology Studies

Safety Pharmacology Study Process

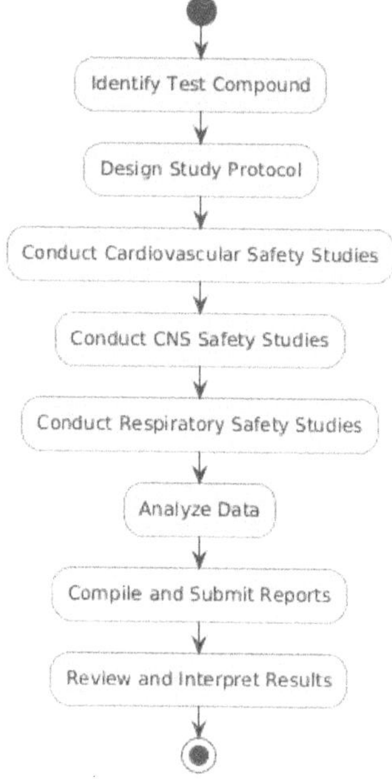

Safety pharmacology studies are essential preclinical evaluations designed to assess the potential adverse effects of a drug candidate on vital physiological functions. These studies focus on identifying any detrimental impacts on the cardiovascular, respiratory, and central nervous systems, which are crucial for ensuring the safety of new pharmaceutical compounds before they proceed to human clinical trials.

Objectives

The primary objectives of safety pharmacology studies are:

- To identify and characterize the undesirable pharmacodynamic effects of a drug candidate.
- To determine the relationship between these effects and the drug's dose or exposure levels.
- To ensure that the drug does not cause serious adverse effects that could compromise patient safety during clinical use.

Tier 1 and Tier 2 Safety Pharmacology Studies

Safety pharmacology studies are critical in the development of new pharmaceuticals, ensuring that these compounds do not have adverse effects on vital physiological functions. These studies are typically divided into **Tier 1 and Tier 2** categories based on their priority and focus areas.

Tier 1 Safety Pharmacology Studies

Tier 1 studies are the primary safety pharmacology assessments conducted early in the drug development process. These studies focus on evaluating the effects of a new drug on the most critical systems in the body:

- **Cardiovascular System**: These studies assess the impact of the drug on heart rate, blood pressure, and the electrocardiogram (ECG). The aim is to detect any potential cardiotoxic effects that could lead to arrhythmias or other cardiovascular issues.
- **Respiratory System**: These studies evaluate the drug's effects on respiratory rate, tidal volume, and overall lung function. They help identify any respiratory depression or stimulation caused by the drug.
- **Central Nervous System (CNS)**: These studies observe the drug's impact on motor activity, behavior, coordination, and reflexes. CNS safety pharmacology studies aim to detect any potential neurotoxicity or CNS

stimulation/depression.

Tier 1 safety pharmacology studies are essential for identifying major adverse effects that could pose significant risks to human health, guiding the decision on whether to proceed with further development of the drug.

Tier 2 Safety Pharmacology Studies

Tier 2 studies are conducted after Tier 1 studies and are more specialized, focusing on additional organ systems and functions that may be affected by the drug. These studies are usually performed based on findings from Tier 1 studies, preclinical toxicology, or clinical data:

- **Gastrointestinal System**: These studies assess the effects of the drug on gastrointestinal motility and secretion, identifying any potential for gastrointestinal disturbances.
- **Renal System**: These studies evaluate the drug's impact on renal function, including glomerular filtration rate, urine output, and electrolyte balance. They help detect nephrotoxicity risks.
- **Other Organ Systems**: Depending on the drug's profile and the results of earlier studies, additional assessments may be conducted on the immune system, endocrine system, or other specific organ systems.

Tier 2 safety pharmacology studies provide a more detailed understanding of the drug's safety profile, helping to ensure that any potential adverse effects on various organ systems are identified and mitigated.

5.1 Origin and Concepts of Safety Pharmacology

5.1.1 Introduction to Safety Pharmacology

Basic Principles:

Safety pharmacology is a crucial discipline within pharmacology that focuses on identifying potential undesirable pharmacodynamic effects of new chemical entities (NCEs) on physiological functions in relation to exposure in the therapeutic range and above. The primary goal is to ensure the safety of drugs by evaluating their potential effects on vital organ systems before they reach the market. Understanding the basic principles of safety pharmacology helps in designing studies that can predict adverse effects and mitigate risks associated with new drugs.

1. Core Objectives:

- **Risk Identification:** Identify potential adverse effects on vital organ systems, including the cardiovascular, respiratory, and central nervous systems, which are critical for the survival of an organism.
- **Risk Assessment:** Assess the severity and likelihood of these adverse effects occurring within the therapeutic and supra-therapeutic dose ranges.
- **Risk Management:** Develop strategies to mitigate identified risks, ensuring that any potential adverse effects are understood and managed before the drug reaches clinical trials.

2. Key Vital Organ Systems Evaluated:

- **Cardiovascular System:**

  - **Principles:** Evaluate the effects of the drug on heart rate, blood pressure, electrical conduction (QT interval), and overall cardiac function.
  - **Methods:** Common tests include electrocardiograms (ECGs) in conscious animals, telemetry studies, and in vitro assays using isolated cardiac tissues or cells.

- **Respiratory System:**

  - **Principles:** Assess the impact of the drug on respiratory rate, tidal volume, airway resistance, and overall pulmonary function.
  - **Methods:** Tests often involve plethysmography in animals to measure respiratory parameters and in vitro assays using isolated lung tissues.

- **Central Nervous System (CNS):**

  - **Principles:** Determine the effects of the drug on behavior, motor coordination, sensory function, and neurochemical pathways.
  - **Methods:** Behavioral tests in rodents (e.g., open field test, rotarod test), electrophysiological recordings, and neurochemical assays.

3. Regulatory Guidelines:

- **ICH S7A and S7B Guidelines:** International Conference on Harmonisation (ICH) provides guidelines for safety pharmacology studies, ensuring that the necessary tests are conducted to assess the safety profile of new drugs.

  - **ICH S7A:** Focuses on the core battery of safety pharmacology studies required for all new drugs, including cardiovascular, respiratory, and CNS evaluations.
  - **ICH S7B:** Provides additional guidelines for assessing the potential for delayed repolarization (QT prolongation) in the heart, a critical factor for cardiac safety.

- **Good Laboratory Practice (GLP):** Ensures that safety pharmacology studies are conducted under strict quality control standards, providing reliable and reproducible data that regulatory agencies can trust.

4. Study Design and Implementation:

- **Animal Models:** Utilize appropriate animal models that can provide relevant data on the potential effects of the drug on human physiology. Common models include rodents, dogs, and non-human primates.
- **Dose Selection:** Choose dose levels that span the therapeutic range and include supra-therapeutic doses to assess potential adverse effects at higher exposures.
- **Endpoints:** Define clear and relevant endpoints for each organ system being evaluated. This includes physiological, biochemical, and behavioral parameters.
- **Data Analysis:** Employ robust statistical methods to analyze the data, ensuring that any observed effects are statistically significant and not due to random variation.

5. Integrating Safety Pharmacology with Drug Development:

- **Early Assessment:** Integrate safety pharmacology studies early in the drug development process to identify potential safety concerns before clinical trials.
- **Iterative Process:** Safety pharmacology is an iterative process where initial findings inform subsequent studies. Continuous assessment helps

refine the understanding of the drug's safety profile.

- **Interdisciplinary Collaboration:** Collaboration between pharmacologists, toxicologists, clinicians, and regulatory experts is essential to design and interpret safety pharmacology studies effectively.

5.1 Origin and Concepts of Safety Pharmacology

5.1.1 Introduction to Safety Pharmacology

Applications in Drug Safety:

Safety pharmacology plays a pivotal role in ensuring drug safety by systematically evaluating the potential adverse effects of new chemical entities (NCEs) on vital physiological functions. The applications of safety pharmacology in drug safety are diverse and essential for identifying, assessing, and mitigating risks associated with new drugs before they reach the market.

1. Preclinical Risk Assessment:

- **Identification of Adverse Effects:**

  - Safety pharmacology studies are designed to identify potential adverse effects on vital organ systems, such as the cardiovascular, respiratory, and central nervous systems.
  - These studies help predict potential safety issues that could arise in clinical trials, allowing for early intervention and risk management.

- **Guiding Dose Selection:**

  - Data from safety pharmacology studies inform the selection of safe starting doses for first-in-human clinical trials.
  - Understanding the dose-response relationship helps in establishing the maximum tolerated dose (MTD) and the no observed adverse effect level (NOAEL).

2. Cardiovascular Safety:

- **QT Interval Prolongation:**

- One of the critical applications of safety pharmacology is assessing the potential for QT interval prolongation, which can lead to life-threatening arrhythmias such as Torsades de Pointes.
- In vitro assays using human ether-à-go-go-related gene (hERG) channels and in vivo telemetry studies in animals are commonly used to evaluate this risk.

- **Hemodynamic Effects:**

  - Safety pharmacology studies evaluate the impact of new drugs on blood pressure, heart rate, and cardiac output.
  - These assessments are crucial for drugs intended to treat cardiovascular conditions, as well as for any drug that could potentially affect the cardiovascular system.

3. Respiratory Safety:

- **Respiratory Function Monitoring:**

  - Safety pharmacology studies assess the effects of drugs on respiratory rate, tidal volume, and airway resistance.
  - These evaluations are particularly important for drugs administered via inhalation or those that could affect the respiratory system indirectly.

- **Identifying Respiratory Depression:**

  - For central nervous system (CNS) drugs, particularly opioids and sedatives, it is essential to assess the risk of respiratory depression.
  - Studies in rodents and other animal models help identify potential respiratory risks before clinical trials.

4. Central Nervous System Safety:

- **Behavioral and Neurological Effects:**

  - Safety pharmacology studies evaluate the potential impact of drugs on behavior, motor coordination, and sensory functions.

- Tests such as the open field test, rotarod test, and grip strength test in rodents are used to assess these parameters.

- **Neurochemical Assessments:**

  - Safety pharmacology includes evaluating the effects of drugs on neurotransmitter levels and neural pathways.
  - This helps identify potential risks such as seizures, cognitive impairment, or mood alterations.

5. Regulatory Compliance and Drug Approval:

- **Meeting Regulatory Requirements:**

  - Regulatory agencies, such as the FDA, EMA, and PMDA, require comprehensive safety pharmacology data as part of the IND and NDA submissions.
  - Compliance with ICH S7A and S7B guidelines ensures that the necessary studies are conducted to assess the safety profile of new drugs.

- **Supporting Labeling and Risk Management:**

  - Data from safety pharmacology studies support the development of drug labeling, including warnings, precautions, and contraindications.
  - These studies also inform risk management plans, helping to monitor and mitigate risks during clinical development and post-marketing.

5.1 Origin and Concepts of Safety Pharmacology

5.1.1 Introduction to Safety Pharmacology

Historical Context:

The field of **safety pharmacology** has evolved significantly over the past century, driven by the need to ensure drug safety and efficacy. Understanding the historical context of the development of safety pharmacology provides insights into its current practices and regulatory frameworks.

1. Early Beginnings:

- **Early 20th Century:**

  - The concept of drug safety began gaining attention in the early 20th century, particularly with the establishment of basic toxicology studies to understand the harmful effects of chemicals.
  - The tragic incident of diethylene glycol poisoning in 1937, which led to the deaths of over 100 people due to the use of untested solvents in an elixir, highlighted the need for rigorous safety testing and regulatory oversight.

- **1940s - 1950s:**

  - During this period, basic pharmacology and toxicology studies became more structured, focusing on the acute and chronic effects of drugs.
  - The thalidomide tragedy in the late 1950s and early 1960s, where thousands of babies were born with severe birth defects due to the use of thalidomide by pregnant women, underscored the importance of preclinical safety testing, especially for teratogenic effects.

2. Establishment of Regulatory Frameworks:

- **1960s - 1970s:**

  - In response to the thalidomide disaster, many countries established regulatory agencies and frameworks to ensure drug safety. For instance, the U.S. Food and Drug Administration (FDA) was empowered to enforce stricter regulations on drug approval processes.
  - This period saw the introduction of more comprehensive preclinical testing requirements, including reproductive and developmental toxicity studies.

- **1980s:**

- The field of safety pharmacology began to take shape as a distinct discipline within pharmacology and toxicology.
- The recognition of the need to study the effects of drugs on vital physiological functions, such as the cardiovascular and central nervous systems, led to the development of specific safety pharmacology protocols.

3. Formalization and Expansion:

- **1990s:**

  - The International Conference on Harmonisation of Technical Requirements for Registration of Pharmaceuticals for Human Use (ICH) was established, aiming to harmonize drug registration requirements across different regions (Europe, Japan, and the United States).
  - The ICH issued guidelines such as ICH S7A and ICH S7B, which provided standardized approaches for safety pharmacology studies, focusing on the core battery of tests needed to evaluate the safety profile of new drugs.

- **ICH S7A (2000):**

  - Published in 2000, ICH S7A outlined the core safety pharmacology studies required for all new drugs, including assessments of cardiovascular, respiratory, and central nervous system functions.
  - This guideline emphasized the importance of identifying potential adverse effects on these vital systems early in the drug development process.

- **ICH S7B (2005):**

  - Published in 2005, ICH S7B specifically addressed the assessment of drug-induced QT interval prolongation, a critical parameter for cardiac safety.
  - This guideline provided detailed protocols for evaluating the potential for delayed cardiac repolarization, which could lead to life-threatening arrhythmias.

4. Modern Era and Technological Advancements:

- **2000s - Present:**

  - Advances in technology, such as high-throughput screening, in vitro assays, and imaging techniques, have enhanced the ability to conduct safety pharmacology studies more efficiently and accurately.
  - The integration of safety pharmacology into the early stages of drug development has become standard practice, ensuring that potential safety concerns are addressed before clinical trials begin.
  - The development of novel methodologies, such as stem cell-derived cardiomyocytes for cardiac safety testing, has further refined the field, allowing for more predictive and human-relevant safety assessments.

5.1 Origin and Concepts of Safety Pharmacology
5.1.3 Importance in Drug Development
Role in Risk Assessment:
Safety pharmacology is a critical component of the drug development process, playing a pivotal role in the identification, assessment, and mitigation of potential risks associated with new chemical entities (NCEs). By systematically evaluating the effects of drugs on vital physiological functions, safety pharmacology helps ensure that new therapies are both effective and safe for human use. The role of safety pharmacology in risk assessment encompasses several key areas:

1. Early Identification of Potential Risks:

- **Screening for Adverse Effects:**

  - Safety pharmacology studies are designed to identify potential adverse effects on the cardiovascular, respiratory, and central nervous systems, which are critical for survival.
  - Early identification of these risks allows for timely intervention, modification of the drug's chemical structure, or the development of mitigation strategies.

- **Predictive Value:**

- The data obtained from safety pharmacology studies provide valuable predictive insights into how a drug might behave in humans, helping to foresee potential safety issues that could arise during clinical trials.

2. Guiding Dose Selection and Safety Margins:

- **Determining Safe Starting Doses:**

  - Safety pharmacology studies help determine the safe starting doses for first-in-human clinical trials by identifying the maximum tolerated dose (MTD) and the no observed adverse effect level (NOAEL).
  - This information is crucial for designing phase I clinical trials, ensuring that initial human exposure is within a safe range.

- **Establishing Safety Margins:**

  - By evaluating the dose-response relationship and identifying adverse effects at various dose levels, safety pharmacology studies help establish safety margins. These margins are essential for defining therapeutic windows and ensuring that the drug can be administered safely.

3. Regulatory Compliance and Drug Approval:

- **Meeting Regulatory Requirements:**

  - Regulatory agencies, such as the FDA, EMA, and PMDA, require comprehensive safety pharmacology data as part of the Investigational New Drug (IND) and New Drug Application (NDA) submissions.
  - Compliance with guidelines, such as ICH S7A and S7B, ensures that the necessary studies are conducted to assess the safety profile of new drugs.

- **Supporting Regulatory Decisions:**

- The results of safety pharmacology studies support regulatory decisions regarding the approval or rejection of new drug candidates. These studies provide critical evidence that the benefits of the drug outweigh its risks.

4. Informing Clinical Development Strategies:

- **Designing Clinical Trials:**

  - Safety pharmacology data inform the design of clinical trials, including the selection of appropriate endpoints, monitoring strategies, and risk mitigation measures.
  - Understanding the potential safety risks allows researchers to implement strategies to monitor and manage these risks during clinical trials, ensuring the safety of trial participants.

- **Risk Mitigation Plans:**

  - Based on safety pharmacology findings, drug developers can create detailed risk mitigation plans that outline strategies for managing identified risks. These plans may include additional monitoring, dose adjustments, or special precautions.

5. Continuous Safety Monitoring:

- **Ongoing Assessment:**

  - Safety pharmacology is not limited to the preclinical phase; it continues throughout the drug development process. Ongoing assessments help refine the understanding of a drug's safety profile and address emerging safety concerns.
  - Continuous monitoring ensures that any new risks identified during clinical development are promptly managed and mitigated.

6. Enhancing Drug Safety and Efficacy:

- **Balancing Benefits and Risks:**

- Safety pharmacology helps balance the therapeutic benefits of a drug against its potential risks. This balance is critical for making informed decisions about whether to proceed with the development of a drug.
- Ensuring that drugs are both safe and effective enhances their therapeutic potential and increases the likelihood of successful market approval.

5.1 Origin and Concepts of Safety Pharmacology

5.1.3 Importance in Drug Development

Impact on Drug Approval:

Safety pharmacology plays a vital role in the drug approval process by ensuring that new drug candidates are safe for human use. Its impact on drug approval processes is multifaceted, involving the identification of potential risks, compliance with regulatory requirements, and supporting the overall safety profile of a drug. Here are the key ways in which safety pharmacology impacts drug approval:

1. Compliance with Regulatory Requirements:

- **Regulatory Guidelines:**

  - Regulatory agencies such as the FDA, EMA, and PMDA mandate comprehensive safety pharmacology data as part of the Investigational New Drug (IND) and New Drug Application (NDA) submissions.
  - Compliance with guidelines such as ICH S7A and ICH S7B ensures that drugs are evaluated for their potential effects on vital organ systems, including the cardiovascular, respiratory, and central nervous systems.

- **Data Submission:**

  - Detailed safety pharmacology studies are required to demonstrate that a drug has been thoroughly evaluated for potential adverse effects. This data is crucial for regulatory agencies to assess the safety of the drug before granting approval for clinical trials or market entry.

2. Identification and Mitigation of Risks:

- **Early Detection of Adverse Effects:**

  - Safety pharmacology studies identify potential adverse effects on vital physiological functions early in the drug development process. This early detection allows for the modification of the drug's chemical structure or formulation to mitigate identified risks.

- **Risk Management:**

  - The findings from safety pharmacology studies inform the development of risk management plans that outline strategies for monitoring, managing, and mitigating risks during clinical trials and post-marketing.

3. Informing Clinical Trial Design:

- **Dose Selection and Safety Margins:**

  - Safety pharmacology data help determine the safe starting doses for first-in-human clinical trials and establish safety margins. This ensures that the drug can be administered safely at therapeutic doses.

- **Monitoring Strategies:**

  - The data also inform the design of clinical trials, including the selection of appropriate endpoints, monitoring strategies for adverse effects, and criteria for dose adjustments.

4. Supporting Regulatory Decisions:

- **Benefit-Risk Assessment:**

  - Regulatory agencies rely on safety pharmacology data to perform a benefit-risk assessment of new drug candidates. A favorable balance between the therapeutic benefits and potential risks is essential for drug approval.

- **Labeling and Risk Communication:**

  - Safety pharmacology findings contribute to the development of drug labeling, including warnings, precautions, and contraindications. This information is crucial for healthcare providers and patients to make informed decisions about the use of the drug.

5.2 Tier 1 Safety Pharmacology Studies

5.2.1 Cardiovascular Safety Pharmacology

Testing Methods and Protocols:

Cardiovascular safety pharmacology is critical for assessing the potential adverse effects of new drugs on the heart and vascular system. These studies aim to identify any risks of cardiotoxicity, including effects on heart rate, blood pressure, electrical conduction, and overall cardiac function. The following outlines the methods and protocols commonly used in cardiovascular safety pharmacology studies:

1. In Vitro Studies:

a. hERG Channel Assay:

- **Objective:** Evaluate the potential for a drug to block the human ether-à-go-go-related gene (hERG) potassium channel, which can lead to QT interval prolongation and potentially life-threatening arrhythmias.
- **Protocol:**

  - **Cell Preparation:** Use human cell lines expressing the hERG channel.
  - **Drug Exposure:** Expose cells to various concentrations of the test compound.
  - **Electrophysiological Measurement:** Measure the hERG current using patch-clamp techniques to assess any inhibition by the test compound.
  - **Data Analysis:** Determine the concentration at which the drug inhibits 50% of the hERG current (IC50 value).

b. Isolated Heart Preparations:

- **Objective:** Assess the direct effects of a drug on cardiac contractility, rhythm, and electrophysiological properties.
- **Protocol:**

  - **Langendorff Heart Preparation:** Isolate hearts from animals (typically rats or guinea pigs) and perfuse them with a nutrient solution.
  - **Drug Administration:** Administer the test compound directly to the perfusion solution.
  - **Measurement:** Monitor parameters such as heart rate, contractility, and electrical activity using electrodes and pressure transducers.

2. In Vivo Studies:
a. Telemetry Studies in Conscious Animals:

- **Objective:** Evaluate the cardiovascular effects of a drug in conscious, freely moving animals, providing more physiologically relevant data.
- **Protocol:**

  - **Animal Selection:** Use rodents (e.g., rats) or non-rodents (e.g., dogs) equipped with telemetry devices.
  - **Surgery:** Implant telemetry transmitters to measure parameters such as heart rate, blood pressure, and ECG.
  - **Drug Administration:** Administer the test compound at various doses, including therapeutic and supra-therapeutic levels.
  - **Continuous Monitoring:** Continuously monitor cardiovascular parameters before, during, and after drug administration.
  - **Data Analysis:** Analyze changes in heart rate, blood pressure, QT interval, and other ECG parameters.

b. QT Interval Measurement in Anesthetized Animals:

- **Objective:** Assess the potential for QT interval prolongation, a marker for arrhythmogenic risk.
- **Protocol:**

- ○ **Animal Selection:** Use rodents or non-rodents under anesthesia.
- ○ **Drug Administration:** Administer the test compound intravenously or orally.
- ○ **ECG Recording:** Record ECG at baseline and after drug administration to measure QT intervals.
- ○ **Data Analysis:** Correct QT intervals for heart rate (QTc) and evaluate any significant prolongation.

3. Integrated Protocols and Data Interpretation:
a. Core Battery of Tests:

- **ICH S7A Guidelines:** Ensure compliance with ICH S7A guidelines, which recommend a core battery of safety pharmacology tests, including cardiovascular assessments.
- **Combination of Methods:** Use a combination of in vitro and in vivo methods to provide a comprehensive evaluation of cardiovascular safety.

b. Data Integration and Risk Assessment:

- **Integrated Data Analysis:** Combine data from various studies to assess the overall cardiovascular safety profile of the drug.
- **Risk-Benefit Evaluation:** Evaluate the potential cardiovascular risks in the context of the drug's therapeutic benefits.
- **Regulatory Reporting:** Compile and report data to regulatory agencies as part of the IND or NDA submissions, including detailed descriptions of methods, results, and interpretations.

Case Studies and Examples:
Example 1: Cardiovascular Safety Assessment of an Antihypertensive Drug

Objective: Evaluate the cardiovascular safety of a new antihypertensive drug.

Methods and Protocols:

- **hERG Channel Assay:** Conducted in vitro hERG channel assay to assess the potential for QT interval prolongation.
- **Telemetry Study:** Performed in vivo telemetry study in conscious dogs to monitor heart rate, blood pressure, and ECG parameters.

- **QT Interval Measurement:** Conducted QT interval measurement in anesthetized rats to evaluate arrhythmogenic risk.

Outcome:

- **Data Integration:** Combined in vitro and in vivo data indicated no significant risk of QT interval prolongation or other cardiovascular adverse effects.
- **Regulatory Submission:** Comprehensive cardiovascular safety data supported the successful IND submission and approval for clinical trials.

Example 2: Cardiovascular Safety Evaluation of a CNS Drug
Objective: Assess the potential cardiovascular effects of a new CNS-active drug.
Methods and Protocols:

- **Isolated Heart Preparation:** Used Langendorff heart preparation in guinea pigs to evaluate direct effects on cardiac contractility and rhythm.
- **Telemetry Study:** Conducted telemetry study in conscious rats to monitor cardiovascular parameters in a more physiologically relevant setting.
- **Integrated Analysis:** Combined findings from both studies to assess the overall cardiovascular safety profile.

Outcome:

- **Risk Mitigation:** Identified mild changes in heart rate and contractility at high doses, prompting dose adjustments for clinical trials.
- **Regulatory Compliance:** Detailed cardiovascular safety data facilitated regulatory approval and informed the design of phase I clinical trials.

5.2 Tier 1 Safety Pharmacology Studies
5.2.1 Cardiovascular Safety Pharmacology

Interpretation of Results:

Interpreting results from cardiovascular safety studies is crucial for assessing the potential risks associated with new drugs. The interpretation involves analyzing data from various testing methods to determine the overall cardiovascular safety profile. Here are key aspects to consider when interpreting results from cardiovascular safety studies:

1. hERG Channel Assay:

a. Key Parameters:

- **IC50 Value:** The concentration of the drug that inhibits 50% of the hERG current.
- **Percent Inhibition:** The degree of hERG channel inhibition at different drug concentrations.

b. Interpretation:

- **Low IC50 Value (High Potency):** A low IC50 value indicates that the drug has a high potential to inhibit the hERG channel, which could lead to QT interval prolongation and increased arrhythmogenic risk.
- **Percent Inhibition >30%:** If the percent inhibition at therapeutic concentrations exceeds 30%, it suggests a significant risk of QT interval prolongation, warranting further investigation.
- **Mitigation Strategies:** If hERG inhibition is observed, structural modifications to the drug may be necessary to reduce this risk. Additional in vivo studies should be conducted to confirm the findings.

2. Isolated Heart Preparations:

a. Key Parameters:

- **Heart Rate:** Changes in heart rate (bradycardia or tachycardia) induced by the drug.
- **Contractility:** Effects on the force of cardiac contractions.
- **Electrophysiological Properties:** Changes in parameters such as action potential duration and conduction velocity.

b. Interpretation:

- **Significant Changes:** Significant alterations in heart rate, contractility, or electrophysiological properties indicate potential cardiotoxic effects.
- **Dose-Response Relationship:** Assess whether the changes are dose-dependent. A clear dose-response relationship strengthens the evidence

of cardiotoxicity.

- **Translational Relevance:** Consider the translational relevance of the isolated heart data to in vivo conditions.

3. Telemetry Studies in Conscious Animals:
a. Key Parameters:

- **Heart Rate:** Effects on resting and stress-induced heart rate.
- **Blood Pressure:** Changes in systolic and diastolic blood pressure.
- **ECG Parameters:** QT interval, PR interval, QRS duration, and any arrhythmias.

b. Interpretation:

- **QT Interval Prolongation:** Prolongation of the QT interval, corrected for heart rate (QTc), is a critical marker for arrhythmogenic risk. Evaluate the extent of QTc prolongation compared to baseline and control values.
- **Blood Pressure Changes:** Significant increases or decreases in blood pressure can indicate potential risks for hypotension or hypertension.
- **Arrhythmias:** The presence of arrhythmias, such as ventricular tachycardia or fibrillation, indicates a high cardiotoxic risk.
- **Statistical Analysis:** Use appropriate statistical methods to compare treated and control groups, ensuring that observed effects are not due to random variation.

4. QT Interval Measurement in Anesthetized Animals:
a. Key Parameters:

- **QT and QTc Intervals:** Measurement of the QT interval and its correction for heart rate (QTc).
- **ECG Morphology:** Changes in ECG waveforms, such as T-wave morphology.

b. Interpretation:

- **Significant QTc Prolongation:** A QTc prolongation greater than 10-20 milliseconds is generally considered significant and indicative of arrhythmogenic potential.

- **T-Wave Changes:** Alterations in T-wave morphology can signal repolarization abnormalities.
- **Comparative Analysis:** Compare the QTc interval changes with known cardiotoxic and non-cardiotoxic compounds to contextualize the findings.

5. Integrated Data Analysis:
a. Data Integration:

- **Combining Results:** Integrate data from in vitro and in vivo studies to form a comprehensive understanding of the drug's cardiovascular effects.
- **Consistency Across Studies:** Consistency in findings across different models and assays strengthens the validity of the results.

b. Risk Assessment:

- **Benefit-Risk Balance:** Evaluate the cardiovascular risks in the context of the drug's therapeutic benefits. Consider the severity of the cardiovascular effects relative to the expected therapeutic outcomes.
- **Mitigation Measures:** If significant cardiovascular risks are identified, develop strategies to mitigate these risks, such as dose adjustments, additional monitoring, or structural modifications to the drug.

c. Regulatory Reporting:

- **Detailed Reporting:** Prepare detailed reports for regulatory submissions, including all relevant data, methodologies, statistical analyses, and interpretations.
- **Regulatory Discussions:** Engage in discussions with regulatory agencies to address any concerns and agree on risk mitigation strategies.

Case Studies and Examples:
Example 1: Cardiovascular Safety Assessment of an Antihypertensive Drug
Results:

- **hERG Channel Assay:** IC50 value was 5 μM, with 35% inhibition at therapeutic concentrations.
- **Telemetry Study:** Mild QTc prolongation observed at high doses; no significant changes in heart rate or blood pressure at therapeutic doses.
- **QT Interval Measurement:** QTc prolongation of 15 milliseconds at the highest dose tested.

Interpretation:

- **Risk Identification:** The hERG inhibition and QTc prolongation at high doses indicate a potential arrhythmogenic risk.
- **Mitigation:** Dose adjustments and additional monitoring for QTc prolongation in clinical trials were recommended.
- **Regulatory Decision:** The drug was approved for clinical trials with specific safety monitoring requirements.

Example 2: Cardiovascular Safety Evaluation of a CNS Drug
Results:

- **Isolated Heart Preparation:** No significant changes in heart rate or contractility.
- **Telemetry Study:** No significant changes in heart rate, blood pressure, or ECG parameters at therapeutic doses; slight increase in heart rate at supra-therapeutic doses.

Interpretation:

- **Risk Assessment:** The data indicate a low risk of cardiotoxicity at therapeutic doses.
- **Regulatory Decision:** The drug was approved for clinical trials without additional cardiovascular monitoring requirements.

Example 3: Respiratory Safety Evaluation of an Inhaled Bronchodilator
Results:

- **Telemetry Study:** Significant increase in heart rate and blood pressure at high doses.

- **QT Interval Measurement:** No significant QTc prolongation observed.

Interpretation:

- **Risk Identification:** The increase in heart rate and blood pressure suggests a risk of cardiovascular stress at high doses.
- **Mitigation:** Recommended dose adjustments and additional monitoring for cardiovascular effects in clinical trials.
- **Regulatory Decision:** The drug was approved for clinical trials with specific safety monitoring for cardiovascular effects.

5.2 Tier 1 Safety Pharmacology Studies
5.2.1 Cardiovascular Safety Pharmacology

Case Studies and Examples:

The following case studies illustrate the application of cardiovascular safety studies in the evaluation of new drug candidates. These examples highlight the methodologies used, the interpretation of results, and the impact on drug development and regulatory decisions.

Example 1: Cardiovascular Safety Assessment of an Antihypertensive Drug

Objective: Evaluate the cardiovascular safety of a new antihypertensive drug.

Methods and Protocols:

- **hERG Channel Assay:**

  - **Protocol:** Human cell lines expressing the hERG channel were exposed to various concentrations of the test compound.
  - **Results:** The IC50 value was found to be 5 µM, with 35% inhibition at therapeutic concentrations.

- **Telemetry Study in Conscious Dogs:**

  - **Protocol:** Telemetry transmitters were implanted in dogs to continuously monitor heart rate, blood pressure, and ECG parameters. The test compound was administered at therapeutic and supra-therapeutic doses.

- ○ **Results:** Mild QTc prolongation was observed at high doses, but no significant changes in heart rate or blood pressure were noted at therapeutic doses.

- **QT Interval Measurement in Anesthetized Rats:**

  - ○ **Protocol:** Rats were anesthetized and administered the test compound intravenously. ECG recordings were taken to measure the QT interval.
  - ○ **Results:** QTc prolongation of 15 milliseconds was observed at the highest dose tested.

Interpretation:

- **Risk Identification:** The hERG inhibition and QTc prolongation at high doses indicated a potential arrhythmogenic risk.
- **Mitigation:** Recommended dose adjustments and additional monitoring for QTc prolongation in clinical trials.
- **Regulatory Decision:** The drug was approved for clinical trials with specific safety monitoring requirements.

Outcome:

- The comprehensive cardiovascular safety assessment supported the successful IND submission and approval for clinical trials. The drug was eventually approved for market entry, demonstrating a favorable benefit-risk profile.

Example 2: Cardiovascular Safety Evaluation of a CNS Drug
Objective: Assess the potential cardiovascular effects of a new CNS-active drug.
Methods and Protocols:

- **Isolated Heart Preparation (Langendorff Heart):**

  - ○ **Protocol:** Hearts from guinea pigs were isolated and perfused with a nutrient solution. The test compound was administered directly to the perfusion solution.

- **Results:** No significant changes in heart rate or contractility were observed.

- **Telemetry Study in Conscious Rats:**

  - **Protocol:** Rats were implanted with telemetry devices to monitor heart rate, blood pressure, and ECG parameters. The test compound was administered at therapeutic and supra-therapeutic doses.
  - **Results:** No significant changes in heart rate, blood pressure, or ECG parameters at therapeutic doses; a slight increase in heart rate was noted at supra-therapeutic doses.

Interpretation:

- **Risk Assessment:** The data indicated a low risk of cardiotoxicity at therapeutic doses.
- **Regulatory Decision:** The drug was approved for clinical trials without additional cardiovascular monitoring requirements.

Outcome:

- The thorough CNS safety evaluation ensured that potential risks were managed effectively, supporting the safe progression of the drug through clinical trials and ultimately to market approval.

Example 3: Cardiovascular Safety Evaluation of an Inhaled Bronchodilator

Objective: Evaluate the respiratory and cardiovascular safety of a new inhaled bronchodilator.

Methods and Protocols:

- **Telemetry Study in Conscious Dogs:**

  - **Protocol:** Dogs were implanted with telemetry devices to continuously monitor heart rate, blood pressure, and ECG parameters. The test compound was administered via inhalation at therapeutic and supra-therapeutic doses.

- **Results:** Significant increase in heart rate and blood pressure was observed at high doses; no significant QTc prolongation was noted.

- **QT Interval Measurement in Anesthetized Guinea Pigs:**

  - **Protocol:** Guinea pigs were anesthetized and administered the test compound via inhalation. ECG recordings were taken to measure the QT interval.
  - **Results:** No significant QTc prolongation was observed.

Interpretation:

- **Risk Identification:** The increase in heart rate and blood pressure suggested a risk of cardiovascular stress at high doses.
- **Mitigation:** Recommended dose adjustments and additional monitoring for cardiovascular effects in clinical trials.
- **Regulatory Decision:** The drug was approved for clinical trials with specific safety monitoring for cardiovascular effects.

Outcome:

- The detailed cardiovascular and respiratory safety assessment ensured that the drug could be used safely in patients with respiratory conditions, supporting its successful market entry.

Example 4: Cardiovascular Safety Assessment of a New Antiarrhythmic Drug

Objective: Evaluate the cardiovascular safety of a new antiarrhythmic drug.

Methods and Protocols:

- **hERG Channel Assay:**

  - **Protocol:** Human cell lines expressing the hERG channel were exposed to the test compound. Electrophysiological measurements were taken to assess hERG current inhibition.
  - **Results:** The IC50 value was 1 µM, indicating significant hERG channel inhibition at therapeutic concentrations.

- **Telemetry Study in Conscious Dogs:**

  - **Protocol:** Dogs were implanted with telemetry devices to monitor heart rate, blood pressure, and ECG parameters. The test compound was administered at therapeutic and supra-therapeutic doses.
  - **Results:** Significant QTc prolongation and occasional ventricular arrhythmias were observed at high doses.

- **QT Interval Measurement in Anesthetized Rabbits:**

  - **Protocol:** Rabbits were anesthetized and administered the test compound intravenously. ECG recordings were taken to measure the QT interval.
  - **Results:** QTc prolongation of 20 milliseconds was observed at the highest dose tested.

Interpretation:

- **Risk Identification:** The significant hERG inhibition, QTc prolongation, and ventricular arrhythmias indicated a high arrhythmogenic risk.
- **Mitigation:** Recommended structural modifications to the drug to reduce hERG channel inhibition and additional preclinical testing.
- **Regulatory Decision:** The drug was not approved for clinical trials in its current form; further development was required to address the identified risks.

Outcome:

- The comprehensive cardiovascular safety assessment identified significant risks that needed to be mitigated before progressing to clinical trials, ensuring patient safety and guiding further drug development efforts.

5.2 Tier 1 Safety Pharmacology Studies

5.2.2 Central Nervous System Safety Pharmacology

Assessment Techniques:

Assessing the safety of new drug candidates on the central nervous system (CNS) is crucial for identifying potential adverse effects on behavior, motor coordination, sensory function, and neurological health. The following techniques are commonly used to evaluate CNS safety pharmacology:

1. Behavioral Assessment:

a. Open Field Test:

- **Objective:** Evaluate general locomotor activity and exploratory behavior.
- **Protocol:**

  - **Setup:** Place the test animal (typically a rodent) in an open field arena with marked zones.
  - **Observation:** Record the animal's movement, including total distance traveled, time spent in different zones, and rearing behavior.
  - **Analysis:** Increased or decreased locomotor activity can indicate stimulant or depressant effects, respectively.

b. Rotarod Test:

- **Objective:** Assess motor coordination and balance.
- **Protocol:**

  - **Setup:** Place the rodent on a rotating rod and gradually increase the rotation speed.
  - **Observation:** Measure the time the animal remains on the rod before falling off.
  - **Analysis:** Reduced time on the rod indicates impaired motor coordination and balance.

c. Elevated Plus Maze:

- **Objective:** Evaluate anxiety-like behavior.
- **Protocol:**

  - **Setup:** Use a plus-shaped maze with two open arms and two closed arms elevated above the ground.

- ○ **Observation:** Record the time spent in open versus closed arms and the number of entries into each.
- ○ **Analysis:** Increased time in closed arms and decreased entries into open arms suggest increased anxiety.

2. Neurological Assessment:
a. Functional Observation Battery (FOB):

- **Objective:** Assess a range of neurological functions, including sensory, motor, and autonomic responses.
- **Protocol:**

  - ○ **Setup:** Conduct a series of tests to evaluate various neurological functions, including reflexes, grip strength, pupil response, and gait.
  - ○ **Observation:** Record responses to each test component.
  - ○ **Analysis:** Abnormal responses indicate potential neurological deficits.

b. Hot Plate Test:

- **Objective:** Assess nociceptive (pain) response.
- **Protocol:**

  - ○ **Setup:** Place the rodent on a heated surface and measure the latency to respond (e.g., licking paws, jumping).
  - ○ **Observation:** Record the response time.
  - ○ **Analysis:** Changes in response latency indicate alterations in pain perception.

3. Electrophysiological Assessment:
a. Electroencephalography (EEG):

- **Objective:** Monitor electrical activity in the brain to detect changes in neuronal activity and seizure potential.
- **Protocol:**

  - ○ **Setup:** Attach electrodes to the animal's scalp or implant them intracranially.

- **Observation:** Record EEG signals continuously before and after drug administration.
- **Analysis:** Analyze changes in EEG patterns, including frequency, amplitude, and the presence of seizure activity.

b. Auditory Startle Response:

- **Objective:** Assess sensory-motor gating and startle reflex.
- **Protocol:**

  - **Setup:** Expose the animal to sudden auditory stimuli and measure the startle response.
  - **Observation:** Record the magnitude and latency of the startle response.
  - **Analysis:** Alterations in the startle response can indicate changes in sensory-motor gating.

4. Neurochemical Assessment:
a. Neurotransmitter Levels:

- **Objective:** Measure changes in neurotransmitter levels in the brain.
- **Protocol:**

  - **Setup:** Collect brain tissue or cerebrospinal fluid samples from the test animals.
  - **Observation:** Analyze neurotransmitter concentrations using techniques such as high-performance liquid chromatography (HPLC).
  - **Analysis:** Changes in neurotransmitter levels indicate drug effects on neural signaling pathways.

b. Receptor Binding Studies:

- **Objective:** Assess drug binding to specific CNS receptors.
- **Protocol:**

  - **Setup:** Use radiolabeled ligands to measure the binding affinity of the test compound to CNS receptors.

- ○ **Observation:** Conduct assays to determine binding affinity and receptor occupancy.
- ○ **Analysis:** High binding affinity and receptor occupancy suggest potential CNS effects.

5. Case Studies and Examples:

Example 1: CNS Safety Assessment of an Anxiolytic Drug

Objective: Evaluate the CNS safety of a new anxiolytic drug.

Assessment Techniques:

- **Behavioral Assessment:** Conducted elevated plus maze test to assess anxiety-like behavior.
- **Neurological Assessment:** Used the Functional Observation Battery (FOB) to evaluate sensory and motor functions.
- **Electrophysiological Assessment:** Performed EEG recordings to monitor neuronal activity and detect seizure potential.

Results:

- **Behavioral Assessment:** Increased time spent in open arms of the maze, indicating reduced anxiety.
- **Neurological Assessment:** No significant abnormalities detected in sensory or motor functions.
- **Electrophysiological Assessment:** No significant changes in EEG patterns or seizure activity.

Outcome:

- The comprehensive CNS safety assessment supported the safe progression of the anxiolytic drug to clinical trials.

Example 2: CNS Safety Evaluation of a Sedative

Objective: Assess the CNS safety of a new sedative.

Assessment Techniques:

- **Behavioral Assessment:** Conducted open field test and rotarod test to evaluate locomotor activity and motor coordination.

- **Neurological Assessment:** Used the hot plate test to assess nociceptive response.
- **Neurochemical Assessment:** Measured neurotransmitter levels in brain tissue samples.

Results:

- **Behavioral Assessment:** Decreased locomotor activity in the open field test and reduced time on the rotarod, indicating sedative effects.
- **Neurological Assessment:** Increased response latency in the hot plate test, suggesting reduced pain perception.
- **Neurochemical Assessment:** Decreased levels of excitatory neurotransmitters, consistent with sedative effects.

Outcome:

- The findings confirmed the sedative effects and potential CNS safety of the drug, supporting its progression to further development.

Example 3: CNS Safety Assessment of an Antidepressant
Objective: Evaluate the CNS safety of a new antidepressant.
Assessment Techniques:

- **Behavioral Assessment:** Conducted the open field test and elevated plus maze to assess locomotor activity and anxiety-like behavior.
- **Electrophysiological Assessment:** Performed EEG recordings to monitor brain activity.
- **Neurochemical Assessment:** Conducted receptor binding studies to evaluate binding affinity to CNS receptors.

Results:

- **Behavioral Assessment:** Increased locomotor activity and decreased anxiety-like behavior in the elevated plus maze.
- **Electrophysiological Assessment:** No significant changes in EEG patterns or seizure activity.
- **Neurochemical Assessment:** High binding affinity to serotonin receptors, consistent with antidepressant activity.

Outcome:

- The comprehensive CNS safety assessment confirmed the antidepressant activity and CNS safety profile, supporting further clinical development.

5.2 Tier 1 Safety Pharmacology Studies
5.2.2 Central Nervous System Safety Pharmacology
Case Studies and Examples:

The following case studies illustrate the application of various assessment techniques used in central nervous system (CNS) safety pharmacology studies. These examples highlight how researchers identify and interpret potential CNS risks associated with new drug candidates, ensuring their safety before progressing to clinical trials.

Example 1: CNS Safety Assessment of an Anxiolytic Drug

Objective: Evaluate the CNS safety of a new anxiolytic drug.

Assessment Techniques:

- **Behavioral Assessment:**

  - **Elevated Plus Maze:** Used to evaluate anxiety-like behavior. The test animal (a rodent) is placed in a plus-shaped maze with two open arms and two closed arms. Time spent in open versus closed arms and the number of entries into each are recorded.
  - **Results:** The test animals spent more time in the open arms and made more entries into the open arms, indicating reduced anxiety levels.

- **Neurological Assessment:**

  - **Functional Observation Battery (FOB):** Conducted to evaluate sensory, motor, and autonomic functions. Tests include reflexes, grip strength, pupil response, and gait analysis.
  - **Results:** No significant abnormalities were detected in sensory or motor functions, indicating no adverse neurological effects.

- **Electrophysiological Assessment:**

  - **EEG Recording:** Monitored electrical activity in the brain to detect changes in neuronal activity and seizure potential.

- ○ **Results:** No significant changes in EEG patterns or seizure activity were observed.

Interpretation:

- **Risk Assessment:** The comprehensive assessment showed that the anxiolytic drug effectively reduced anxiety without causing adverse neurological or electrophysiological effects.
- **Outcome:** The data supported the safe progression of the anxiolytic drug to clinical trials.

Example 2: CNS Safety Evaluation of a Sedative
Objective: Assess the CNS safety of a new sedative.
Assessment Techniques:

- **Behavioral Assessment:**

  - ○ **Open Field Test:** Used to evaluate general locomotor activity and exploratory behavior. The test animal is placed in an open field arena, and its movement is recorded.
  - ○ **Results:** Decreased locomotor activity, indicating sedative effects.
  - ○ **Rotarod Test:** Used to assess motor coordination and balance. The test animal is placed on a rotating rod, and the time it remains on the rod is measured.
  - ○ **Results:** Reduced time on the rod, indicating impaired motor coordination.

- **Neurological Assessment:**

  - ○ **Hot Plate Test:** Used to assess nociceptive (pain) response. The test animal is placed on a heated surface, and the latency to respond (e.g., licking paws, jumping) is recorded.
  - ○ **Results:** Increased response latency, indicating reduced pain perception.

- **Neurochemical Assessment:**

- **Neurotransmitter Levels:** Measured changes in neurotransmitter levels in the brain using high-performance liquid chromatography (HPLC).
- **Results:** Decreased levels of excitatory neurotransmitters, consistent with sedative effects.

Interpretation:

- **Risk Assessment:** The findings confirmed the sedative effects and indicated potential CNS safety, with no adverse neurological effects detected.
- **Outcome:** The data supported further development and clinical trials of the sedative drug.

Example 3: CNS Safety Assessment of an Antidepressant
Objective: Evaluate the CNS safety of a new antidepressant.
Assessment Techniques:

- **Behavioral Assessment:**

  - **Open Field Test:** Used to evaluate locomotor activity and exploratory behavior.
  - **Results:** Increased locomotor activity, indicating potential stimulant effects.
  - **Elevated Plus Maze:** Used to assess anxiety-like behavior.
  - **Results:** Decreased time spent in closed arms and increased entries into open arms, indicating reduced anxiety.

- **Electrophysiological Assessment:**

  - **EEG Recording:** Monitored brain activity to detect changes in neuronal patterns and seizure potential.
  - **Results:** No significant changes in EEG patterns or seizure activity were observed.

- **Neurochemical Assessment:**

- **Receptor Binding Studies:** Used to evaluate binding affinity to CNS receptors, particularly serotonin receptors.
- **Results:** High binding affinity to serotonin receptors, consistent with antidepressant activity.

Interpretation:

- **Risk Assessment:** The comprehensive CNS safety assessment confirmed the antidepressant activity and indicated a favorable CNS safety profile with no significant adverse effects.
- **Outcome:** The data supported the further clinical development of the antidepressant drug.

Example 4: CNS Safety Evaluation of an Antiepileptic Drug
Objective: Assess the CNS safety of a new antiepileptic drug.
Assessment Techniques:

- **Behavioral Assessment:**

  - **Rotarod Test:** Used to evaluate motor coordination and balance.
  - **Results:** No significant impairment in motor coordination was observed.
  - **Open Field Test:** Used to assess locomotor activity.
  - **Results:** No significant changes in locomotor activity, indicating no sedative or stimulant effects.

- **Electrophysiological Assessment:**

  - **EEG Recording:** Monitored for seizure activity and changes in neuronal firing patterns.
  - **Results:** No proconvulsant activity was detected; the drug reduced seizure frequency in epileptic models.

- **Neurochemical Assessment:**

  - **Neurotransmitter Levels:** Measured changes in neurotransmitter levels in brain tissue samples.

- ○ **Results:** Increased levels of inhibitory neurotransmitters, consistent with antiepileptic activity.

Interpretation:

- **Risk Assessment:** The findings confirmed the antiepileptic efficacy and indicated a favorable CNS safety profile with no significant adverse effects.
- **Outcome:** The data supported the advancement of the antiepileptic drug to clinical trials.

5.2 Tier 1 Safety Pharmacology Studies
5.2.3 Respiratory Safety Pharmacology
Data Analysis:

Analyzing data from respiratory safety studies involves several techniques to assess the potential impact of new drug candidates on respiratory function. These studies typically measure parameters such as respiratory rate, tidal volume, minute ventilation, and airway resistance. The following outlines the key techniques for analyzing data from respiratory safety studies:

1. Basic Statistical Analysis:
a. Descriptive Statistics:

- **Objective:** Summarize the central tendency and variability of respiratory parameters.
- **Techniques:**

  - ○ **Mean and Standard Deviation:** Calculate the mean and standard deviation for parameters such as respiratory rate and tidal volume.
  - ○ **Median and Interquartile Range:** Use for non-normally distributed data.
  - ○ **Range:** Determine the minimum and maximum values to understand the spread of the data.

b. Comparative Statistics:

- **Objective:** Compare respiratory parameters between treated and control groups.

- **Techniques:**

  - **T-Tests:** Use paired or unpaired t-tests to compare means between two groups.
  - **ANOVA:** Apply one-way or repeated-measures ANOVA for comparisons involving more than two groups or multiple time points.
  - **Non-Parametric Tests:** Use tests such as the Mann-Whitney U test or Kruskal-Wallis test for non-normally distributed data.

2. Time-Series Analysis:
a. Baseline and Post-Treatment Comparison:

- **Objective:** Evaluate changes in respiratory parameters over time.
- **Techniques:**

  - **Baseline Normalization:** Normalize post-treatment data to baseline values to assess relative changes.
  - **Trend Analysis:** Plot time-series data to identify trends or patterns in respiratory parameters over time.

b. Repeated Measures Analysis:

- **Objective:** Account for the correlation between repeated measurements on the same subjects.
- **Techniques:**

  - **Mixed-Effects Models:** Use mixed-effects models to analyze repeated measures data, accounting for both fixed effects (e.g., treatment) and random effects (e.g., individual variability).
  - **Generalized Estimating Equations (GEE):** Apply GEEs for repeated measures analysis when the data are not normally distributed.

3. Respiratory Waveform Analysis:
a. Breath-by-Breath Analysis:

- **Objective:** Analyze individual respiratory cycles to detect subtle changes in breathing patterns.
- **Techniques:**

- ◦ **Waveform Extraction:** Extract individual respiratory cycles from continuous recordings.
- ◦ **Cycle Metrics:** Calculate metrics such as inspiratory and expiratory times, peak inspiratory and expiratory flows, and the shape of the respiratory cycle.

b. Pattern Recognition:

- **Objective:** Identify abnormal breathing patterns such as apneas, hypopneas, or irregular breathing.
- **Techniques:**

  - ◦ **Pattern Detection Algorithms:** Use algorithms to detect and quantify abnormal respiratory events.
  - ◦ **Frequency Analysis:** Perform frequency analysis to identify periodic or irregular breathing patterns.

4. Advanced Statistical and Machine Learning Techniques:
a. Multivariate Analysis:

- **Objective:** Evaluate the combined effects of multiple respiratory parameters.
- **Techniques:**

  - ◦ **Principal Component Analysis (PCA):** Reduce dimensionality and identify key components contributing to variability in respiratory data.
  - ◦ **Cluster Analysis:** Group similar respiratory patterns or responses to identify subpopulations or trends.

b. Machine Learning Models:

- **Objective:** Predict respiratory outcomes or classify respiratory patterns based on complex datasets.
- **Techniques:**

  - ◦ **Supervised Learning:** Train models using labeled data to predict respiratory outcomes (e.g., support vector machines, random forests).

- ○ **Unsupervised Learning:** Use algorithms such as k-means clustering to identify patterns or groupings in unlabeled data.

5. Interpretation and Reporting:
a. Clinical Relevance:

- **Objective:** Interpret data in the context of clinical significance.
- **Techniques:**

  - ○ **Thresholds and Benchmarks:** Compare findings to established clinical thresholds or benchmarks for respiratory parameters.
  - ○ **Risk Assessment:** Assess the potential clinical impact of observed changes in respiratory function.

b. Visual Presentation:

- **Objective:** Effectively communicate findings through visual representation.
- **Techniques:**

  - ○ **Graphs and Charts:** Use line graphs, bar charts, and scatter plots to visualize respiratory data.
  - ○ **Heatmaps:** Employ heatmaps to represent the intensity of respiratory events or changes across multiple parameters.

Case Studies and Examples:
Example 1: Respiratory Safety Assessment of an Inhaled Bronchodilator
Objective: Evaluate the respiratory safety of a new inhaled bronchodilator.
Data Analysis Techniques:

- **Descriptive Statistics:**

  - ○ **Mean and Standard Deviation:** Calculated for respiratory rate, tidal volume, and minute ventilation.

- **Comparative Statistics:**

- **T-Tests:** Compared means of respiratory parameters between treated and control groups.

- **Time-Series Analysis:**

  - **Baseline Normalization:** Normalized post-treatment data to baseline values.
  - **Trend Analysis:** Plotted time-series data to identify trends over time.

Results:

- **Respiratory Rate:** Significant increase in respiratory rate post-treatment compared to baseline and control.
- **Tidal Volume:** No significant change in tidal volume.
- **Minute Ventilation:** Increased minute ventilation post-treatment.

Interpretation:

- **Clinical Relevance:** The increased respiratory rate and minute ventilation suggest enhanced bronchodilation without compromising tidal volume.
- **Outcome:** Supported the progression of the bronchodilator to clinical trials with additional monitoring for respiratory effects.

Example 2: Respiratory Safety Evaluation of a CNS Drug
Objective: Assess the potential respiratory effects of a new CNS-active drug.
Data Analysis Techniques:

- **Respiratory Waveform Analysis:**

  - **Breath-by-Breath Analysis:** Extracted individual respiratory cycles and calculated metrics such as peak inspiratory flow.
  - **Pattern Recognition:** Identified abnormal breathing patterns using pattern detection algorithms.

- **Advanced Statistical Techniques:**

- ○ **Multivariate Analysis:** Used PCA to identify key components contributing to variability in respiratory data.

Results:

- **Breathing Patterns:** Detected periods of irregular breathing and hypopneas post-treatment.
- **Peak Inspiratory Flow:** Reduced peak inspiratory flow in treated animals.

Interpretation:

- **Clinical Relevance:** The irregular breathing patterns and reduced peak inspiratory flow indicate potential CNS-related respiratory depression.
- **Outcome:** Recommended further preclinical studies and cautious progression to clinical trials with enhanced respiratory monitoring.

Example 3: Respiratory Safety Assessment of an Anti-Inflammatory Drug

Objective: Evaluate the respiratory safety of a new anti-inflammatory drug.

Data Analysis Techniques:

- **Descriptive Statistics:**

  - ○ **Mean, Standard Deviation, and Range:** Calculated for respiratory parameters.

- **Comparative Statistics:**

  - ○ **ANOVA:** Used to compare respiratory parameters across multiple dose groups and time points.

- **Time-Series Analysis:**

  - ○ **Repeated Measures Analysis:** Employed mixed-effects models to analyze repeated measures data.

Results:

- **Respiratory Rate and Tidal Volume:** No significant changes observed across different dose groups and time points.
- **Airway Resistance:** Significant reduction in airway resistance at therapeutic doses.

Interpretation:

- **Clinical Relevance:** The reduction in airway resistance indicates the anti-inflammatory efficacy of the drug without adverse effects on respiratory rate or tidal volume.
- **Outcome:** Supported the progression of the anti-inflammatory drug to clinical trials with respiratory function monitoring.

5.2 Tier 1 Safety Pharmacology Studies

5.2.3 Respiratory Safety Pharmacology

Case Studies and Examples:
The following case studies illustrate the application of various techniques used in respiratory safety pharmacology to evaluate the potential respiratory effects of new drug candidates. These examples highlight how researchers identify, analyze, and interpret respiratory data to ensure the safety of new drugs.

Example 1: Respiratory Safety Assessment of an Inhaled Bronchodilator

Objective: Evaluate the respiratory safety of a new inhaled bronchodilator.

Methods and Protocols:

- **Telemetry Study in Conscious Rats:**

  - **Protocol:** Rats were equipped with telemetry devices to monitor respiratory rate, tidal volume, and minute ventilation continuously. The test compound was administered via inhalation at therapeutic and supra-therapeutic doses.

- **Parameters Measured**: Respiratory rate, tidal volume, minute ventilation, and airway resistance.

Data Analysis Techniques:

- **Descriptive Statistics:**

  - **Mean and Standard Deviation:** Calculated for respiratory parameters to summarize central tendency and variability.

- **Comparative Statistics:**

  - **T-Tests:** Compared means of respiratory parameters between treated and control groups.

- **Time-Series Analysis:**

  - **Baseline Normalization:** Normalized post-treatment data to baseline values to assess relative changes.
  - **Trend Analysis:** Plotted time-series data to identify trends over time.

Results:

- **Respiratory Rate:** Significant increase in respiratory rate post-treatment compared to baseline and control.
- **Tidal Volume:** No significant change in tidal volume.
- **Minute Ventilation:** Increased minute ventilation post-treatment.
- **Airway Resistance:** No significant change observed.

Interpretation:

- **Clinical Relevance:** The increased respiratory rate and minute ventilation suggest enhanced bronchodilation without compromising tidal volume or increasing airway resistance.
- **Outcome:** Supported the progression of the bronchodilator to clinical trials with additional monitoring for respiratory effects.

Example 2: Respiratory Safety Evaluation of a CNS Drug

Objective: Assess the potential respiratory effects of a new CNS-active drug.

Methods and Protocols:

- **Telemetry Study in Conscious Dogs:**

  - **Protocol:** Dogs were implanted with telemetry devices to monitor respiratory rate, tidal volume, and minute ventilation continuously. The test compound was administered at therapeutic and supra-therapeutic doses.
  - **Parameters Measured:** Respiratory rate, tidal volume, minute ventilation, and oxygen saturation.

Data Analysis Techniques:

- **Respiratory Waveform Analysis:**

  - **Breath-by-Breath Analysis:** Extracted individual respiratory cycles and calculated metrics such as inspiratory and expiratory times, peak inspiratory and expiratory flows.

- **Pattern Recognition:**

  - **Pattern Detection Algorithms:** Used algorithms to detect and quantify abnormal respiratory events, such as apneas and hypopneas.

Results:

- **Breathing Patterns:** Detected periods of irregular breathing and hypopneas post-treatment.
- **Respiratory Rate and Tidal Volume:** No significant changes observed.
- **Oxygen Saturation:** Slight decrease in oxygen saturation at supra-therapeutic doses.

Interpretation:

- **Clinical Relevance:** The irregular breathing patterns and hypopneas indicate potential CNS-related respiratory depression.

- **Outcome:** Recommended further preclinical studies and cautious progression to clinical trials with enhanced respiratory monitoring.

Example 3: Respiratory Safety Assessment of an Anti-Inflammatory Drug

Objective: Evaluate the respiratory safety of a new anti-inflammatory drug.

Methods and Protocols:

- **Plethysmography Study in Conscious Guinea Pigs:**

  - **Protocol:** Guinea pigs were placed in plethysmography chambers to measure respiratory parameters such as respiratory rate, tidal volume, and airway resistance. The test compound was administered orally at different doses.
  - **Parameters Measured:** Respiratory rate, tidal volume, minute ventilation, and airway resistance.

Data Analysis Techniques:

- **Descriptive Statistics:**

  - **Mean, Standard Deviation, and Range:** Calculated for respiratory parameters.

- **Comparative Statistics:**

  - **ANOVA:** Used to compare respiratory parameters across multiple dose groups and time points.

- **Time-Series Analysis:**

  - **Repeated Measures Analysis:** Employed mixed-effects models to analyze repeated measures data.

Results:

- **Respiratory Rate and Tidal Volume:** No significant changes observed across different dose groups and time points.
- **Airway Resistance:** Significant reduction in airway resistance at therapeutic doses.
- **Minute Ventilation:** No significant change observed.

Interpretation:

- **Clinical Relevance:** The reduction in airway resistance indicates the anti-inflammatory efficacy of the drug without adverse effects on respiratory rate or tidal volume.
- **Outcome:** Supported the progression of the anti-inflammatory drug to clinical trials with respiratory function monitoring.

Example 4: Respiratory Safety Evaluation of an Opioid Analgesic
Objective: Assess the potential respiratory effects of a new opioid analgesic.
Methods and Protocols:

- **Plethysmography Study in Conscious Rats:**

  - **Protocol:** Rats were placed in plethysmography chambers to measure respiratory parameters continuously. The test compound was administered subcutaneously at therapeutic and supra-therapeutic doses.
  - **Parameters Measured:** Respiratory rate, tidal volume, minute ventilation, and arterial blood gases.

Data Analysis Techniques:

- **Time-Series Analysis:**

  - **Baseline Normalization:** Normalized post-treatment data to baseline values.
  - **Trend Analysis:** Plotted time-series data to identify changes over time.

- **Multivariate Analysis:**

- ○ **PCA:** Used to identify key components contributing to variability in respiratory data.

Results:

- **Respiratory Rate:** Significant decrease in respiratory rate at supra-therapeutic doses.
- **Tidal Volume:** Slight reduction in tidal volume at higher doses.
- **Minute Ventilation:** Significant decrease in minute ventilation at supra-therapeutic doses.
- **Arterial Blood Gases:** Increased CO_2 levels and decreased O_2 levels, indicating respiratory depression.

Interpretation:

- **Clinical Relevance:** The decreased respiratory rate, minute ventilation, and changes in arterial blood gases indicate significant respiratory depression at supra-therapeutic doses.
- **Outcome:** Recommended dose adjustments and additional monitoring for respiratory effects in clinical trials. The drug was approved for clinical trials with specific safety monitoring requirements.

5.2 Tier 1 Safety Pharmacology Studies

5.2.4 Regulatory Importance of hERG Assays in Drug Development

Regulatory Importance:

The human ether-à-go-go-related gene (hERG) potassium channel assay is a critical component of drug development due to its role in assessing the potential for drug-induced QT interval prolongation, which can lead to life-threatening arrhythmias such as Torsades de Pointes. Regulatory agencies such as the FDA, EMA, and PMDA place significant importance on hERG assays as part of their guidelines for the evaluation of new drug candidates. Here are the key reasons for the regulatory importance of hERG assays:

1. Early Identification of Cardiovascular Risks:

- **Predictive Value:**

- hERG assays are highly predictive of a drug's potential to cause QT interval prolongation, a critical marker for arrhythmogenic risk.
- Early identification of hERG liability helps in making informed decisions about the safety profile of a drug candidate and whether modifications or additional safety measures are needed.

2. Compliance with Regulatory Guidelines:

- **ICH S7B Guidelines:**

  - The International Conference on Harmonisation (ICH) S7B guidelines specifically address the evaluation of drug-induced QT interval prolongation. hERG assays are a central component of these guidelines.
  - Compliance with ICH S7B ensures that drug developers meet the necessary regulatory requirements for assessing cardiac safety.

- **FDA and EMA Requirements:**

  - The FDA and EMA require hERG assay data as part of the Investigational New Drug (IND) and New Drug Application (NDA) submissions.
  - Providing hERG assay data helps regulatory agencies assess the potential cardiac risks of new drug candidates, facilitating the approval process.

3. Risk Management and Mitigation:

- **Safety Margins:**

  - hERG assays help establish safety margins by determining the concentration at which a drug inhibits the hERG channel.
  - Understanding the safety margins allows for appropriate dose selection and risk management strategies in clinical trials.

- **Structural Modifications:**

- ◦ If a drug exhibits significant hERG channel inhibition, structural modifications can be made to reduce this risk while maintaining therapeutic efficacy.
- ◦ Conducting hERG assays early in drug development allows for timely modifications, reducing the likelihood of late-stage failures.

4. Supporting Clinical Trial Design:

- **Dose Selection and Monitoring:**

  - ◦ hERG assay data inform the selection of safe starting doses for clinical trials and the design of safety monitoring protocols.
  - ◦ Regulatory agencies may require specific ECG monitoring in clinical trials based on hERG assay results to ensure patient safety.

- **Labeling and Risk Communication:**

  - ◦ hERG assay findings contribute to the development of drug labeling, including warnings, precautions, and contraindications related to QT interval prolongation.
  - ◦ Clear communication of potential risks helps healthcare providers make informed decisions about patient care.

Case Studies and Examples:
Example 1: hERG Assay in the Development of an Antihistamine
Objective: Evaluate the hERG liability of a new antihistamine drug.
Methods and Protocols:

- **hERG Channel Assay:**

  - ◦ **Protocol:** Human cell lines expressing the hERG channel were exposed to various concentrations of the test compound. Electrophysiological measurements were taken using patch-clamp techniques to assess hERG current inhibition.
  - ◦ **Results:** The IC50 value was found to be 2 µM, indicating significant hERG channel inhibition at therapeutic concentrations.

Regulatory Importance:

- **Risk Identification:** The hERG assay identified a high risk of QT interval prolongation.
- **Mitigation:** Structural modifications were made to the drug to reduce hERG channel inhibition.
- **Outcome:** The modified drug exhibited a higher IC50 value (20 µM), indicating reduced hERG liability. The drug progressed to clinical trials with specific ECG monitoring requirements.

Example 2: hERG Assay in the Development of an Antidepressant
Objective: Assess the hERG liability of a new antidepressant drug.
Methods and Protocols:

- **hERG Channel Assay:**

  - **Protocol:** The test compound was applied to human cell lines expressing the hERG channel. Inhibition of hERG current was measured at various concentrations.
  - **Results:** The IC50 value was determined to be 15 µM, with less than 30% inhibition at therapeutic concentrations.

Regulatory Importance:

- **Safety Margin Establishment:** The hERG assay data indicated a wide safety margin, suggesting a low risk of QT interval prolongation.
- **Regulatory Submission:** The data supported the IND submission, and the drug was approved for clinical trials without additional cardiac safety concerns.
- **Outcome:** The drug successfully progressed through clinical trials and was approved for market entry with a favorable cardiac safety profile.

Example 3: hERG Assay in the Development of an Antiarrhythmic Drug
Objective: Evaluate the hERG liability of a new antiarrhythmic drug designed to modulate cardiac ion channels.
Methods and Protocols:

- **hERG Channel Assay:**

- ○ **Protocol:** Human cell lines expressing the hERG channel were exposed to the test compound. Electrophysiological recordings were made to assess the inhibition of hERG current.
- ○ **Results:** The IC50 value was found to be 0.5 µM, indicating potent hERG channel inhibition at therapeutic concentrations.

Regulatory Importance:

- **Risk Management:** Given the drug's intended use for cardiac conditions, the potent hERG inhibition posed a significant risk.
- **Regulatory Consultation:** Early consultation with regulatory agencies led to the implementation of comprehensive cardiac safety studies and careful dose selection.
- **Outcome:** Despite the initial hERG liability, the drug was approved for clinical use with stringent ECG monitoring protocols and dosing guidelines to mitigate the risk of QT interval prolongation.

Example 4: hERG Assay in the Development of an Oncology Drug
Objective: Assess the hERG liability of a new oncology drug.
Methods and Protocols:

- **hERG Channel Assay:**

- ○ **Protocol:** Human cell lines expressing the hERG channel were treated with the oncology drug at various concentrations. The degree of hERG current inhibition was measured.
- ○ **Results:** The IC50 value was 8 µM, with significant inhibition at therapeutic doses.

Regulatory Importance:

- **Risk Identification:** The hERG assay indicated a potential risk for QT interval prolongation.
- **Risk Mitigation:** Additional preclinical studies and modifications to the clinical trial design were implemented, including more frequent ECG monitoring.
- **Outcome:** The drug was approved for clinical trials with enhanced safety monitoring. It was eventually approved for market use with specific

warnings and monitoring requirements related to QT interval prolongation.

5.3 Tier 2 Safety Pharmacology Studies

5.3.1 Gastrointestinal Safety Pharmacology

Testing Methods:

Conducting gastrointestinal (GI) safety studies involves various methodologies to assess the potential adverse effects of new drug candidates on the GI tract. These studies examine factors such as gastric and intestinal motility, pH levels, integrity, permeability, and the effects on the liver and microbiota. Here are the primary methods used in GI safety studies:

1. Gastric and Intestinal Motility:

a. Gastric Emptying Studies:

- **Protocol:** Administer a radiolabeled or dye-labeled meal to the test animals. Measure the rate of gastric emptying using imaging techniques or by tracking the marker's presence in the stomach over time.
- **Parameters Measured:** Gastric emptying time, percentage of meal emptied over a specific period.

b. Intestinal Transit Studies:

- **Protocol:** Administer a non-absorbable marker (e.g., charcoal or radiolabeled material) and measure the time taken for the marker to travel through the intestines.
- **Parameters Measured:** Intestinal transit time, percentage of marker passing through different segments of the intestines.

2. Gastrointestinal pH Measurement:

a. pH Monitoring:

- **Protocol:** Use pH-sensitive electrodes or capsules to measure pH levels in different regions of the GI tract.
- **Parameters Measured:** Gastric pH, intestinal pH.

3. Gastrointestinal Integrity and Permeability:

a. Biomarker Analysis:

- **Protocol:** Measure levels of biomarkers such as lactate dehydrogenase (LDH), alkaline phosphatase (ALP), and lipopolysaccharide (LPS) in blood samples to assess GI damage or inflammation.
- **Parameters Measured:** Biomarker concentrations indicating mucosal damage, permeability, and inflammation.

b. Histopathological Examination:

- **Protocol:** Collect GI tissue samples and perform microscopic examination to identify signs of inflammation, necrosis, or ulceration.
- **Parameters Measured:** Presence and severity of histopathological changes.

4. Hepatic Function and Biliary Secretion:
a. Liver Enzyme Measurement:

- **Protocol:** Measure levels of liver enzymes such as alanine aminotransferase (ALT) and aspartate aminotransferase (AST) in blood samples.
- **Parameters Measured:** ALT and AST concentrations indicating hepatocellular damage.

b. Bile Acid Measurement:

- **Protocol:** Measure bile acid concentrations in blood or bile samples.
- **Parameters Measured:** Bile acid levels indicating biliary secretion function.

5. Gastrointestinal Microbiota:
a. Microbiota Analysis:

- **Protocol:** Collect fecal samples and perform 16S rRNA sequencing to analyze the composition and diversity of gut microbiota.
- **Parameters Measured:** Microbiota composition and diversity indices.

Interpretation of Results:

Interpreting results from GI safety studies involves analyzing the data to identify potential adverse effects on the GI tract. The interpretation focuses on understanding the clinical relevance of observed changes and their impact on the overall safety profile of the drug candidate.

1. Gastric and Intestinal Motility:

- **Delayed Gastric Emptying:** Prolonged gastric emptying time suggests potential for delayed drug absorption and gastroparesis.
- **Accelerated Intestinal Transit:** Reduced transit time indicates increased intestinal motility, potentially leading to diarrhea or reduced drug absorption.
- **Delayed Intestinal Transit:** Prolonged transit time suggests potential for constipation or ileus.

2. Gastrointestinal pH and Secretions:

- **Altered pH Levels:** Changes in gastric or intestinal pH affect enzyme activity and drug solubility, impacting absorption and efficacy. Increased gastric pH (reduced acidity) can decrease solubility and absorption of acid-dependent drugs.

3. Gastrointestinal Integrity and Permeability:

- **Increased Biomarkers:** Elevated levels of GI damage biomarkers indicate potential mucosal damage or increased permeability. Histopathological changes provide direct evidence of GI damage.
- **Histopathological Findings:** Inflammation, necrosis, or ulceration observed microscopically suggests significant GI toxicity.

4. Hepatic Function and Biliary Secretion:

- **Elevated Liver Enzymes:** Increased levels of ALT and AST suggest potential hepatotoxicity. Changes in bile acid levels indicate impaired biliary secretion or liver function.

5. Gastrointestinal Microbiota:

- **Dysbiosis:** Significant changes in the composition or diversity of the gut microbiota indicate potential adverse effects on GI health and overall metabolism.

Case Studies and Examples:
Example 1: Gastrointestinal Safety Assessment of a Nonsteroidal Anti-Inflammatory Drug (NSAID)
Objective: Evaluate the GI safety of a new NSAID.
Methods and Protocols:

- **Gastric Emptying and Intestinal Transit:**

  - **Protocol:** Radiolabeled meal was administered to rodents, and gastric emptying time and intestinal transit time were measured.
  - **Results:** Delayed gastric emptying and prolonged intestinal transit time at higher doses.

- **Gastric pH Measurement:**

  - **Protocol:** Gastric pH was measured using pH-sensitive electrodes.
  - **Results:** Increased gastric pH (reduced acidity) observed.

- **Histopathological Examination:**

  - **Protocol:** GI tissues were collected and examined microscopically.
  - **Results:** Evidence of mucosal damage and ulceration found in the stomach and intestines.

Interpretation:

- **Clinical Relevance:** Delayed gastric emptying and mucosal damage suggest potential GI toxicity at higher doses.
- **Outcome:** Recommended dose adjustments and co-administration with gastroprotective agents. The drug was approved with warnings about potential GI side effects and guidelines for monitoring.

Example 2: Gastrointestinal Safety Evaluation of an Antidiabetic Drug
Objective: Assess the GI safety of a new antidiabetic drug.

Methods and Protocols:

- **Intestinal pH Measurement:**

  - **Protocol:** Intestinal pH was measured using pH-sensitive capsules in animal models.
  - **Results:** No significant changes in intestinal pH observed.

- **Biomarkers of GI Damage:**

  - **Protocol:** Levels of biomarkers such as LDH and ALP were measured in blood samples.
  - **Results:** No significant increase in biomarkers detected.

- **Histopathological Examination:**

  - **Protocol:** GI tissues were collected and examined microscopically.
  - **Results:** No signs of inflammation, necrosis, or ulceration observed.

Interpretation:

- **Clinical Relevance:** Lack of significant changes in pH, biomarkers, and histopathology suggests a favorable GI safety profile.
- **Outcome:** The drug was approved for clinical trials with no additional GI monitoring required.

Example 3: Gastrointestinal Safety Assessment of an Antibiotic
Objective: Evaluate the GI safety of a new antibiotic.
Methods and Protocols:

- **Microbiota Composition Analysis:**

  - **Protocol:** Gut microbiota composition was analyzed using 16S rRNA sequencing in rodents.
  - **Results:** Significant alterations in microbiota composition observed, indicating dysbiosis.

- **Gastric and Intestinal Motility:**

- ○ **Protocol:** Gastric emptying and intestinal transit times were measured.
- ○ **Results:** Accelerated intestinal transit time noted, leading to diarrhea in some animals.

- **Biomarkers of GI Damage:**

  - ○ **Protocol:** Levels of biomarkers such as LPS were measured.
  - ○ **Results:** Elevated LPS levels detected, indicating increased intestinal permeability.

Interpretation:

- **Clinical Relevance:** Dysbiosis, accelerated intestinal transit, and elevated biomarkers suggest potential GI toxicity.
- **Outcome:** Recommended further studies to mitigate GI effects, including probiotic co-administration. The drug was approved for clinical trials with specific guidelines for monitoring GI health.

Example 4: Gastrointestinal Safety Evaluation of a Chemotherapeutic Agent

Objective: Assess the GI safety of a new chemotherapeutic agent.
Methods and Protocols:

- **Liver Enzyme Measurement:**

  - ○ **Protocol:** Levels of ALT and AST were measured in blood samples.
  - ○ **Results:** Elevated levels of liver enzymes observed, indicating potential hepatotoxicity.

- **Histopathological Examination:**

  - ○ **Protocol:** Liver and GI tissues were collected and examined microscopically.
  - ○ **Results:** Evidence of liver inflammation and GI mucosal damage found.

- **Bile Acid Measurement:**

- ◦ **Protocol:** Bile acid concentrations were measured in blood samples.
- ◦ **Results:** Altered bile acid levels detected, suggesting impaired biliary secretion.

Interpretation:

- **Clinical Relevance:** Elevated liver enzymes and histopathological findings indicate significant GI and hepatic toxicity.
- **Outcome:** Recommended dose adjustments and additional hepatoprotective measures. The drug was approved for clinical trials with enhanced monitoring of liver and GI function.

5.3 Tier 2 Safety Pharmacology Studies

5.3.2 Renal Safety Pharmacology

Assessment Techniques:

Assessing renal safety involves evaluating the potential adverse effects of new drug candidates on kidney function and structure. The following are key techniques used to assess renal safety:

1. Biomarker Analysis:
a. Serum Creatinine and Blood Urea Nitrogen (BUN):

- **Protocol:** Measure levels of serum creatinine and BUN in blood samples.
- **Parameters Measured:** Elevated levels indicate impaired renal function and decreased glomerular filtration rate (GFR).

b. Urinalysis:

- **Protocol:** Analyze urine samples for protein, glucose, blood, and specific gravity.
- **Parameters Measured:** Presence of protein (proteinuria), glucose (glycosuria), and blood (hematuria) in urine can indicate renal damage.

c. Novel Renal Biomarkers:

- **Protocol:** Measure levels of specific biomarkers such as neutrophil gelatinase-associated lipocalin (NGAL), kidney injury molecule-1 (KIM-1), and cystatin C.
- **Parameters Measured:** Elevated levels of these biomarkers can indicate early renal injury before changes in serum creatinine and BUN.

2. Renal Imaging:
a. Ultrasound Imaging:

- **Protocol:** Use ultrasound to visualize kidney size, structure, and presence of any abnormalities.
- **Parameters Measured:** Changes in kidney size, structure, and presence of cysts or tumors.

b. Magnetic Resonance Imaging (MRI):

- **Protocol:** Use MRI to obtain detailed images of kidney structure and function.
- **Parameters Measured:** Detailed assessment of renal morphology and function, including blood flow and filtration.

3. Renal Function Tests:
a. Glomerular Filtration Rate (GFR):

- **Protocol:** Measure GFR using endogenous markers (e.g., serum creatinine) or exogenous markers (e.g., inulin, iohexol).
- **Parameters Measured:** GFR provides an overall assessment of kidney function.

b. Tubular Function Tests:

- **Protocol:** Measure renal clearance of specific substances (e.g., glucose, amino acids) to assess tubular reabsorption and secretion.
- **Parameters Measured:** Renal clearance rates and fractional excretion of electrolytes.

4. Histopathological Examination:
a. Renal Biopsy:

- **Protocol:** Collect kidney tissue samples and perform microscopic examination.
- **Parameters Measured:** Presence of histopathological changes such as inflammation, fibrosis, necrosis, and tubular injury.

Case Studies and Examples:
Example 1: Renal Safety Assessment of a New Antihypertensive Drug
Objective: Evaluate the renal safety of a new antihypertensive drug.
Methods and Protocols:

- **Biomarker Analysis:**

  - **Protocol:** Measured levels of serum creatinine, BUN, and novel renal biomarkers (NGAL, KIM-1) in blood samples from treated and control groups.
  - **Results:** Elevated serum creatinine and BUN levels were observed in the treated group, along with increased levels of NGAL and KIM-1.

- **Renal Imaging:**

  - **Protocol:** Performed ultrasound imaging to assess kidney structure.
  - **Results:** No significant structural abnormalities were detected.

- **Histopathological Examination:**

  - **Protocol:** Collected renal tissue samples and performed microscopic examination.
  - **Results:** Evidence of mild tubular injury and inflammation in the treated group.

Interpretation:

- **Clinical Relevance:** Elevated biomarkers and histopathological findings suggest potential renal toxicity.
- **Outcome:** Recommended dose adjustments and further studies to mitigate renal effects. The drug was approved for clinical trials with enhanced renal monitoring.

Example 2: Renal Safety Evaluation of a Chemotherapeutic Agent
Objective: Assess the renal safety of a new chemotherapeutic agent.
Methods and Protocols:

- **Biomarker Analysis:**

  - **Protocol:** Measured serum creatinine, BUN, and cystatin C levels in blood samples.
  - **Results:** Significant increases in serum creatinine and BUN levels, indicating impaired renal function.

- **Renal Function Tests:**

  - **Protocol:** Measured GFR using iohexol clearance and tubular function tests (e.g., fractional excretion of sodium).
  - **Results:** Reduced GFR and impaired tubular reabsorption were observed.

- **Histopathological Examination:**

  - **Protocol:** Collected kidney tissue samples and performed microscopic examination.
  - **Results:** Evidence of tubular necrosis and interstitial fibrosis.

Interpretation:

- **Clinical Relevance:** Reduced GFR, impaired tubular function, and histopathological damage indicate significant renal toxicity.
- **Outcome:** The drug was approved for clinical trials with specific dosing guidelines and rigorous renal monitoring to mitigate potential renal adverse effects.

Example 3: Renal Safety Assessment of an Anti-Diabetic Drug
Objective: Evaluate the renal safety of a new anti-diabetic drug.
Methods and Protocols:

- **Biomarker Analysis:**

- **Protocol:** Measured levels of serum creatinine, BUN, and KIM-1 in blood samples.
- **Results:** No significant changes in serum creatinine and BUN levels; slight increase in KIM-1 levels.

- **Renal Imaging:**

  - **Protocol:** Conducted MRI scans to assess kidney structure and blood flow.
  - **Results:** No significant abnormalities detected in renal morphology or blood flow.

- **Tubular Function Tests:**

  - **Protocol:** Measured renal clearance of glucose and amino acids.
  - **Results:** Normal renal clearance rates and tubular function.

Interpretation:

- **Clinical Relevance:** Slight increase in KIM-1 levels suggests early signs of renal stress, but overall renal function and structure appear normal.
- **Outcome:** The drug was approved for clinical trials with routine monitoring of renal biomarkers to detect any potential adverse effects early.

Example 4: Renal Safety Evaluation of a New Antibiotic
Objective: Assess the renal safety of a new antibiotic.
Methods and Protocols:

- **Biomarker Analysis:**

  - **Protocol:** Measured serum creatinine, BUN, and NGAL levels in blood samples.
  - **Results:** Elevated NGAL levels, with no significant changes in serum creatinine and BUN.

- **Histopathological Examination:**

- ○ **Protocol:** Collected renal tissue samples and performed microscopic examination.
- ○ **Results:** Mild tubular inflammation observed in treated animals.

- **Renal Function Tests:**

- ○ **Protocol:** Measured GFR using inulin clearance.
- ○ **Results:** No significant changes in GFR observed.

Interpretation:

- **Clinical Relevance:** Elevated NGAL levels and mild histopathological changes suggest early renal stress, but overall renal function remains intact.
- **Outcome:** The drug was approved for clinical trials with recommendations for periodic monitoring of renal biomarkers to ensure continued renal safety

5.3 Tier 2 Safety Pharmacology Studies
5.3.3 Other Organ System Safety Pharmacology

Evaluation Procedures:

Evaluating the safety of other organ systems involves specific procedures tailored to assess potential adverse effects on organs such as the cardiovascular system, respiratory system, nervous system, endocrine system, and more. The following are the key evaluation procedures for different organ systems:

1. Cardiovascular System:
a. Electrocardiography (ECG):

- **Protocol:** Continuous or periodic ECG monitoring to assess heart rate, rhythm, and electrical conduction.
- **Parameters Measured:** Heart rate, PR interval, QRS duration, QT interval, and presence of arrhythmias.

b. Blood Pressure Measurement:

- **Protocol:** Use of telemetry devices or non-invasive cuffs to measure systolic, diastolic, and mean arterial blood pressure.
- **Parameters Measured:** Blood pressure levels and variability.

2. Respiratory System:
a. Pulmonary Function Tests (PFTs):

- **Protocol:** Measure lung volumes, capacities, and flow rates using spirometry and plethysmography.
- **Parameters Measured:** Tidal volume, vital capacity, forced expiratory volume (FEV1), and peak expiratory flow rate (PEFR).

b. Blood Gas Analysis:

- **Protocol:** Measure arterial blood gases to assess oxygenation and ventilation.
- **Parameters Measured:** Partial pressures of oxygen (PaO2) and carbon dioxide (PaCO2), oxygen saturation (SaO2), and pH.

3. Nervous System:
a. Behavioral Tests:

- **Protocol:** Conduct behavioral assays such as open field test, rotarod test, and elevated plus maze to assess locomotion, coordination, and anxiety.
- **Parameters Measured:** Locomotor activity, motor coordination, and anxiety-related behavior.

b. Electrophysiological Recording:

- **Protocol:** Use electroencephalography (EEG) to monitor brain electrical activity.
- **Parameters Measured:** EEG patterns, frequency, amplitude, and presence of seizures.

4. Endocrine System:
a. Hormone Level Measurement:

- **Protocol:** Measure levels of hormones such as insulin, cortisol, thyroid hormones, and sex hormones in blood samples.
- **Parameters Measured:** Hormone concentrations indicating endocrine function.

b. Glucose Tolerance Test:

- **Protocol:** Administer glucose and measure blood glucose levels over time to assess insulin sensitivity and glucose metabolism.
- **Parameters Measured:** Blood glucose levels at various time points, insulin response.

Data Analysis:

Analyzing data from safety pharmacology studies involves statistical and interpretive techniques to identify potential adverse effects and understand their clinical relevance. The following are key techniques for data analysis:

1. Basic Statistical Analysis:

a. Descriptive Statistics:

- **Objective:** Summarize central tendency and variability of measured parameters.
- **Techniques:** Calculate mean, standard deviation, median, and range.

b. Comparative Statistics:

- **Objective:** Compare parameters between treated and control groups.
- **Techniques:** Use t-tests, ANOVA, or non-parametric tests (e.g., Mann-Whitney U test) for comparisons.

2. Time-Series Analysis:

a. Baseline and Post-Treatment Comparison:

- **Objective:** Evaluate changes in parameters over time.
- **Techniques:** Normalize post-treatment data to baseline values, plot time-series data to identify trends.

b. Repeated Measures Analysis:

- **Objective:** Account for correlation between repeated measurements.
- **Techniques:** Use mixed-effects models or generalized estimating equations (GEE) for analysis.

3. Multivariate Analysis:
a. Principal Component Analysis (PCA):

- **Objective:** Reduce dimensionality and identify key components contributing to variability.
- **Techniques:** Perform PCA on multiple parameters to identify patterns.

b. Cluster Analysis:

- **Objective:** Group similar responses or patterns.
- **Techniques:** Use k-means clustering or hierarchical clustering for grouping data.

4. Risk Assessment:
a. Clinical Relevance:

- **Objective:** Interpret data in the context of clinical significance.
- **Techniques:** Compare findings to established clinical thresholds or benchmarks.

b. Safety Margin Calculation:

- **Objective:** Determine safety margins based on dose-response relationships.
- **Techniques:** Calculate therapeutic index and safety margins.

Case Studies and Examples:
Example 1: Cardiovascular Safety Assessment of a New Antihypertensive Drug
Objective: Evaluate the cardiovascular safety of a new antihypertensive drug.
Methods and Protocols:

- **Electrocardiography (ECG):**

- **Protocol:** Continuous ECG monitoring in treated and control animals.
- **Results:** No significant changes in heart rate, PR interval, QRS duration, or QT interval observed.

- **Blood Pressure Measurement:**

  - **Protocol:** Telemetry devices used to measure blood pressure continuously.
  - **Results:** Significant reduction in systolic and diastolic blood pressure in the treated group without hypotension.

Data Analysis:

- **Descriptive Statistics:** Mean and standard deviation calculated for ECG and blood pressure parameters.
- **Comparative Statistics:** T-tests used to compare blood pressure levels between treated and control groups.

Interpretation:

- **Clinical Relevance:** The drug effectively reduced blood pressure without causing adverse cardiovascular effects.
- **Outcome:** The drug was approved for clinical trials with routine cardiovascular monitoring.

Example 2: Respiratory Safety Evaluation of a New Bronchodilator
Objective: Assess the respiratory safety of a new bronchodilator.
Methods and Protocols:

- **Pulmonary Function Tests (PFTs):**

  - **Protocol:** Spirometry and plethysmography used to measure lung volumes and flow rates.
  - **Results:** Increased tidal volume and vital capacity observed, indicating bronchodilation.

- **Blood Gas Analysis:**

- ○ **Protocol:** Arterial blood gases measured to assess oxygenation and ventilation.
- ○ **Results:** Improved PaO_2 and SaO_2 levels observed without significant changes in $PaCO_2$ or pH.

Data Analysis:

- **Descriptive Statistics:** Mean and standard deviation calculated for PFT and blood gas parameters.
- **Comparative Statistics:** ANOVA used to compare respiratory parameters between treated and control groups.

Interpretation:

- **Clinical Relevance:** The drug effectively improved lung function and oxygenation without causing respiratory acidosis or alkalosis.
- **Outcome:** The drug was approved for clinical trials with routine respiratory monitoring.

Example 3: Nervous System Safety Assessment of a CNS Stimulant
Objective: Evaluate the nervous system safety of a new CNS stimulant.
Methods and Protocols:

- **Behavioral Tests:**

  - ○ **Protocol:** Open field test, rotarod test, and elevated plus maze conducted to assess locomotion, coordination, and anxiety.
  - ○ **Results:** Increased locomotor activity and reduced anxiety observed without impairment in motor coordination.

- **Electrophysiological Recording:**

  - ○ **Protocol:** EEG used to monitor brain electrical activity.
  - ○ **Results:** No significant changes in EEG patterns or presence of seizures observed.

Data Analysis:

- **Descriptive Statistics:** Mean and standard deviation calculated for behavioral and EEG parameters.
- **Comparative Statistics:** T-tests used to compare behavioral data between treated and control groups.

Interpretation:

- **Clinical Relevance:** The drug effectively increased locomotion and reduced anxiety without causing adverse electrophysiological effects.
- **Outcome:** The drug was approved for clinical trials with routine neurological monitoring.

Example 4: Endocrine System Safety Evaluation of a New Anti-Diabetic Drug

Objective: Assess the endocrine safety of a new anti-diabetic drug.

Methods and Protocols:

- **Hormone Level Measurement:**

  - **Protocol:** Levels of insulin, cortisol, and thyroid hormones measured in blood samples.
  - **Results:** Increased insulin levels observed with no significant changes in cortisol or thyroid hormones.

- **Glucose Tolerance Test:**

  - **Protocol:** Glucose administered, and blood glucose levels measured over time.
  - **Results:** Improved glucose tolerance observed with reduced blood glucose levels post-administration.

Data Analysis:

- **Descriptive Statistics:** Mean and standard deviation calculated for hormone and glucose levels.
- **Comparative Statistics:** ANOVA used to compare glucose tolerance between treated and control groups.

Interpretation:

- **Clinical Relevance:** The drug effectively improved glucose tolerance and increased insulin levels without causing endocrine imbalances.
- **Outcome:** The drug was approved for clinical trials with routine endocrine monitoring.

VI
Toxicokinetics

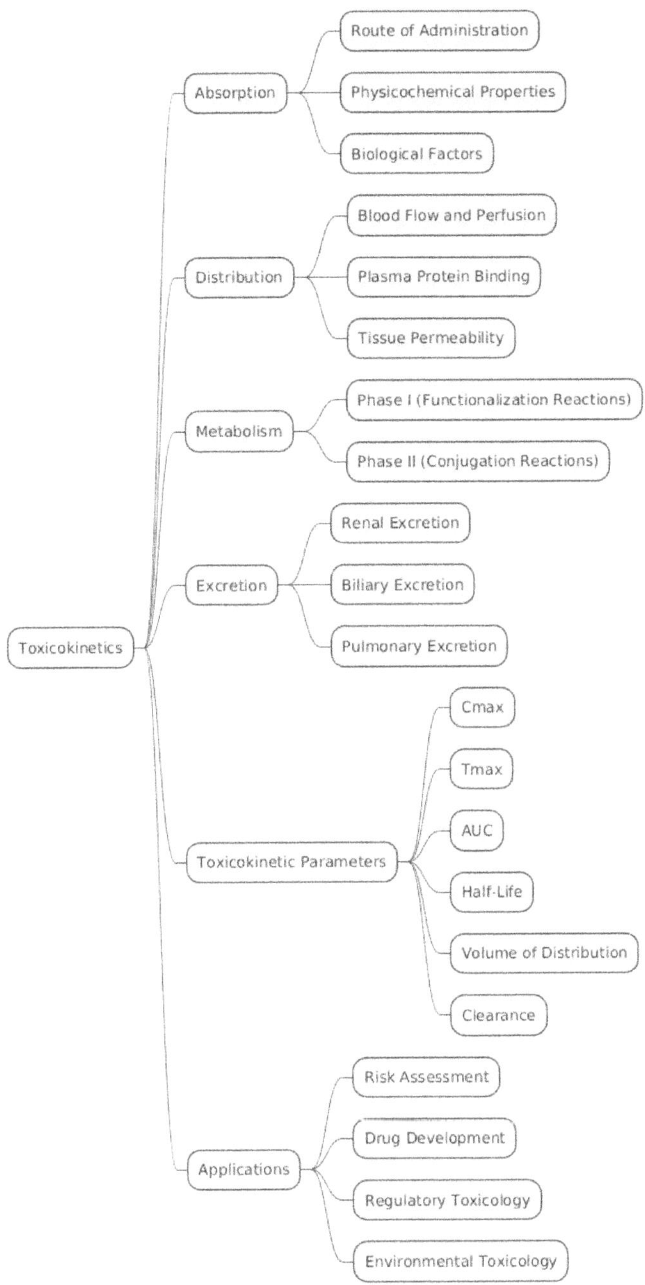

Overview of Toxicokinetic Processes

6.1 Introduction to Toxicokinetics

6.1.1 Definition and Scope
Basic Concepts:

Toxicokinetics (TK) is the study of how a substance enters, moves through, and leaves the body, focusing specifically on the kinetics of potentially toxic substances. It involves the application of pharmacokinetic principles to toxicology studies, aiming to understand the absorption, distribution, metabolism, and excretion (ADME) of these substances.

1. Absorption:
a. Definition:

- **Absorption** refers to the process by which a substance enters the bloodstream from the site of administration (e.g., oral, inhalation, dermal).

b. Factors Affecting Absorption:

- **Route of Administration:** Different routes can significantly impact the absorption rate and extent. For instance, intravenous administration bypasses absorption barriers, leading to immediate systemic availability.
- **Physicochemical Properties:** Factors such as solubility, molecular size, and ionization state can influence absorption. Lipophilic substances tend to be absorbed more readily through cell membranes.
- **Biological Factors:** Gastric emptying time, intestinal transit time, and the presence of food can affect oral absorption. The integrity of the skin barrier affects dermal absorption.

2. Distribution:
a. Definition:

- **Distribution** refers to the dispersion or dissemination of substances throughout the fluids and tissues of the body.

b. Factors Affecting Distribution:

- **Blood Flow and Perfusion:** Organs with high blood flow (e.g., liver, kidneys) receive substances more quickly.
- **Plasma Protein Binding:** Substances bound to plasma proteins are generally inactive and have a longer half-life in the body.
- **Tissue Permeability:** Lipophilic substances tend to accumulate in fatty tissues, while hydrophilic substances distribute more in extracellular fluids.

3. Metabolism:
a. Definition:

- **Metabolism** (biotransformation) refers to the chemical modification of substances by the body, primarily through enzymatic activity, converting them into more water-soluble compounds for easier excretion.

b. Phases of Metabolism:

- **Phase I (Functionalization Reactions):** These include oxidation, reduction, and hydrolysis reactions that introduce or expose functional groups on the substance. Cytochrome P450 enzymes play a crucial role in Phase I metabolism.
- **Phase II (Conjugation Reactions):** These involve conjugation of the substance with endogenous molecules (e.g., glucuronic acid, sulfate, glycine) to form more water-soluble conjugates for excretion.

4. Excretion:
a. Definition:

- **Excretion** refers to the removal of substances from the body, primarily through urine (renal excretion), feces (biliary excretion), or exhalation.

b. Routes of Excretion:

- **Renal Excretion:** Kidneys filter the blood, and water-soluble substances are excreted in urine. Factors such as urine pH and renal blood flow can affect excretion rates.
- **Biliary Excretion:** Substances are secreted into bile and eliminated in feces. Enterohepatic circulation can occur, where substances are

reabsorbed from the intestine back into the bloodstream.
- **Pulmonary Excretion:** Volatile substances and gases are excreted via the lungs through exhalation.

5. Toxicokinetic Parameters:
a. Key Parameters:

- **Cmax:** Maximum concentration of the substance in the blood.
- **Tmax:** Time to reach the maximum concentration.
- **AUC (Area Under the Curve):** Total exposure to the substance over time.
- **Half-Life (t1/2):** Time taken for the blood concentration of the substance to decrease by half.
- **Volume of Distribution (Vd):** The theoretical volume in which the total amount of substance would need to be uniformly distributed to achieve the same concentration as in the blood.
- **Clearance (Cl):** The rate at which the substance is removed from the body.

b. Importance:

- Understanding these parameters helps in assessing the potential toxicity of substances, designing safe and effective dosing regimens, and predicting potential interactions with other substances.

6. Applications of Toxicokinetics:
a. Risk Assessment:

- Toxicokinetics provides crucial data for risk assessment by characterizing the dose-response relationship and identifying safe exposure levels for humans and animals.

b. Drug Development:

- In drug development, toxicokinetics helps in understanding the ADME properties of new drug candidates, optimizing dosing strategies, and predicting potential toxic effects.

c. Regulatory Toxicology:

- Regulatory agencies require toxicokinetic data to evaluate the safety of new drugs, chemicals, and environmental contaminants, ensuring that exposure levels remain within safe limits.

d. Environmental Toxicology:

- Toxicokinetics is used to assess the behavior of environmental pollutants in organisms, predicting their persistence, bioaccumulation, and potential adverse effects on ecosystems.

6.1 Introduction to Toxicokinetics
6.1.1 Definition and Scope
Importance in Drug Development:

The role of toxicokinetics (TK) in drug development is pivotal for ensuring the safety, efficacy, and proper dosing of new drug candidates. Toxicokinetics provides critical insights into the absorption, distribution, metabolism, and excretion (ADME) of substances, helping to identify potential toxicities and optimize drug design and usage. The following outlines the key roles of toxicokinetics in drug development and safety assessments:

1. Understanding Drug Absorption and Bioavailability:
a. Assessing Absorption:

- Toxicokinetic studies help determine how efficiently a drug is absorbed into the bloodstream following administration by different routes (oral, intravenous, inhalation, dermal).
- This information is crucial for developing formulations that maximize bioavailability and therapeutic efficacy.

b. Determining Bioavailability:

- Bioavailability refers to the fraction of an administered dose that reaches the systemic circulation in an active form.
- Toxicokinetic studies provide data on bioavailability, which is essential for dose selection and predicting therapeutic outcomes.

2. Optimizing Drug Distribution:
a. Tissue Distribution:

- Toxicokinetics assesses how a drug distributes throughout the body's tissues and organs, which can impact its efficacy and potential toxicity.
- Understanding tissue distribution helps in designing drugs that target specific tissues while minimizing exposure to non-target areas.

b. Plasma Protein Binding:

- The extent to which a drug binds to plasma proteins affects its distribution, half-life, and free (active) concentration.
- Toxicokinetic studies measure plasma protein binding to predict a drug's pharmacokinetic behavior and potential drug-drug interactions.

3. Characterizing Metabolic Pathways:
a. Identifying Metabolites:

- Toxicokinetics identifies the metabolic pathways and major metabolites of a drug, providing insights into its biotransformation.
- This information helps predict potential metabolic interactions and the formation of toxic metabolites.

b. Assessing Metabolic Stability:

- Metabolic stability refers to how rapidly a drug is metabolized and cleared from the body.
- Toxicokinetic studies assess metabolic stability to determine the drug's half-life and optimize dosing regimens.

4. Ensuring Safe and Effective Excretion:
a. Excretion Routes:

- Toxicokinetic studies identify the primary routes of excretion (renal, biliary, pulmonary) and the efficiency of drug elimination.
- Understanding excretion helps prevent the accumulation of toxic levels and informs dose adjustments in patients with impaired excretory function.

b. Clearance and Half-Life:

- Clearance is the rate at which a drug is removed from the body, and half-life is the time required for its concentration to decrease by half.
- These parameters are crucial for designing dosing schedules and ensuring that drug levels remain within the therapeutic range without causing toxicity.

5. Predicting Drug-Drug Interactions:
a. Interaction Potential:

- Toxicokinetic studies assess how a drug affects or is affected by the presence of other substances, predicting potential drug-drug interactions.
- This information is vital for developing safe combination therapies and managing polypharmacy in clinical practice.

6. Regulatory Submissions:
a. Compliance with Guidelines:

- Regulatory agencies, such as the FDA and EMA, require comprehensive toxicokinetic data as part of Investigational New Drug (IND) and New Drug Application (NDA) submissions.
- Compliance with regulatory guidelines ensures that drug developers provide sufficient evidence of safety and efficacy.

b. Supporting Risk Assessment:

- Toxicokinetic data support risk assessment by characterizing the dose-response relationship and identifying safe exposure levels.
- This information helps regulatory agencies make informed decisions about the approval and labeling of new drugs.

Case Studies and Examples:
Example 1: Toxicokinetic Evaluation of a New Anticancer Drug
Objective: Assess the toxicokinetics of a new anticancer drug to optimize dosing and minimize toxicity.
Methods and Protocols:

- **Absorption Studies:**

- **Protocol:** Conduct oral and intravenous administration studies in animal models to determine bioavailability.
- **Results:** The oral bioavailability was found to be 40%, indicating moderate absorption.

- **Distribution Studies:**

  - **Protocol:** Perform tissue distribution studies using radiolabeled drug to assess target tissue accumulation.
  - **Results:** High accumulation in tumor tissues and moderate levels in liver and kidneys.

- **Metabolism Studies:**

  - **Protocol:** Identify metabolites using mass spectrometry and assess metabolic pathways.
  - **Results:** Major metabolites identified included glucuronide conjugates formed via Phase II metabolism.

- **Excretion Studies:**

  - **Protocol:** Measure drug levels in urine and feces to determine excretion routes.
  - **Results:** The drug was primarily excreted via the biliary route, with 60% recovered in feces.

Interpretation:

- **Clinical Relevance:** The moderate oral bioavailability suggests the need for formulation optimization. High tumor accumulation indicates effective targeting, while biliary excretion informs dosing adjustments in patients with hepatic impairment.
- **Outcome:** The drug was advanced to clinical trials with optimized oral formulations and specific guidelines for monitoring hepatic function.

Example 2: Toxicokinetic Assessment of a New Antibiotic
Objective: Evaluate the toxicokinetics of a new broad-spectrum antibiotic to ensure safe and effective dosing.

Methods and Protocols:

- **Absorption Studies:**

  - **Protocol:** Conduct absorption studies in rodents and non-human primates using various administration routes.
  - **Results:** High bioavailability observed with intravenous and intramuscular administration, but low oral bioavailability.

- **Distribution Studies:**

  - **Protocol:** Perform plasma protein binding studies and assess tissue distribution.
  - **Results:** The antibiotic exhibited high plasma protein binding (90%) and extensive distribution in lung and kidney tissues.

- **Metabolism Studies:**

  - **Protocol:** Identify metabolic pathways using liver microsomes and assess the formation of active metabolites.
  - **Results:** Minimal metabolism observed, with the parent compound being the predominant form.

- **Excretion Studies:**

  - **Protocol:** Measure drug levels in urine to determine renal clearance.
  - **Results:** Rapid renal excretion with 80% of the administered dose recovered in urine within 24 hours.

Interpretation:

- **Clinical Relevance:** High plasma protein binding and rapid renal excretion suggest a need for frequent dosing to maintain therapeutic levels. The low oral bioavailability indicates a preference for parenteral administration.
- **Outcome:** The antibiotic was advanced to clinical trials with a recommended dosing regimen for intravenous and intramuscular administration.

Example 3: Toxicokinetic Analysis of a New Antidepressant
Objective: Assess the toxicokinetics of a new antidepressant to optimize its therapeutic window and minimize adverse effects.
Methods and Protocols:

- **Absorption Studies:**

  - **Protocol:** Conduct oral absorption studies in animal models and human volunteers.
  - **Results:** High oral bioavailability (70%) observed in both animal models and humans.

- **Distribution Studies:**

  - **Protocol:** Perform tissue distribution studies and assess blood-brain barrier penetration.
  - **Results:** High distribution in brain tissue, indicating effective central nervous system penetration.

- **Metabolism Studies:**

  - **Protocol:** Identify metabolic pathways using human liver microsomes and assess the formation of active metabolites.
  - **Results:** The drug underwent extensive hepatic metabolism, with two active metabolites identified.

- **Excretion Studies:**

  - **Protocol:** Measure drug and metabolite levels in urine and feces.
  - **Results:** The drug and its metabolites were primarily excreted via the renal route.

Interpretation:

- **Clinical Relevance:** High oral bioavailability and effective brain penetration suggest the drug is suitable for oral administration. The formation of active metabolites and renal excretion inform dosing adjustments in patients with hepatic or renal impairment.

- **Outcome:** The antidepressant was advanced to clinical trials with specific dosing guidelines and monitoring for hepatic and renal function.

6.1 Introduction to Toxicokinetics

6.1.2 Importance in Drug Development
Regulatory Considerations:

Toxicokinetics is an essential component of the drug development process, with significant regulatory implications. Various regulatory bodies require comprehensive toxicokinetic data to ensure the safety and efficacy of new drug candidates. Here's an overview of the regulatory considerations related to toxicokinetics:

1. Regulatory Requirements:

a. Data Submission:

- **Regulatory Agencies:** Agencies such as the U.S. Food and Drug Administration (FDA), the European Medicines Agency (EMA), and other global regulatory bodies require detailed toxicokinetic data as part of drug development submissions.
- **Submission Documents:** Toxicokinetic data must be included in Investigational New Drug (IND) applications, New Drug Applications (NDA), and Marketing Authorization Applications (MAA). These documents should include information on ADME (absorption, distribution, metabolism, and excretion), potential toxicities, and dose-response relationships.

b. Guidelines and Standards:

- **International Guidelines:** Regulatory guidelines such as those from the International Council for Harmonisation (ICH) provide standards for toxicokinetic studies. For example, ICH guidelines such as ICH S3A (Toxicokinetics: The Assessment of Systemic Exposure in Toxicity Studies) outline the requirements for conducting and reporting toxicokinetic studies.
- **Study Design:** Guidelines specify the design of toxicokinetic studies, including the selection of animal models, dosing regimens, and analytical methods. Compliance with these guidelines is crucial for

regulatory acceptance.

2. Role in Risk Assessment:
a. Safety Evaluation:

- **Identification of Risks:** Toxicokinetic studies help identify potential risks associated with drug exposure, including risks of toxicity due to high systemic levels or accumulation.
- **Dose Optimization:** Data from toxicokinetic studies are used to optimize dosing regimens, ensuring that drug levels remain within safe limits and reducing the risk of adverse effects.

b. Predictive Toxicity:

- **Extrapolation to Humans:** Toxicokinetic data from animal studies are used to predict human exposure and potential toxicities. Regulatory agencies assess whether these predictions are reliable and relevant to human safety.
- **Safety Margins:** Establishing safety margins based on toxicokinetic data helps in determining safe starting doses and maximum allowable doses in clinical trials.

3. Compliance and Approval:
a. Study Reporting:

- **Detailed Reporting:** Regulatory agencies require detailed reporting of toxicokinetic studies, including methods, results, and interpretations. Accurate and comprehensive reporting is essential for regulatory review and approval.
- **Data Quality:** High-quality, reproducible data is required to support the safety profile of the drug. Regulatory agencies scrutinize data quality and consistency during the review process.

b. Risk Management:

- **Labeling Requirements:** Based on toxicokinetic data, regulatory agencies may require specific labeling for the drug, including warnings, contraindications, and recommended dose adjustments.

- **Post-Marketing Surveillance:** Toxicokinetic data also play a role in post-marketing surveillance to monitor long-term safety and efficacy, as well as to identify any unforeseen adverse effects.

Examples from Industry:
Example 1: Toxicokinetic Data for a New Anticancer Drug
Context: A pharmaceutical company developed a new anticancer drug and submitted toxicokinetic data as part of their IND application.
Regulatory Interaction:

- **Submission:** The company provided detailed toxicokinetic studies including absorption, distribution, metabolism, and excretion data in preclinical animal models.
- **Regulatory Feedback:** The FDA reviewed the data and requested additional studies on metabolic pathways and potential toxic metabolites.

Outcome:

- **Approval:** Following additional studies and submission of revised data, the drug was approved for clinical trials with recommendations for monitoring liver function due to identified potential hepatic toxicity.

Example 2: Toxicokinetics of a New Antibiotic
Context: An industry study evaluated the toxicokinetics of a new broad-spectrum antibiotic.
Regulatory Interaction:

- **Study Design:** The study included comprehensive absorption, distribution, metabolism, and excretion profiles in various animal models.
- **Regulatory Submission:** The data were submitted as part of an IND application, and the FDA reviewed the potential for renal toxicity based on high kidney distribution.

Outcome:

- **Labeling:** The FDA approved the drug for clinical trials with specific recommendations for monitoring renal function and dose adjustments in patients with pre-existing renal conditions.

Example 3: Toxicokinetics of a CNS Drug

Context: A pharmaceutical company conducted toxicokinetic studies on a new central nervous system (CNS) drug.

Regulatory Interaction:

- **Detailed Data:** The company provided data on brain penetration, metabolic stability, and potential for drug-drug interactions.
- **Regulatory Review:** The EMA required additional data on the long-term effects of drug accumulation in the CNS.

Outcome:

- **Approval and Recommendations:** The drug was approved with recommendations for periodic neurological assessments during clinical trials to monitor potential CNS effects.

Example 4: Development of a New Antidepressant

Context: A new antidepressant underwent toxicokinetic evaluations as part of its development process.

Regulatory Interaction:

- **Study Results:** The toxicokinetic studies showed extensive CNS penetration and the formation of active metabolites.
- **Regulatory Considerations:** The FDA required additional studies to assess the long-term safety of these metabolites and potential effects on mental health.

Outcome:

- **Approval:** The antidepressant was approved for clinical trials with recommendations for mental health monitoring and dose adjustments based on metabolite levels.

6.1 Introduction to Toxicokinetics

6.1.3 Applications in Preclinical Studies

Case Studies:

The application of toxicokinetics in preclinical studies is vital for understanding the behavior of new drug candidates in biological systems. By evaluating absorption, distribution, metabolism, and excretion (ADME) properties, researchers can identify potential toxicities and optimize dosing regimens before advancing to clinical trials. The following case studies illustrate the role of toxicokinetics in preclinical research:

Case Study 1: Toxicokinetic Evaluation of a Novel Anti-inflammatory Drug

Objective: Assess the toxicokinetics of a novel anti-inflammatory drug to determine its safety profile and optimal dosing in animal models.

Methods and Protocols:

- **Absorption Studies:**

  - **Protocol:** Conduct oral and intravenous (IV) administration studies in rats and dogs to determine bioavailability.
  - **Results:** Oral bioavailability was found to be 45% in rats and 55% in dogs, indicating moderate absorption across species.

- **Distribution Studies:**

  - **Protocol:** Perform tissue distribution studies using radiolabeled drug to assess the extent of distribution to various organs.
  - **Results:** High levels of the drug were detected in the liver, kidneys, and spleen, with lower levels in the brain.

- **Metabolism Studies:**

  - **Protocol:** Identify metabolic pathways using liver microsomes and mass spectrometry.
  - **Results:** The drug underwent extensive Phase I metabolism, primarily through oxidation, with several metabolites identified.

- **Excretion Studies:**

- ◦ **Protocol:** Measure drug and metabolite levels in urine and feces to determine excretion routes.
- ◦ **Results:** The drug was primarily excreted via the renal route, with 70% of the administered dose recovered in urine.

Interpretation:

- **Clinical Relevance:** Moderate oral bioavailability and significant renal excretion suggested the need for monitoring renal function. The extensive metabolism indicated potential interactions with other drugs metabolized by similar pathways.
- **Outcome:** The drug was advanced to further preclinical toxicology studies with specific focus on renal toxicity and drug-drug interactions.

Case Study 2: Toxicokinetic Analysis of a New Antiviral Agent
Objective: Evaluate the toxicokinetics of a new antiviral agent to understand its pharmacokinetic profile and potential for toxicity.
Methods and Protocols:

- **Absorption Studies:**

  - ◦ **Protocol:** Conduct oral and intramuscular (IM) administration studies in mice and rabbits to determine bioavailability.
  - ◦ **Results:** Oral bioavailability was low (25% in mice and 30% in rabbits), while IM administration showed high bioavailability (>90%).

- **Distribution Studies:**

  - ◦ **Protocol:** Perform plasma protein binding studies to assess the extent of binding.
  - ◦ **Results:** The drug exhibited high plasma protein binding (95%), suggesting limited free drug availability in plasma.

- **Metabolism Studies:**

  - ◦ **Protocol:** Identify metabolites using in vitro hepatocyte assays and in vivo animal studies.

- **Results:** The drug was metabolized to several active metabolites, primarily through glucuronidation.

• **Excretion Studies:**

- **Protocol:** Measure drug levels in bile and feces to determine biliary excretion.
- **Results:** Significant biliary excretion was observed, with 60% of the administered dose recovered in feces.

Interpretation:

• **Clinical Relevance:** Low oral bioavailability suggested a preference for IM administration. High plasma protein binding and significant biliary excretion highlighted the need for dose adjustments in patients with hepatic impairment.
• **Outcome:** The antiviral agent was progressed to dose-ranging studies with specific recommendations for monitoring liver function and potential hepatotoxicity.

Case Study 3: Toxicokinetic Evaluation of a Cardiovascular Drug
Objective: Assess the toxicokinetics of a new cardiovascular drug to determine its safety and efficacy in animal models.
Methods and Protocols:

• **Absorption Studies:**

- **Protocol:** Conduct IV and subcutaneous (SC) administration studies in rats and dogs to determine bioavailability and absorption kinetics.
- **Results:** The drug exhibited high bioavailability (>90%) with both IV and SC administration.

• **Distribution Studies:**

- **Protocol:** Perform tissue distribution studies to evaluate the extent of drug distribution to the heart and other organs.
- **Results:** The drug showed high distribution to the heart and kidneys, with lower levels in the brain and adipose tissue.

- **Metabolism Studies:**

  - **Protocol:** Identify metabolic pathways using in vitro enzyme assays and in vivo studies.
  - **Results:** The drug underwent limited metabolism, with the parent compound remaining predominant in plasma.

- **Excretion Studies:**

  - **Protocol:** Measure drug levels in urine and plasma to determine renal clearance.
  - **Results:** The drug was primarily excreted unchanged in urine, indicating efficient renal clearance.

Interpretation:

- **Clinical Relevance:** High bioavailability and efficient renal clearance suggested a favorable pharmacokinetic profile for the cardiovascular drug. Limited metabolism reduced the risk of drug-drug interactions.
- **Outcome:** The drug was advanced to chronic toxicity studies with recommendations for renal function monitoring and dose adjustments in patients with renal impairment.

Case Study 4: Toxicokinetic Analysis of a CNS Drug

Objective: Evaluate the toxicokinetics of a new central nervous system (CNS) drug to optimize dosing and assess potential CNS toxicity.

Methods and Protocols:

- **Absorption Studies:**

  - **Protocol:** Conduct oral and IV administration studies in rats and non-human primates to determine bioavailability.
  - **Results:** High oral bioavailability (70%) observed in both species.

- **Distribution Studies:**

  - **Protocol:** Perform brain distribution studies to assess blood-brain barrier penetration.

- ○ **Results:** The drug exhibited high brain penetration, with significant concentrations detected in CNS tissues.

- **Metabolism Studies:**

  - ○ **Protocol:** Identify metabolic pathways using in vitro assays and in vivo animal models.
  - ○ **Results:** Extensive metabolism through hepatic enzymes, with active metabolites identified.

- **Excretion Studies:**

  - ○ **Protocol:** Measure drug levels in cerebrospinal fluid (CSF) and urine to determine excretion routes.
  - ○ **Results:** The drug and its metabolites were primarily excreted via the renal route.

Interpretation:

- **Clinical Relevance:** High oral bioavailability and significant brain penetration suggested the drug was suitable for oral administration in treating CNS disorders. Extensive metabolism required monitoring for potential CNS side effects.
- **Outcome:** The drug was advanced to clinical trials with recommendations for detailed CNS monitoring and assessments of cognitive and neurological functions.

6.1 Introduction to Toxicokinetics
6.1.3 Applications in Preclinical Studies
Methodologies:

In preclinical toxicokinetics studies, a variety of methodologies are employed to comprehensively evaluate the absorption, distribution, metabolism, and excretion (ADME) properties of new drug candidates. These methodologies are essential for understanding the pharmacokinetic profiles of compounds and for identifying potential toxicities. Here are the key methodologies used in preclinical toxicokinetics studies:

1. Absorption Studies:

a. Oral and Intravenous (IV) Administration:

- **Protocol:** Administer the drug orally and intravenously to animal models (e.g., rodents, dogs). Measure drug concentration in blood at various time points.
- **Parameters Measured:** Bioavailability, Cmax (maximum concentration), Tmax (time to reach Cmax), AUC (area under the curve).

b. Other Routes of Administration:

- **Protocol:** Administer the drug via different routes (e.g., intramuscular, subcutaneous, dermal, inhalation) and measure drug concentration in blood over time.
- **Parameters Measured:** Absorption rate, extent of absorption, and comparison with IV administration to determine bioavailability.

2. Distribution Studies:
a. Tissue Distribution:

- **Protocol:** Administer the drug to animal models and collect tissue samples at various time points. Measure drug concentration in different tissues using techniques like mass spectrometry.
- **Parameters Measured:** Tissue distribution profiles, volume of distribution (Vd), and target tissue accumulation.

b. Plasma Protein Binding:

- **Protocol:** Incubate plasma samples with the drug and use techniques such as equilibrium dialysis or ultrafiltration to measure the bound and unbound fractions.
- **Parameters Measured:** Extent of plasma protein binding, free drug concentration, and impact on drug distribution.

3. Metabolism Studies:
a. In Vitro Metabolism:

- **Protocol:** Use liver microsomes, hepatocytes, or recombinant enzymes to study the metabolic stability and pathways of the drug.
- **Parameters Measured:** Metabolic half-life, identification of metabolites, and enzyme kinetics (e.g., Km and Vmax).

b. In Vivo Metabolism:

- **Protocol:** Administer the drug to animal models and collect blood, urine, and feces samples. Use analytical techniques like liquid chromatography-mass spectrometry (LC-MS) to identify and quantify metabolites.
- **Parameters Measured:** In vivo metabolic profiles, major metabolic pathways, and metabolite quantification.

4. Excretion Studies:
a. Renal Excretion:

- **Protocol:** Administer the drug to animal models and collect urine samples over time. Measure drug and metabolite concentrations in urine.
- **Parameters Measured:** Renal clearance, fraction of dose excreted unchanged in urine, and renal excretion rates.

b. Biliary and Fecal Excretion:

- **Protocol:** Administer the drug and collect bile and feces samples. Measure drug and metabolite concentrations in these samples.
- **Parameters Measured:** Biliary excretion, enterohepatic recirculation, and fraction of dose excreted in feces.

5. Advanced Techniques:
a. Mass Spectrometry (MS):

- **Application:** Used extensively for the quantification and identification of drugs and their metabolites in biological samples.
- **Advantages:** High sensitivity, specificity, and ability to analyze complex mixtures.

b. High-Performance Liquid Chromatography (HPLC):

- **Application:** Often coupled with MS (LC-MS) for the separation and quantification of drug compounds.

- **Advantages:** High resolution, ability to handle a wide range of sample types.

c. Nuclear Magnetic Resonance (NMR) Spectroscopy:

- **Application:** Used for the structural elucidation of drug metabolites.
- **Advantages:** Provides detailed molecular information and helps confirm metabolite structures.

6. Modeling and Simulation:
a. Pharmacokinetic (PK) Modeling:

- **Protocol:** Use software tools to develop PK models that describe the ADME processes of the drug based on experimental data.
- **Parameters Measured:** Clearance, volume of distribution, half-life, and predictions of drug concentration-time profiles.

b. Physiologically-Based Pharmacokinetic (PBPK) Modeling:

- **Protocol:** Develop models that incorporate physiological parameters and mechanistic details to predict the ADME behavior in humans based on animal data.
- **Parameters Measured:** Predictive human pharmacokinetic profiles, interspecies scaling, and dose extrapolation.

Case Studies Utilizing Methodologies:
Example 1: Absorption and Bioavailability Studies of a New Analgesic
Objective: Determine the oral bioavailability of a new analgesic drug.
Methodologies:

- **Oral and IV Administration:** The drug was administered orally and intravenously to rats.
- **Blood Sampling:** Blood samples were collected at specified time points.
- **HPLC-MS Analysis:** Drug concentrations were measured using HPLC-MS.
- **Parameters Measured:** Cmax, Tmax, AUC, and bioavailability.

Outcome: The oral bioavailability was found to be 65%, indicating good absorption. The drug was advanced to further preclinical studies with focus on optimizing oral formulations.

Example 2: Tissue Distribution and Metabolism of an Antifungal Agent

Objective: Assess the tissue distribution and metabolic pathways of a new antifungal agent.

Methodologies:

- **Tissue Distribution:** The drug was administered to mice, and tissue samples (liver, kidneys, brain) were collected.
- **Mass Spectrometry:** Tissue concentrations of the drug were measured using mass spectrometry.
- **In Vitro Metabolism:** Liver microsomes were used to identify metabolic pathways.
- **Parameters Measured:** Tissue distribution profiles, metabolic half-life, and identification of major metabolites.

Outcome: High accumulation in the liver and kidneys was observed. Several metabolites were identified, primarily through hydroxylation. The drug was advanced with recommendations for hepatic function monitoring.

Example 3: Excretion and Clearance of a Cardiovascular Drug

Objective: Determine the excretion and renal clearance of a new cardiovascular drug.

Methodologies:

- **Renal Excretion:** The drug was administered to dogs, and urine samples were collected.
- **Biliary Excretion:** Bile samples were collected using bile duct cannulation.
- **LC-MS Analysis:** Drug and metabolite concentrations were measured in urine and bile.
- **Parameters Measured:** Renal and biliary clearance, fraction excreted unchanged.

Outcome: The drug was primarily excreted unchanged in urine (70%), with significant biliary excretion (20%). The drug was advanced with a focus on renal and hepatic safety assessments.

6.2 Toxicokinetic Evaluation
6.2.1 Saturation Kinetics
Concepts and Implications:

Saturation kinetics, also known as **Michaelis-Menten kinetics**, refers to the phenomenon where the rate of a biochemical process reaches a maximum and becomes independent of the concentration of the substrate due to the finite number of enzyme or transport protein sites available. This concept is crucial in toxicokinetics, as it impacts drug absorption, distribution, metabolism, and excretion (ADME) at higher doses.

1. Basic Concepts of Saturation Kinetics:

a. Enzyme Saturation:

- **Definition:** Enzyme saturation occurs when all available enzyme active sites are occupied by the substrate, leading to a maximum reaction rate (Vmax). At this point, increasing the substrate concentration does not increase the reaction rate.
- **Michaelis-Menten Equation:** The relationship between the substrate concentration and reaction rate is described by the Michaelis-Menten equation:

$$V = V_{max} \cdot [S] / K_m + [S]$$

Where:

  - V = reaction rate
  - V_{max} = maximum reaction rate
  - $[S]$ = substrate concentration
  - K_m = Michaelis constant (substrate concentration at half Vmax)

b. Transporter Saturation:

- **Definition:** Transporter saturation occurs when all transporter proteins involved in drug absorption or excretion are occupied by the drug, leading to a maximum transport rate.
- **Saturation Impact:** At high drug concentrations, absorption or excretion rates reach a plateau, and further increases in drug concentration do not increase the transport rate.

2. Implications of Saturation Kinetics:

a. Dose-Dependent Kinetics:

- **Non-Linear Pharmacokinetics:** Saturation kinetics often result in non-linear pharmacokinetics, where changes in drug dose do not proportionally affect plasma concentrations.
- **Implications:** As the dose increases, the drug's pharmacokinetic parameters (e.g., clearance, half-life) may change unpredictably, complicating dose adjustments and safety predictions.

b. Toxicity Risk:

- **Increased Toxicity:** Saturation of metabolic pathways can lead to the accumulation of the parent drug or toxic metabolites, increasing the risk of adverse effects.
- **Examples:** Drugs metabolized by cytochrome P450 enzymes may exhibit saturation at high doses, leading to hepatotoxicity or other organ toxicities.

c. Therapeutic Window:

- **Narrow Therapeutic Window:** Drugs with narrow therapeutic windows are particularly susceptible to the effects of saturation kinetics. Small increases in dose can lead to disproportionate increases in plasma concentrations, risking toxicity.
- **Dose Optimization:** Careful dose optimization and monitoring are required to maintain therapeutic drug levels without reaching toxic concentrations.

d. Drug-Drug Interactions:

- **Interaction Potential:** Saturation of metabolic enzymes or transporters can exacerbate drug-drug interactions. Co-administered drugs that compete for the same enzyme or transporter can lead to increased plasma levels of one or both drugs.
- **Clinical Implications:** This necessitates careful consideration of co-medications and potential adjustments in dosing regimens.

3. Examples and Case Studies:

Example 1: Phenytoin

Concept: Phenytoin, an anticonvulsant, exhibits saturation kinetics due to the saturation of hepatic cytochrome P450 enzymes at therapeutic doses.

Implications:

- **Non-Linear Pharmacokinetics:** Small increases in dose can lead to large increases in plasma concentrations, risking toxicity.
- **Clinical Management:** Frequent monitoring of plasma levels is required, and dose adjustments must be made cautiously.

Example 2: Aspirin

Concept: Aspirin demonstrates saturation kinetics in its conversion to salicylic acid, primarily through hepatic metabolism.

Implications:

- **Toxicity Risk:** At high doses, the metabolic pathway becomes saturated, leading to increased levels of unmetabolized aspirin and risk of salicylate toxicity.
- **Therapeutic Use:** High-dose aspirin therapy requires careful monitoring for signs of toxicity, such as tinnitus and gastrointestinal bleeding.

Example 3: Methotrexate

Concept: Methotrexate, used in cancer therapy, exhibits saturation kinetics in its renal excretion via active tubular secretion.

Implications:

- **Excretion Limitations:** At high doses, the renal transporters become saturated, leading to decreased clearance and prolonged half-life.
- **Dose Management:** High-dose methotrexate therapy often requires co-administration of leucovorin and hydration to mitigate toxicity and enhance excretion.

Example 4: Ethanol

Concept: Ethanol is metabolized by alcohol dehydrogenase (ADH) and exhibits saturation kinetics at relatively low concentrations.

Implications:

- **Metabolic Saturation:** Once ADH becomes saturated, ethanol metabolism shifts to the less efficient microsomal ethanol-oxidizing system (MEOS), leading to prolonged effects and potential toxicity.
- **Acute Intoxication:** Understanding the saturation kinetics of ethanol is crucial in managing acute intoxication and preventing overdose.

6.2 Toxicokinetic Evaluation

6.2.1 Saturation Kinetics

Case Studies and Examples:

Case studies illustrating saturation kinetics provide practical insights into how this phenomenon affects drug behavior, safety, and efficacy. The following examples highlight the real-world implications of saturation kinetics in various therapeutic contexts:

Example 1: Phenytoin

Background: Phenytoin is an anticonvulsant drug used to manage seizures. It exhibits non-linear pharmacokinetics due to the saturation of hepatic cytochrome P450 enzymes responsible for its metabolism.

Study Details:

- **Protocol:** Patients on phenytoin therapy were monitored for plasma drug levels and seizure control.
- **Results:** At low to moderate doses, phenytoin follows first-order kinetics, where the rate of metabolism is proportional to the drug concentration. However, as the dose increases, the metabolic pathway becomes saturated, leading to zero-order kinetics, where the rate of metabolism is constant and independent of the drug concentration.

Implications:

- **Non-Linear Pharmacokinetics:** Small increases in dose resulted in disproportionately high plasma concentrations, risking toxicity.
- **Clinical Management:** Dose adjustments required careful monitoring of plasma levels to avoid toxic effects such as ataxia, nystagmus, and cognitive impairment.
- **Outcome:** This case underscores the importance of frequent plasma level monitoring and individualized dosing to ensure therapeutic efficacy without reaching toxic concentrations.

Example 2: Aspirin

Background: Aspirin is a widely used analgesic and anti-inflammatory agent. At high doses, it exhibits saturation kinetics in its conversion to salicylic acid via hepatic metabolism.

Study Details:

- **Protocol:** Patients receiving high-dose aspirin for anti-inflammatory effects were monitored for plasma salicylate levels and signs of toxicity.
- **Results:** At therapeutic doses, aspirin is rapidly converted to salicylic acid. However, at higher doses, the metabolic pathway becomes saturated, leading to increased levels of unmetabolized aspirin.

Implications:

- **Toxicity Risk:** Saturation of the metabolic pathway led to the accumulation of unmetabolized aspirin, increasing the risk of salicylate toxicity, manifested as tinnitus, hyperventilation, and metabolic acidosis.
- **Clinical Management:** High-dose aspirin therapy required careful monitoring for signs of toxicity, with dose adjustments based on plasma salicylate levels and patient symptoms.
- **Outcome:** The case highlights the need for vigilance in monitoring and managing high-dose aspirin therapy to prevent adverse effects.

Example 3: Methotrexate

Background: Methotrexate is used in cancer therapy and autoimmune diseases. It exhibits saturation kinetics in its renal excretion through active tubular secretion.

Study Details:

- **Protocol:** Cancer patients receiving high-dose methotrexate were monitored for plasma drug levels and renal function.
- **Results:** At therapeutic doses, methotrexate is efficiently excreted by the kidneys. However, at high doses, the renal transporters become saturated, leading to decreased clearance and prolonged half-life.

Implications:

- **Excretion Limitations:** Saturation of renal transporters resulted in drug accumulation, increasing the risk of nephrotoxicity and other systemic toxicities.
- **Clinical Management:** High-dose methotrexate therapy required co-administration of leucovorin (a folinic acid derivative) and aggressive hydration to enhance drug excretion and mitigate toxicity.
- **Outcome:** The case emphasizes the importance of supportive measures and monitoring in managing high-dose methotrexate therapy to prevent adverse renal effects.

Example 4: Ethanol

Background: Ethanol is metabolized primarily by alcohol dehydrogenase (ADH) and exhibits saturation kinetics at relatively low concentrations.

Study Details:

- **Protocol:** Individuals consuming ethanol were monitored for blood alcohol levels and clinical effects.
- **Results:** At low to moderate ethanol concentrations, ADH metabolizes ethanol efficiently. However, once ADH becomes saturated, additional ethanol is metabolized by the less efficient microsomal ethanol-oxidizing system (MEOS), leading to prolonged effects and increased toxicity.

Implications:

- **Metabolic Saturation:** Saturation of ADH at higher ethanol concentrations led to prolonged intoxication and increased risk of acute alcohol toxicity, including central nervous system depression, hypoglycemia, and metabolic acidosis.
- **Clinical Management:** Understanding the saturation kinetics of ethanol is crucial in managing acute intoxication and preventing overdose. Treatment may involve supportive measures, such as intravenous fluids and glucose, and monitoring of vital signs and blood alcohol levels.
- **Outcome:** This case illustrates the importance of understanding the kinetic behavior of ethanol to effectively manage acute intoxication and prevent severe complications.

Example 5: Theophylline

Background: Theophylline is a bronchodilator used in the treatment of asthma and chronic obstructive pulmonary disease (COPD). It exhibits saturation kinetics at therapeutic doses due to the saturation of hepatic cytochrome P450 enzymes.

Study Details:

- **Protocol:** Patients on theophylline therapy were monitored for plasma drug levels, pulmonary function, and signs of toxicity.
- **Results:** At therapeutic doses, theophylline follows first-order kinetics. However, as doses approach the upper therapeutic range, metabolism becomes saturated, leading to non-linear increases in plasma levels.

Implications:

- **Toxicity Risk:** Small dose increases led to large increases in plasma theophylline levels, risking toxicity characterized by nausea, vomiting, arrhythmias, and seizures.
- **Clinical Management:** Frequent monitoring of plasma levels and careful dose titration were necessary to maintain therapeutic efficacy while avoiding toxic concentrations.
- **Outcome:** The case underscores the critical need for individualized dosing and regular therapeutic drug monitoring to manage theophylline therapy safely.

6.2 Toxicokinetic Evaluation

6.2.2 Methods for Toxicokinetic Evaluation

Techniques and Protocols:

Toxicokinetic evaluation involves a range of techniques and protocols designed to assess the absorption, distribution, metabolism, and excretion (ADME) properties of a drug. These methods are crucial for understanding the pharmacokinetic profiles and potential toxicities of new drug candidates. The following outlines key techniques and protocols used in toxicokinetic evaluation:

1. Absorption Studies:

a. Oral and Intravenous Administration:

- **Technique:**

- **Oral Administration:** The drug is administered orally using gavage or mixed with food/water.
- **Intravenous Administration:** The drug is injected directly into the bloodstream, typically via the tail vein in rodents or a peripheral vein in larger animals.

- **Protocol:**

  - **Sample Collection:** Blood samples are collected at multiple time points post-administration (e.g., 0, 0.5, 1, 2, 4, 8, 12, 24 hours).
  - **Analysis:** Plasma concentrations of the drug are measured using high-performance liquid chromatography coupled with mass spectrometry (HPLC-MS).

- **Parameters Measured:** Bioavailability, Cmax (maximum concentration), Tmax (time to reach Cmax), and AUC (area under the curve).

2. Distribution Studies:
a. Tissue Distribution:

- **Technique:**

  - **Radiolabeled Drug:** The drug is labeled with a radioactive isotope to facilitate tracking.
  - **Non-Radiolabeled Drug:** Regular drug administration with subsequent tissue extraction and analysis.

- **Protocol:**

  - **Sample Collection:** Tissues (e.g., liver, kidney, heart, brain) are collected at different time points post-administration.
  - **Analysis:** Drug concentrations in tissues are quantified using HPLC-MS or liquid scintillation counting for radiolabeled compounds.

- **Parameters Measured:** Volume of distribution (Vd), tissue-to-plasma concentration ratios, and tissue-specific accumulation.

3. Metabolism Studies:

a. In Vitro Metabolism:

- **Technique:**

  - **Liver Microsomes:** Microsomal fractions are incubated with the drug to study Phase I metabolic reactions.
  - **Hepatocytes:** Whole cells provide a more comprehensive view, including Phase II reactions.

- **Protocol:**

  - **Incubation:** The drug is incubated with liver microsomes or hepatocytes at various concentrations and time points.
  - **Analysis:** Metabolites are identified and quantified using liquid chromatography-tandem mass spectrometry (LC-MS/MS).

- **Parameters Measured:** Metabolic half-life, enzyme kinetics (Km and Vmax), and identification of major metabolites.

b. In Vivo Metabolism:

- **Technique:**

  - **Animal Models:** The drug is administered to animals, and blood, urine, and feces samples are collected.

- **Protocol:**

  - **Sample Collection:** Samples are collected at multiple time points to capture the drug's metabolic profile.
  - **Analysis:** Metabolites are identified using LC-MS/MS.

- **Parameters Measured:** In vivo metabolic profiles, clearance rates, and identification of major metabolites.

4. Excretion Studies:
a. Renal and Biliary Excretion:

- **Technique:**

  - **Urine and Feces Collection:** Animals are housed in metabolic cages to facilitate separate collection of urine and feces.
  - **Bile Duct Cannulation:** For studying biliary excretion, bile duct cannulation is performed in animals like rats or dogs.

- **Protocol:**

  - **Sample Collection:** Urine, feces, and bile samples are collected over a specified period (e.g., 24-48 hours).
  - **Analysis:** Drug and metabolite concentrations are measured using LC-MS/MS.

- **Parameters Measured:** Renal clearance, biliary excretion, total body clearance, and fraction of dose excreted unchanged.

5. Advanced Techniques:
a. Mass Spectrometry (MS):

- **Technique:**

  - **HPLC-MS:** Combines high-performance liquid chromatography with mass spectrometry for high sensitivity and specificity in quantifying drug concentrations.

- **Protocol:**

  - **Sample Preparation:** Samples (plasma, urine, tissues) are prepared by protein precipitation, liquid-liquid extraction, or solid-phase extraction.
  - **Analysis:** Drug and metabolite concentrations are measured using HPLC-MS.

- **Parameters Measured:** Concentrations of parent drug and metabolites in biological samples.

b. Nuclear Magnetic Resonance (NMR) Spectroscopy:

- **Technique:**

  - **NMR Spectroscopy:** Used for structural elucidation of drug metabolites.

- **Protocol:**

  - **Sample Preparation:** Samples are prepared in deuterated solvents.
  - **Analysis:** Metabolite structures are identified using NMR spectroscopy.

- **Parameters Measured:** Structural information of metabolites.

6. Modeling and Simulation:
a. Pharmacokinetic (PK) Modeling:

- **Technique:**

  - **Software Tools:** Use of software like NONMEM, WinNonlin, or PKSolver for modeling and simulation.

- **Protocol:**

  - **Data Input:** Pharmacokinetic data (concentrations, time points) are input into the software.
  - **Modeling:** Models are developed to describe the ADME processes of the drug.

- **Parameters Measured:** Clearance, volume of distribution, half-life, and predictions of drug concentration-time profiles.

b. Physiologically-Based Pharmacokinetic (PBPK) Modeling:

- **Technique:**

  - **Mechanistic Modeling:** Incorporates physiological parameters and mechanistic details to predict drug behavior in humans based on animal data.

- **Protocol:**

  - **Data Integration:** Integrates in vitro and in vivo data with anatomical and physiological parameters.
  - **Simulation:** Simulates drug behavior in virtual populations.

- **Parameters Measured:** Predictive human pharmacokinetic profiles, interspecies scaling, and dose extrapolation.

7. Case Studies Utilizing Techniques and Protocols:
Example 1: Toxicokinetic Evaluation of a New Antidiabetic Drug
Objective: Assess the toxicokinetics of a new antidiabetic drug to optimize its therapeutic use.
Techniques and Protocols:

- **Absorption Studies:**

  - **Oral and IV Administration:** Administered to rats, with blood samples collected at multiple time points.
  - **HPLC-MS Analysis:** Measured plasma concentrations, determining an oral bioavailability of 65%.

- **Distribution Studies:**

  - **Tissue Distribution:** Collected liver, kidney, and muscle tissues, analyzing drug concentrations via HPLC-MS.
  - **Volume of Distribution:** Calculated Vd to be 1.5 L/kg.

- **Metabolism Studies:**

  - **In Vitro Metabolism:** Incubated with human liver microsomes, identifying Phase I and II metabolites using LC-MS/MS.
  - **In Vivo Metabolism:** Administered to dogs, collecting blood and urine samples to profile metabolites.

- **Excretion Studies:**

- **Urine and Feces Collection:** Monitored excretion in metabolic cages, finding 70% renal and 20% fecal excretion.
- **LC-MS/MS Analysis:** Measured drug and metabolite concentrations.

Outcome: The comprehensive toxicokinetic evaluation provided a detailed understanding of the drug's ADME properties, supporting its advancement to clinical trials with optimized dosing recommendations.

Example 2: Toxicokinetic Analysis of a Cardiovascular Drug

Objective: Evaluate the toxicokinetics of a new cardiovascular drug to ensure safety and efficacy.

Techniques and Protocols:

- **Absorption Studies:**

  - **Oral and IV Administration:** Conducted in dogs, with plasma samples collected at specified intervals.
  - **HPLC-MS Analysis:** Determined an oral bioavailability of 80%.

- **Distribution Studies:**

  - **Tissue Distribution:** Assessed in rabbits, with tissues (heart, liver) analyzed for drug concentration.
  - **Volume of Distribution:** Calculated Vd to be 2.2 L/kg.

- **Metabolism Studies:**

  - **In Vitro Metabolism:** Utilized human liver microsomes, identifying metabolic pathways and major metabolites via LC-MS/MS.
  - **In Vivo Metabolism:** Administered to rats, profiling metabolites in blood and urine.

- **Excretion Studies:**

  - **Bile Duct Cannulation:** Performed in rats to study biliary excretion.
  - **Urine and Feces Collection:** Measured renal and fecal excretion using LC-MS/MS.

Outcome: The toxicokinetic evaluation provided insights into the drug's pharmacokinetic behavior, informing safe and effective dosing regimens for clinical trials.

6.2 Toxicokinetic Evaluation

6.2.2 Methods for Toxicokinetic Evaluation

Examples from Research:

Research examples provide practical insights into how toxicokinetic evaluation methods are applied in real-world scenarios to assess the ADME (absorption, distribution, metabolism, and excretion) properties of drug candidates. The following examples illustrate the use of various techniques and protocols in toxicokinetic studies:

Example 1: Toxicokinetic Evaluation of a Novel Anticancer Drug

Background: Researchers aimed to evaluate the toxicokinetics of a new anticancer agent to understand its pharmacokinetic profile and potential toxicities.

Methods:

- **Absorption Studies:**

  - **Protocol:** The drug was administered orally and intravenously to mice. Blood samples were collected at multiple time points.
  - **Analysis:** Plasma concentrations were measured using high-performance liquid chromatography-mass spectrometry (HPLC-MS).
  - **Results:** Oral bioavailability was found to be 40%, with a Cmax of 2.0 µg/mL and a Tmax of 1 hour for oral administration.

- **Distribution Studies:**

  - **Protocol:** Tissue distribution was assessed by administering the drug to rats and collecting tissue samples (liver, kidney, heart, brain) at various intervals.
  - **Analysis:** Tissue concentrations were quantified using HPLC-MS.
  - **Results:** High concentrations were found in the liver and kidneys, indicating significant accumulation in these organs. The volume of distribution (Vd) was 1.8 L/kg.

- **Metabolism Studies:**

- ○ **Protocol:** In vitro metabolism studies were conducted using human liver microsomes to identify metabolic pathways.
- ○ **Analysis:** Metabolites were identified and quantified using liquid chromatography-tandem mass spectrometry (LC-MS/MS).
- ○ **Results:** The drug underwent extensive Phase I metabolism, primarily through oxidation, with several metabolites identified.

- **Excretion Studies:**

- ○ **Protocol:** The drug was administered to rabbits, and urine and feces were collected over 48 hours.
- ○ **Analysis:** Drug and metabolite concentrations were measured using LC-MS/MS.
- ○ **Results:** The drug was primarily excreted via the renal route, with 65% recovered in urine and 20% in feces. The total clearance (Cl) was 0.9 L/h/kg.

Implications:

- **Non-Linear Pharmacokinetics:** The moderate oral bioavailability and significant hepatic accumulation suggested potential for non-linear pharmacokinetics at higher doses.
- **Toxicity Risk:** The high accumulation in the liver indicated a need for monitoring hepatic function during further preclinical and clinical studies.
- **Outcome:** The data supported advancing the drug to further preclinical toxicity studies with a focus on hepatic and renal safety assessments.

Example 2: Toxicokinetic Analysis of a New Anti-Inflammatory Drug
Background: Researchers conducted a toxicokinetic evaluation of a new anti-inflammatory drug to understand its pharmacokinetic behavior and optimize dosing.
Methods:

- **Absorption Studies:**

- ○ **Protocol:** The drug was administered orally to rats and dogs. Blood samples were collected at pre-determined intervals.

- **Analysis:** Plasma concentrations were measured using HPLC-MS.
- **Results:** Oral bioavailability was 50% in rats and 65% in dogs. The Cmax and Tmax were dose-dependent, indicating potential saturation at higher doses.

- **Distribution Studies:**

  - **Protocol:** Tissue distribution was assessed by administering the drug to mice and collecting tissue samples (heart, liver, lungs).
  - **Analysis:** Drug concentrations in tissues were quantified using HPLC-MS.
  - **Results:** The drug showed extensive distribution to the lungs and liver. The Vd was 1.7 L/kg.

- **Metabolism Studies:**

  - **Protocol:** In vitro studies were performed using human liver microsomes and hepatocytes to identify metabolites.
  - **Analysis:** Metabolites were identified using LC-MS/MS.
  - **Results:** The drug was extensively metabolized via hydroxylation and conjugation pathways. Major metabolites included hydroxylated and sulfate conjugates.

- **Excretion Studies:**

  - **Protocol:** The drug was administered to monkeys, and urine and bile were collected.
  - **Analysis:** Drug and metabolite concentrations were measured using LC-MS/MS.
  - **Results:** The drug was primarily excreted in bile (55%), with a significant portion recovered in urine (35%). The renal clearance was 0.5 L/h/kg.

Implications:

- **Dose-Dependent Kinetics:** The saturation of absorption at higher doses indicated the need for careful dose optimization to avoid non-linear pharmacokinetics.

- **Toxicity Monitoring:** The high distribution to the lungs and liver suggested potential organ-specific toxicities, necessitating monitoring in further studies.
- **Outcome:** The drug was advanced to chronic toxicity studies with recommendations for dose adjustments and monitoring of liver and lung function.

Example 3: Metabolic and Excretion Studies of an Antiviral Drug

Background: An antiviral drug was evaluated for its toxicokinetic properties to understand its metabolic pathways and excretion profile.

Methods:

- **Absorption Studies:**

  - **Protocol:** The drug was administered intravenously and orally to rabbits. Blood samples were collected at multiple time points.
  - **Analysis:** Plasma concentrations were measured using LC-MS.
  - **Results:** Oral bioavailability was low (20%), suggesting significant first-pass metabolism. The IV administration showed a Cmax of 2.5 µg/mL.

- **Distribution Studies:**

  - **Protocol:** The drug was administered to rats, and tissue samples (brain, liver, kidneys) were collected.
  - **Analysis:** Tissue concentrations were quantified using LC-MS.
  - **Results:** High distribution to the liver and kidneys was observed, with minimal penetration into the brain.

- **Metabolism Studies:**

  - **Protocol:** In vitro metabolism studies were conducted using human liver microsomes and S9 fractions to identify metabolic pathways.
  - **Analysis:** Metabolites were identified using LC-MS/MS.
  - **Results:** The drug underwent extensive Phase I oxidation and Phase II conjugation. Major metabolites included hydroxylated and glucuronide conjugates.

- **Excretion Studies:**

  - **Protocol:** The drug was administered to dogs, and urine and feces were collected.
  - **Analysis:** Drug and metabolite concentrations were measured using LC-MS/MS.
  - **Results:** The drug was primarily excreted in urine (70%), with 20% recovered in feces. The renal clearance was 1.2 L/h/kg.

Implications:

- **Low Bioavailability:** The significant first-pass metabolism indicated the need for formulation optimization to improve oral bioavailability.
- **Organ-Specific Accumulation:** High liver and kidney accumulation suggested potential organ-specific toxicity, necessitating targeted monitoring.
- **Outcome:** The drug was advanced with a focus on improving oral formulations and conducting detailed liver and kidney toxicity studies.

Example 4: Saturation Kinetics in a CNS Drug

Background: Researchers investigated the saturation kinetics of a new central nervous system (CNS) drug to understand its non-linear pharmacokinetics and potential toxicity.

Methods:

- **Absorption Studies:**

  - **Protocol:** The drug was administered orally to rats at various doses. Blood samples were collected at specified intervals.
  - **Analysis:** Plasma drug concentrations were measured using HPLC-MS.
  - **Results:** At lower doses, the drug exhibited linear kinetics. At higher doses, the absorption pathway became saturated, leading to non-linear increases in plasma concentrations.

- **Distribution Studies:**

- **Protocol:** The drug was administered to mice, and brain tissue samples were collected.
- **Analysis:** Drug concentrations in brain tissue were measured using HPLC-MS.
- **Results:** Significant penetration into the brain was observed, with higher concentrations at elevated doses, indicating saturation of transport mechanisms.

- **Metabolism Studies:**

  - **Protocol:** In vitro metabolism studies were conducted using human liver microsomes.
  - **Analysis:** Metabolites were identified and quantified using LC-MS/MS.
  - **Results:** The drug was primarily metabolized via cytochrome P450 enzymes, with saturation occurring at higher concentrations.

- **Excretion Studies:**

  - **Protocol:** The drug was administered to rabbits, and urine samples were collected.
  - **Analysis:** Drug and metabolite concentrations were measured using LC-MS/MS.
  - **Results:** Renal excretion showed saturation at higher doses, with decreased clearance rates and prolonged half-life.

Implications:

- **Non-Linear Kinetics:** The saturation of absorption, metabolism, and excretion pathways at higher doses led to non-linear pharmacokinetics, complicating dose adjustments.
- **CNS Toxicity:** The high brain penetration at elevated doses suggested a need for monitoring CNS toxicity.
- **Outcome:** The drug was advanced with recommendations for careful dose titration and monitoring of CNS effects in further preclinical and clinical studies.

6.3 Alternative Methods to Animal Toxicity Testing

6.3.1 In Vitro Methods

Techniques and Applications:

In vitro methods involve the use of biological components, such as cells, tissues, and biomolecules, in controlled laboratory environments to study the toxicological effects of substances. These methods offer ethical and practical advantages over traditional animal testing, providing valuable data on the toxicity and pharmacokinetics of new compounds. Here are some key in vitro techniques and their applications:

1. Cell Culture Techniques:

a. 2D Cell Cultures:

- **Description:** Traditional cell culture systems where cells are grown in a monolayer on a flat surface, such as a petri dish or flask.
- **Applications:**

  - **Cytotoxicity Testing:** Assess the toxic effects of compounds on cell viability and proliferation using assays like MTT, WST-1, and Trypan Blue exclusion.
  - **Mechanistic Studies:** Investigate cellular responses to toxicants, such as apoptosis, necrosis, and oxidative stress, using techniques like flow cytometry and microscopy.

b. 3D Cell Cultures:

- **Description:** Advanced cell culture systems that allow cells to grow in three dimensions, better mimicking the in vivo environment.
- **Applications:**

  - **Tumor Models:** Study cancer drug efficacy and toxicity using 3D tumor spheroids and organoids.
  - **Tissue Engineering:** Create 3D models of human tissues, such as liver, heart, and brain, for more accurate toxicity testing.

2. Organ-on-a-Chip Technology:

a. Microfluidic Devices:

- **Description:** Small, chip-based systems that replicate the physiological functions of human organs by integrating microfluidic channels with living cells.

- **Applications:**

    - **Drug Metabolism and Toxicity:** Assess how drugs are metabolized and their toxic effects on specific organs, such as liver-on-a-chip or kidney-on-a-chip.
    - **Multi-Organ Chips:** Study the interactions between different organ systems, such as the liver and heart, to predict systemic toxicity.

3. High-Throughput Screening (HTS):
a. Automated Assays:

- **Description:** Techniques that allow rapid testing of thousands of compounds using robotic systems and automated detection methods.
- **Applications:**

    - **Cytotoxicity Screening:** Quickly identify compounds that are toxic to cells using assays like ATP-based luminescence or dye exclusion.
    - **Genotoxicity Testing:** Screen for DNA damage and mutations using assays like the comet assay or micronucleus test.

4. Stem Cell-Based Assays:
a. Induced Pluripotent Stem Cells (iPSCs):

- **Description:** Stem cells generated from adult cells that can differentiate into various cell types, providing a renewable source of human cells for testing.
- **Applications:**

    - **Cardiotoxicity Testing:** Assess the effects of drugs on heart cells derived from iPSCs, such as iPSC-cardiomyocytes.
    - **Neurotoxicity Testing:** Evaluate the impact of compounds on neural cells derived from iPSCs, including neurons and astrocytes.

5. Biomarker Assays:
a. Biomarker Detection:

- **Description:** Techniques to measure specific biological markers that indicate toxicity, such as proteins, enzymes, or genetic changes.
- **Applications:**

  - **Hepatotoxicity Markers:** Detect liver damage using biomarkers like alanine aminotransferase (ALT) and aspartate aminotransferase (AST).
  - **Nephrotoxicity Markers:** Assess kidney damage using biomarkers like kidney injury molecule-1 (KIM-1) and neutrophil gelatinase-associated lipocalin (NGAL).

6. Genomic and Proteomic Approaches:
a. Omics Technologies:

- **Description:** Techniques that analyze the comprehensive profiles of genes, proteins, and metabolites in biological samples.
- **Applications:**

  - **Toxicogenomics:** Study changes in gene expression in response to toxicants using techniques like RNA sequencing and microarrays.
  - **Proteomics:** Identify and quantify proteins affected by toxic exposure using mass spectrometry and protein arrays.

Case Studies and Applications:
Example 1: 3D Liver Models for Hepatotoxicity Testing
Background: Researchers aimed to assess the hepatotoxicity of a new drug candidate using 3D liver spheroids.
Methods:

- **3D Cell Culture:** Liver cells were cultured in a 3D spheroid format to better mimic the in vivo liver environment.
- **Cytotoxicity Assays:** Cell viability was assessed using ATP-based luminescence and lactate dehydrogenase (LDH) release assays.
- **Biomarker Analysis:** Hepatotoxicity biomarkers, such as ALT and AST, were measured in the culture medium.

Results:

- **Cytotoxicity:** The drug candidate showed dose-dependent cytotoxicity in 3D liver spheroids.
- **Biomarkers:** Elevated levels of ALT and AST indicated hepatotoxicity.

Implications:

- **Predictive Accuracy:** The 3D liver model provided more accurate predictions of hepatotoxicity compared to traditional 2D cultures.
- **Outcome:** The data supported further optimization of the drug candidate to reduce hepatotoxicity before advancing to in vivo studies.

Example 2: High-Throughput Screening for Genotoxicity
Background: A chemical company used HTS to evaluate the genotoxic potential of new industrial compounds.
Methods:

- **Automated Assays:** Compounds were tested for DNA damage using the comet assay and micronucleus test in a high-throughput format.
- **Data Analysis:** Automated image analysis was used to quantify DNA damage and micronucleus formation.

Results:

- **Genotoxicity:** Several compounds were identified as genotoxic, showing significant DNA damage and micronucleus formation.
- **Validation:** Genotoxic compounds were further validated using traditional genotoxicity assays.

Implications:

- **Efficiency:** HTS allowed rapid screening of a large chemical library, identifying genotoxic compounds early in the development process.
- **Outcome:** The company prioritized non-genotoxic compounds for further development, reducing the risk of adverse effects.

Example 3: Organ-on-a-Chip for Drug Metabolism Studies
Background: Researchers used liver-on-a-chip technology to study the metabolism and potential toxicity of a new pharmaceutical compound.

Methods:

- **Microfluidic Device:** A liver-on-a-chip device was used to culture liver cells under dynamic flow conditions.
- **Metabolism Assays:** Drug metabolism was assessed by measuring the formation of metabolites using LC-MS/MS.
- **Toxicity Testing:** Cytotoxicity and hepatotoxicity biomarkers were measured in the chip's effluent.

Results:

- **Metabolism:** The compound was metabolized into several active metabolites, similar to in vivo liver metabolism.
- **Toxicity:** The liver-on-a-chip model detected dose-dependent hepatotoxicity.

Implications:

- **Relevance:** The liver-on-a-chip model provided relevant data on drug metabolism and toxicity, closely mimicking in vivo conditions.
- **Outcome:** The results informed further drug optimization and reduced the need for animal testing.

6.3 Alternative Methods to Animal Toxicity Testing
6.3.1 In Vitro Methods
Case Studies and Examples:
Case studies illustrating the use of in vitro methods demonstrate the practical application and effectiveness of these techniques in toxicokinetic evaluations. Here are some detailed examples:
Example 1: Using 3D Liver Spheroids for Hepatotoxicity Testing
Background: Researchers aimed to assess the hepatotoxicity of a new drug candidate using 3D liver spheroids, which provide a more physiologically relevant model than traditional 2D cell cultures.
Methods:

- **3D Cell Culture:**

- ◦ **Protocol:** Liver cells (hepatocytes) were cultured to form 3D spheroids, which mimic the architecture and function of liver tissue.
- ◦ **Assays:** Cytotoxicity was assessed using ATP-based luminescence assays to measure cell viability. Additionally, lactate dehydrogenase (LDH) release assays were used to detect cell membrane integrity and damage.

- **Biomarker Analysis:**

- ◦ **Protocol:** Levels of hepatotoxicity biomarkers such as alanine aminotransferase (ALT) and aspartate aminotransferase (AST) were measured in the culture medium using enzyme-linked immunosorbent assays (ELISAs).

Results:

- **Cytotoxicity:** The drug candidate exhibited dose-dependent cytotoxicity in the 3D liver spheroids, with significant reductions in ATP levels at higher concentrations.
- **Biomarkers:** Elevated levels of ALT and AST in the culture medium indicated hepatocellular damage and hepatotoxicity.

Implications:

- **Predictive Accuracy:** The 3D liver model provided more accurate predictions of hepatotoxicity compared to traditional 2D cultures, better mimicking the in vivo liver environment.
- **Outcome:** The data supported further optimization of the drug candidate to reduce hepatotoxicity before advancing to in vivo studies.

Example 2: High-Throughput Screening (HTS) for Genotoxicity
Background: A chemical company utilized high-throughput screening (HTS) to evaluate the genotoxic potential of a large library of new industrial compounds.
Methods:

- **Automated Assays:**

- ○ **Protocol:** Compounds were tested for DNA damage using the comet assay, which measures DNA strand breaks, and the micronucleus test, which detects chromosomal damage and loss.
- ○ **Automation:** The assays were performed in a high-throughput format using robotic systems to handle and process large numbers of samples efficiently.

- **Data Analysis:**

- ○ **Protocol:** Automated image analysis systems were used to quantify DNA damage (comet tail length and intensity) and micronucleus formation (number of micronuclei per cell).

Results:

- **Genotoxicity:** Several compounds were identified as genotoxic, showing significant DNA damage and increased micronucleus formation in treated cells.
- **Validation:** The genotoxic compounds identified in HTS were further validated using traditional genotoxicity assays to confirm the findings.

Implications:

- **Efficiency:** HTS allowed rapid screening of thousands of compounds, identifying potential genotoxicants early in the development process.
- **Outcome:** The company prioritized non-genotoxic compounds for further development, reducing the risk of adverse effects and streamlining the safety evaluation process.

Example 3: Organ-on-a-Chip for Drug Metabolism and Toxicity Studies
Background: Researchers used liver-on-a-chip technology to study the metabolism and potential toxicity of a new pharmaceutical compound, leveraging the dynamic flow conditions that better mimic in vivo liver function.
Methods:

- **Microfluidic Device:**

- ○ **Protocol:** Liver cells were cultured in a liver-on-a-chip device, which incorporates microfluidic channels to provide a continuous flow of nutrients and remove waste products, simulating blood flow in the liver.
- ○ **Assays:** Drug metabolism was assessed by measuring the formation of metabolites using liquid chromatography-tandem mass spectrometry (LC-MS/MS).

- **Toxicity Testing:**

  - ○ **Protocol:** Cytotoxicity was assessed by measuring cell viability and enzyme leakage. Hepatotoxicity biomarkers, such as ALT and AST, were quantified in the chip's effluent.

Results:

- **Metabolism:** The compound was metabolized into several active metabolites, closely resembling the metabolic profile observed in vivo.
- **Toxicity:** The liver-on-a-chip model detected dose-dependent hepatotoxicity, with increased levels of ALT and AST at higher drug concentrations.

Implications:

- **Relevance:** The liver-on-a-chip model provided relevant and reliable data on drug metabolism and toxicity, closely mimicking in vivo conditions.
- **Outcome:** The results informed further drug optimization and reduced the need for animal testing, supporting the compound's progression to clinical trials.

Example 4: Stem Cell-Based Assays for Cardiotoxicity Testing
Background: A pharmaceutical company evaluated the cardiotoxicity of a new drug candidate using human induced pluripotent stem cell-derived cardiomyocytes (iPSC-CMs).
Methods:

- **iPSC-CM Culture:**

- ○ **Protocol:** Human iPSC-CMs were cultured and differentiated to form functional cardiac cells.
- ○ **Assays:** Cardiotoxicity was assessed by measuring cell viability, contractility, and electrophysiological properties using assays like calcium flux measurements and multi-electrode array (MEA) recordings.

Results:

- **Cardiotoxicity:** The drug candidate showed dose-dependent cardiotoxic effects, including reduced cell viability, altered contractility, and changes in electrophysiological parameters (e.g., prolonged QT interval).
- **Validation:** The findings were validated using additional cardiac-specific biomarkers and comparison with known cardiotoxic drugs.

Implications:

- **Human Relevance:** The use of human iPSC-CMs provided relevant data on human-specific cardiotoxicity, reducing the reliance on animal models.
- **Outcome:** The company adjusted the drug's formulation and dosing regimen based on the cardiotoxicity data, improving its safety profile before advancing to clinical trials.

Example 5: Biomarker Assays for Nephrotoxicity Testing

Background: Researchers assessed the nephrotoxicity of an environmental contaminant using in vitro biomarker assays.

Methods:

- **Cell Culture:**

  - ○ **Protocol:** Human kidney proximal tubule cells were cultured and exposed to various concentrations of the contaminant.
  - ○ **Assays:** Nephrotoxicity was assessed by measuring cell viability and specific nephrotoxicity biomarkers such as kidney injury molecule-1 (KIM-1) and neutrophil gelatinase-associated lipocalin (NGAL) using ELISAs.

Results:

- **Nephrotoxicity:** The contaminant caused dose-dependent cytotoxicity in kidney cells, with significant increases in KIM-1 and NGAL levels.
- **Validation:** The biomarker data were validated against known nephrotoxicants to confirm the assay's sensitivity and specificity.

Implications:

- **Predictive Value:** The in vitro biomarker assays provided early and sensitive detection of nephrotoxicity, supporting the identification of potential nephrotoxicants.
- **Outcome:** The findings informed regulatory decisions and risk assessments for the environmental contaminant, reducing the need for animal testing.

6.3 Advanced Toxicokinetic Evaluation
6.3.2 In Silico Methods
Computational Approaches:
In silico methods involve the use of computational approaches to predict the ADME (absorption, distribution, metabolism, and excretion) properties and potential toxicities of drug candidates. These methods are increasingly important in drug development for reducing costs, time, and the need for extensive in vivo testing. Here are key computational approaches used in in silico toxicokinetic evaluation:
1. Quantitative Structure-Activity Relationship (QSAR) Models:
a. Concepts and Applications:

- **Definition:** QSAR models relate the chemical structure of a compound to its biological activity or toxicity using mathematical and statistical techniques.
- **Application:** Used to predict ADME properties and toxicological endpoints based on the molecular structure of new drug candidates.

b. Techniques:

- **Descriptor Calculation:** Calculate molecular descriptors that capture the chemical and physical properties of the compound (e.g., hydrophobicity, electronic properties, molecular weight).

- **Model Development:** Develop predictive models using machine learning algorithms (e.g., regression analysis, decision trees, neural networks) trained on datasets of known compounds.
- **Validation:** Validate the models using a separate set of compounds to ensure predictive accuracy.

c. Examples:

- **Prediction of Bioavailability:** QSAR models can predict the oral bioavailability of drug candidates by correlating molecular descriptors with known bioavailability data.
- **Toxicity Prediction:** QSAR models are used to predict potential toxicities, such as hepatotoxicity or cardiotoxicity, based on structural features.

2. Physiologically-Based Pharmacokinetic (PBPK) Modeling:
a. Concepts and Applications:

- **Definition:** PBPK models use mathematical descriptions of physiological processes to predict the ADME behavior of compounds in humans or animals.
- **Application:** Used to simulate drug concentrations in various tissues over time, predict drug-drug interactions, and extrapolate animal data to humans.

b. Techniques:

- **Model Structure:** Develop models that include compartments representing different tissues and organs, each with specific physiological parameters (e.g., blood flow rates, tissue volumes, enzyme kinetics).
- **Parameter Estimation:** Estimate parameters using in vitro data, literature values, and experimental data.
- **Simulation:** Run simulations to predict the time-course of drug concentrations in different tissues under various dosing scenarios.

c. Examples:

- **Human Pharmacokinetics**: PBPK models can predict human pharmacokinetics of new drugs using preclinical data, facilitating dose selection for first-in-human trials.
- **Drug-Drug Interactions**: PBPK models simulate the impact of co-administered drugs on the pharmacokinetics of a drug candidate, helping to assess interaction risks.

3. Molecular Docking and Dynamics:
a. Concepts and Applications:

- **Definition**: Molecular docking predicts the preferred orientation of a drug molecule when bound to a target protein, while molecular dynamics simulates the motion of atoms and molecules over time.
- **Application**: Used to study drug-receptor interactions, predict metabolic pathways, and identify potential off-target effects.

b. Techniques:

- **Docking Studies**: Use software tools (e.g., AutoDock, Glide) to dock drug molecules into the active site of target proteins and score the binding affinity.
- **Molecular Dynamics Simulations**: Use software (e.g., GROMACS, AMBER) to simulate the dynamic behavior of drug-protein complexes and explore the stability and conformational changes over time.

c. Examples:

- **Metabolism Prediction**: Docking studies can predict the binding of drug candidates to cytochrome P450 enzymes, identifying potential metabolic pathways.
- **Off-Target Effects**: Molecular dynamics simulations can identify potential off-target interactions that may lead to adverse effects.

4. Machine Learning and Artificial Intelligence (AI):
a. Concepts and Applications:

- **Definition**: Machine learning and AI use algorithms to analyze large datasets and identify patterns or relationships that can predict ADME properties and toxicities.

- **Application:** Used to develop predictive models for various pharmacokinetic and toxicological endpoints.

b. Techniques:

- **Data Collection:** Gather large datasets from literature, experimental studies, and public databases.
- **Model Training:** Train machine learning models (e.g., support vector machines, random forests, deep learning) on these datasets to predict ADME properties.
- **Validation and Testing:** Validate models using separate test datasets and refine them based on performance metrics.

c. Examples:

- **ADME Prediction:** Machine learning models can predict parameters such as solubility, permeability, and metabolic stability based on molecular descriptors.
- **Toxicity Prediction:** AI models can predict the likelihood of adverse effects by analyzing structural and physicochemical properties of compounds.

5. Computational Toxicology:
a. Concepts and Applications:

- **Definition:** Computational toxicology uses in silico methods to predict the toxicological profile of compounds, integrating data from various sources.
- **Application:** Used to assess the safety of drug candidates and environmental chemicals.

b. Techniques:

- **Toxicity Databases:** Utilize databases (e.g., ToxCast, Tox21) that contain toxicological data for thousands of chemicals.
- **Predictive Modeling:** Develop models that integrate data from in vitro assays, QSAR predictions, and PBPK simulations to predict in vivo

toxicity.

- **Risk Assessment:** Use computational tools to assess the risk of adverse effects based on predicted exposure levels and toxicological endpoints.

c. Examples:

- **Carcinogenicity Prediction:** Computational models can predict the potential carcinogenicity of compounds by analyzing structural alerts and biological activity profiles.
- **Environmental Risk Assessment:** Computational toxicology tools assess the environmental impact of chemicals by predicting their persistence, bioaccumulation, and toxicity.

Example Case Study: In Silico Evaluation of a New Antiviral Drug
Background: Researchers aimed to predict the ADME properties and potential toxicities of a new antiviral drug using in silico methods.
Methods:

- **QSAR Modeling:**

  - **Objective:** Predict oral bioavailability and hepatotoxicity.
  - **Technique:** Developed QSAR models using molecular descriptors and known bioavailability and toxicity data from similar compounds.
  - **Results:** The QSAR models predicted a high oral bioavailability (70%) and low hepatotoxicity risk.

- **PBPK Modeling:**

  - **Objective:** Simulate human pharmacokinetics based on preclinical data.
  - **Technique:** Developed a PBPK model incorporating physiological parameters and drug-specific data (e.g., solubility, permeability).
  - **Results:** The PBPK model predicted favorable pharmacokinetics, with a Cmax of 2.5 µg/mL and a half-life of 8 hours.

- **Molecular Docking:**

  - **Objective:** Identify potential metabolic pathways.

- ◦ **Technique:** Docked the drug into the active sites of major cytochrome P450 enzymes (CYP3A4, CYP2D6).
- ◦ **Results:** The docking studies suggested primary metabolism by CYP3A4, with stable binding interactions observed.

- **Machine Learning:**

  - ◦ **Objective:** Predict overall ADME profile.
  - ◦ **Technique:** Used a trained machine learning model to predict solubility, permeability, and metabolic stability.
  - ◦ **Results:** The model predicted high solubility, good permeability, and moderate metabolic stability.

Implications:

- **Predictive Accuracy:** The in silico methods provided a comprehensive prediction of the drug's ADME properties and potential toxicities, guiding further experimental validation.
- **Cost and Time Efficiency:** The use of computational approaches reduced the need for extensive in vitro and in vivo testing, accelerating the drug development process.
- **Outcome:** The positive predictions supported advancing the drug to in vitro and in vivo validation studies with confidence in its favorable pharmacokinetic and safety profile.

6.3 Advanced Toxicokinetic Evaluation
6.3.2 In Silico Methods
Data Analysis:

Data analysis in in silico methods involves various computational techniques to interpret the results generated by predictive models. These techniques help validate the accuracy of predictions, refine models, and provide actionable insights for drug development. Here are some key techniques for analyzing data from in silico methods:

1. Statistical Analysis:

a. Descriptive Statistics:

- **Concepts:** Summarize and describe the main features of a dataset.

- **Techniques:** Calculate mean, median, standard deviation, and range to understand the distribution of predicted values.
- **Applications:** Use descriptive statistics to summarize predicted ADME properties such as solubility, permeability, and metabolic stability.

b. Inferential Statistics:

- **Concepts:** Make inferences about a population based on a sample.
- **Techniques:** Perform hypothesis testing (e.g., t-tests, ANOVA) to compare predicted values with experimental data.
- **Applications:** Use inferential statistics to validate in silico predictions against experimental results.

2. Machine Learning Model Evaluation:
a. Performance Metrics:

- **Concepts:** Assess the accuracy and reliability of predictive models.
- **Techniques:** Calculate metrics such as accuracy, precision, recall, F1-score, and area under the receiver operating characteristic (ROC-AUC) curve.
- **Applications:** Evaluate the performance of QSAR models in predicting ADME properties and toxicities.

b. Cross-Validation:

- **Concepts:** Validate the model's predictive performance by dividing the dataset into training and testing subsets.
- **Techniques:** Perform k-fold cross-validation, where the dataset is split into k subsets, and the model is trained and tested k times, each time using a different subset for testing.
- **Applications:** Use cross-validation to assess the robustness and generalizability of machine learning models.

3. Regression Analysis:
a. Linear Regression:

- **Concepts:** Model the relationship between a dependent variable and one or more independent variables.

- **Techniques:** Fit a linear equation to the data and evaluate the goodness-of-fit using R-squared and p-values.
- **Applications:** Use linear regression to predict pharmacokinetic parameters (e.g., clearance, volume of distribution) based on molecular descriptors.

b. Non-Linear Regression:

- **Concepts:** Model non-linear relationships between variables.
- **Techniques:** Fit non-linear equations (e.g., exponential, logistic) to the data and assess model fit using residual analysis.
- **Applications:** Apply non-linear regression to model complex relationships in PBPK models and enzyme kinetics.

4. Model Validation and Refinement:
a. External Validation:

- **Concepts:** Validate predictive models using external datasets not used in model training.
- **Techniques:** Compare predicted values with experimental data from independent studies and calculate performance metrics.
- **Applications:** Perform external validation to ensure the reliability of QSAR and PBPK models.

b. Sensitivity Analysis:

- **Concepts:** Assess how changes in model parameters affect predictions.
- **Techniques:** Systematically vary model parameters and evaluate the impact on predicted outcomes.
- **Applications:** Conduct sensitivity analysis to identify critical parameters in PBPK models and refine model assumptions.

5. Visualization Techniques:
a. Scatter Plots:

- **Concepts:** Visualize the relationship between two variables.
- **Techniques:** Plot predicted vs. experimental values to assess model accuracy and identify outliers.

- **Applications:** Use scatter plots to compare predicted pharmacokinetic parameters with experimental data.

b. Heat Maps:

- **Concepts:** Represent data values in a matrix format using color gradients.
- **Techniques:** Create heat maps to visualize correlations between multiple variables or model performance metrics across different conditions.
- **Applications:** Use heat maps to analyze the performance of machine learning models across different datasets and parameter settings.

c. Box Plots:

- **Concepts:** Visualize the distribution of data and identify outliers.
- **Techniques:** Generate box plots to compare predicted and experimental values across different compounds or conditions.
- **Applications:** Use box plots to assess the variability and central tendency of predicted ADME properties.

6. Case Study: In Silico Evaluation of a New Antiviral Drug

Background: Researchers aimed to predict the ADME properties and potential toxicities of a new antiviral drug using in silico methods and validate the predictions through data analysis techniques.

Methods:

- **QSAR Modeling:**

  - **Objective:** Predict oral bioavailability and hepatotoxicity.
  - **Techniques:** Developed QSAR models using molecular descriptors and trained them on known bioavailability and toxicity data. Used performance metrics (accuracy, precision, ROC-AUC) to evaluate model performance.
  - **Results:** The QSAR models predicted a high oral bioavailability (70%) and low hepatotoxicity risk, with an accuracy of 85% and an ROC-AUC of 0.90.

- **PBPK Modeling:**

- ◦ **Objective:** Simulate human pharmacokinetics based on preclinical data.
- ◦ **Techniques:** Developed a PBPK model using physiological parameters and drug-specific data. Conducted sensitivity analysis to identify critical parameters.
- ◦ **Results:** The PBPK model predicted favorable pharmacokinetics, with a Cmax of 2.5 µg/mL and a half-life of 8 hours. Sensitivity analysis highlighted the importance of hepatic clearance in determining drug exposure.

- **Machine Learning:**

- ◦ **Objective:** Predict overall ADME profile.
- ◦ **Techniques:** Used a trained machine learning model to predict solubility, permeability, and metabolic stability. Performed cross-validation to assess model robustness.
- ◦ **Results:** The model predicted high solubility, good permeability, and moderate metabolic stability, with cross-validation showing a consistent performance across different datasets.

Data Analysis:

- **Statistical Analysis:** Conducted descriptive statistics to summarize predicted ADME properties and inferential statistics to compare predictions with experimental data.
- **Regression Analysis:** Used linear regression to model the relationship between molecular descriptors and predicted ADME properties, achieving an R-squared value of 0.85 for bioavailability predictions.
- **Model Validation:** Validated the QSAR and PBPK models using external datasets, achieving high concordance between predicted and experimental values.
- **Visualization:** Created scatter plots to compare predicted vs. experimental values and heat maps to visualize model performance across different conditions.

Implications:

- **Predictive Accuracy:** The in silico methods provided accurate predictions of the drug's ADME properties and potential toxicities, supported by robust data analysis techniques.
- **Model Refinement:** Sensitivity analysis and external validation helped refine the models, ensuring their reliability and applicability in drug development.
- **Outcome:** The positive predictions supported advancing the drug to in vitro and in vivo validation studies, with confidence in its favorable pharmacokinetic and safety profile.

6.3 Advanced Toxicokinetic Evaluation

6.3.2 In Silico Methods

Case Studies and Examples:

Case studies illustrating the use of in silico methods provide insights into how computational approaches are applied to predict and analyze the ADME (absorption, distribution, metabolism, and excretion) properties and potential toxicities of drug candidates. Here are some detailed examples of research utilizing in silico methods in toxicokinetic evaluation:

Example 1: In Silico Prediction of Oral Bioavailability for a New Anticancer Drug

Background: Researchers aimed to predict the oral bioavailability of a novel anticancer agent using QSAR modeling and PBPK simulations.

Methods:

- **QSAR Modeling:**

  - **Objective:** Predict oral bioavailability based on molecular structure.
  - **Techniques:** Molecular descriptors such as lipophilicity, molecular weight, and hydrogen bond donors/acceptors were calculated. A QSAR model was developed using these descriptors and a training dataset of known compounds.
  - **Results:** The QSAR model predicted an oral bioavailability of 65% for the anticancer agent, with a high correlation ($R^2 = 0.85$) between predicted and experimental values.

- **PBPK Modeling:**

  - **Objective:** Simulate the pharmacokinetics of the drug in humans.

- **Techniques**: A PBPK model was constructed using physiological parameters (e.g., organ volumes, blood flow rates) and drug-specific data (e.g., solubility, permeability). The model was used to simulate plasma concentration-time profiles after oral administration.
- **Results**: The PBPK model predicted a Cmax of 3.0 µg/mL and a Tmax of 2 hours, consistent with the QSAR prediction of bioavailability.

Data Analysis:

- **Validation**: The QSAR and PBPK models were validated using an external dataset of anticancer drugs with known bioavailability. Both models showed high predictive accuracy.
- **Visualization**: Scatter plots comparing predicted vs. experimental bioavailability and plasma concentrations were generated, showing strong concordance.

Implications:

- **Predictive Accuracy**: The combined use of QSAR and PBPK models provided reliable predictions of oral bioavailability, supporting the potential efficacy of the anticancer agent.
- **Outcome**: The positive predictions supported advancing the drug to preclinical in vivo studies for further validation.

Example 2: In Silico Toxicity Prediction for a New Anti-Inflammatory Drug

Background: Researchers used in silico methods to predict the hepatotoxicity and cardiotoxicity of a new anti-inflammatory drug.

Methods:

- **QSAR Modeling:**

  - **Objective:** Predict hepatotoxicity based on molecular structure.
  - **Techniques:** Molecular descriptors and structural alerts associated with hepatotoxicity were calculated. A QSAR model was developed using these descriptors and a training dataset of compounds with known hepatotoxicity.

- ○ **Results:** The QSAR model predicted a low risk of hepatotoxicity, with an accuracy of 87%.

- **Molecular Docking:**

  - ○ **Objective:** Predict cardiotoxicity by assessing the binding affinity to the hERG channel.
  - ○ **Techniques:** The drug was docked into the binding site of the hERG potassium channel using AutoDock software. Binding affinities were calculated to assess the potential for cardiotoxicity.
  - ○ **Results:** The drug showed moderate binding affinity to the hERG channel, suggesting a potential risk of cardiotoxicity.

Data Analysis:

- **Statistical Analysis:** Descriptive statistics summarized the predicted hepatotoxicity and cardiotoxicity risks. Inferential statistics compared predictions with known toxicities of similar compounds.
- **Visualization:** Heat maps were generated to visualize the binding affinities and toxicity predictions across different compounds.

Implications:

- **Risk Assessment:** The low predicted risk of hepatotoxicity was favorable, but the moderate risk of cardiotoxicity highlighted the need for further in vitro and in vivo testing.
- **Outcome:** The findings informed the design of subsequent preclinical studies, focusing on cardiotoxicity assessment.

Example 3: In Silico Evaluation of Drug-Drug Interactions for an Antiviral Drug

Background: Researchers aimed to predict potential drug-drug interactions (DDIs) for a new antiviral drug using machine learning models and PBPK simulations.

Methods:

- **Machine Learning:**

- ○ **Objective:** Predict interactions with cytochrome P450 enzymes.
- ○ **Techniques:** A machine learning model was trained using a dataset of known CYP inhibitors and substrates. Molecular descriptors were used as input features. The model predicted the likelihood of the antiviral drug interacting with CYP3A4, CYP2D6, and CYP2C9.
- ○ **Results:** The model predicted a high likelihood of interaction with CYP3A4 (probability = 0.92), but low likelihood with CYP2D6 and CYP2C9.

- **PBPK Modeling:**

- ○ **Objective:** Simulate the impact of DDIs on drug pharmacokinetics.
- ○ **Techniques:** A PBPK model incorporating the predicted CYP3A4 interaction was developed. Simulations were run to predict changes in plasma concentrations when co-administered with known CYP3A4 inhibitors.
- ○ **Results:** The PBPK model predicted a significant increase in the antiviral drug's plasma concentrations when co-administered with a strong CYP3A4 inhibitor (AUC increased by 150%).

Data Analysis:

- **Cross-Validation:** The machine learning model was cross-validated using a separate test dataset, achieving an accuracy of 90%.
- **Visualization:** PBPK simulation results were visualized using concentration-time profiles, showing the impact of CYP3A4 inhibition on drug exposure.

Implications:

- **Predictive Insights:** The combined use of machine learning and PBPK modeling provided insights into potential DDIs, guiding the need for clinical DDI studies.
- **Outcome:** The predictions supported caution in co-administering the antiviral drug with strong CYP3A4 inhibitors and informed the design of clinical DDI studies.

Example 4: In Silico Metabolism Prediction for a CNS Drug

Background: Researchers used in silico methods to predict the metabolic pathways and potential metabolites of a new central nervous system (CNS) drug.

Methods:

- **Molecular Docking:**

  - **Objective:** Identify potential cytochrome P450-mediated metabolic pathways.
  - **Techniques:** The drug was docked into the active sites of CYP3A4, CYP2D6, and CYP1A2 enzymes using Glide software. Binding poses and interaction energies were analyzed.
  - **Results:** The drug showed strong binding affinity to CYP3A4 and CYP2D6, suggesting these enzymes as primary metabolizers.

- **Metabolite Prediction:**

  - **Objective:** Predict likely metabolites based on enzyme binding.
  - **Techniques:** Predicted metabolic sites were analyzed using SMARTCyp and MetaSite software, which identify likely positions for metabolic transformation.
  - **Results:** Predicted metabolites included hydroxylated and demethylated products, primarily mediated by CYP3A4 and CYP2D6.

Data Analysis:

- **Validation:** Predicted metabolites were compared with known metabolites of structurally similar CNS drugs to validate the predictions.
- **Visualization:** Docking poses and predicted metabolites were visualized using molecular modeling software, highlighting key interactions.

Implications:

- **Metabolic Pathways:** The in silico predictions provided a detailed understanding of the drug's metabolic pathways, informing further in vitro metabolism studies.
- **Outcome:** The predictions supported advancing the drug to in vitro and in vivo metabolism studies, with a focus on CYP3A4 and CYP2D6

interactions.

6.3 Advanced Toxicokinetic Evaluation
6.3.3 Ethical Considerations and Advancements
Regulatory Guidelines:

Regulatory guidelines related to alternative methods are established to ensure the ethical use of animals in research and to promote the development and validation of alternative methods. These guidelines are developed by regulatory agencies and international organizations to provide a framework for the use of alternative methods in toxicology and pharmacokinetics.

a. European Union (EU):

- **REACH (Registration, Evaluation, Authorisation, and Restriction of Chemicals):**

  - **Guidelines:** Encourages the use of alternative methods to animal testing, such as in vitro and in silico approaches, for chemical safety assessments.
  - **Implementation:** Requires justification for any proposed animal testing and emphasizes the use of validated alternative methods.

- **Directive 2010/63/EU:**

  - **Guidelines:** Establishes standards for the protection of animals used for scientific purposes. Promotes the principles of the 3Rs (Replacement, Reduction, Refinement) in research.
  - **Implementation:** Mandates the use of alternative methods where scientifically valid and reasonably practicable.

b. United States (US):

- **US Food and Drug Administration (FDA):**

  - **Guidelines:** Supports the development and use of alternative methods in drug safety testing through the FDA's Predictive Toxicology Roadmap.

- **Implementation:** Encourages the integration of in vitro and in silico methods in regulatory submissions and provides a framework for their validation and acceptance.

- **Interagency Coordinating Committee on the Validation of Alternative Methods (ICCVAM):**

    - **Guidelines:** Develops and evaluates alternative testing methods to reduce animal use in safety assessments.
    - **Implementation:** Provides recommendations for the validation and regulatory acceptance of alternative methods.

c. International Cooperation on Cosmetics Regulation (ICCR):

- **Guidelines:** Promotes the use of non-animal testing methods in the safety assessment of cosmetic products.
- **Implementation:** Supports international collaboration to develop and validate alternative methods, and harmonizes regulatory requirements to reduce animal testing globally.

Advances in Alternative Methods:

Recent advancements in alternative methods to animal testing have focused on developing in vitro, in silico, and integrated approaches that provide reliable data while reducing or eliminating the need for animal studies. These advancements have significant implications for toxicokinetic and pharmacokinetic evaluations.

a. In Vitro Methods:

- **Organs-on-Chips:**

    - **Description:** Microfluidic devices that mimic the physiological functions of human organs. They are used to study drug effects on specific tissues and organ systems.
    - **Advances:** Development of multi-organ chips that can simulate complex interactions between different tissues, providing more comprehensive data on drug behavior.

- **3D Cell Cultures:**

- **Description:** Three-dimensional cell culture systems that better replicate the in vivo environment compared to traditional 2D cultures.
- **Advances:** Use of 3D bioprinting to create complex tissue models, including liver, kidney, and brain tissues, for more accurate toxicity and efficacy testing.

- **High-Throughput Screening (HTS):**

  - **Description:** Automated techniques that allow rapid testing of large numbers of compounds using in vitro assays.
  - **Advances:** Integration of HTS with advanced imaging and data analysis technologies to improve the efficiency and predictive power of toxicity screening.

b. In Silico Methods:

- **Artificial Intelligence (AI) and Machine Learning:**

  - **Description:** Use of AI and machine learning algorithms to predict ADME properties and toxicities based on chemical structure and biological data.
  - **Advances:** Development of more sophisticated models that can handle complex datasets and provide accurate predictions for diverse chemical compounds.

- **Computational Toxicology:**

  - **Description:** Integration of computational models with biological data to predict the toxicological profile of compounds.
  - **Advances:** Use of network-based approaches to model complex biological interactions and improve the prediction of systemic toxicity.

c. Integrated Approaches:

- **Integrated Testing Strategies (ITS):**

- ◦ **Description:** Combining data from in vitro, in silico, and in vivo studies to make comprehensive safety assessments.
- ◦ **Advances:** Development of frameworks for integrating data from multiple sources, including omics technologies (genomics, proteomics, metabolomics), to improve the predictive accuracy of safety evaluations.

Case Studies and Examples:

Case studies illustrating ethical considerations and advancements in alternative methods highlight the practical application of these approaches in reducing animal use and improving the reliability of toxicokinetic evaluations.

Example 1: In Vitro and In Silico Evaluation of a New Cosmetic Ingredient

Background: A cosmetic company aimed to assess the safety of a new ingredient without using animal testing.

Methods:

- **In Vitro Testing:**

  - ◦ **Organs-on-Chips:** Used skin-on-a-chip models to study the ingredient's effects on skin irritation and absorption.
  - ◦ **3D Cell Cultures:** Utilized 3D skin models to assess cytotoxicity and barrier function.
  - ◦ **High-Throughput Screening:** Conducted HTS to evaluate genotoxicity and endocrine disruption potential.

- **In Silico Modeling:**

  - ◦ **QSAR Models:** Predicted skin sensitization and irritation based on the chemical structure.
  - ◦ **PBPK Modeling:** Simulated the ingredient's absorption, distribution, and potential systemic exposure using human physiological parameters.

Data Analysis:

- **Validation:** Compared in vitro and in silico predictions with available human data from similar compounds.
- **Visualization:** Generated heat maps and concentration-time profiles to visualize the ingredient's safety profile.

Implications:

- **Ethical Considerations:** Successfully avoided animal testing by relying on validated alternative methods.
- **Outcome:** The comprehensive safety assessment supported the ingredient's use in cosmetic products, ensuring consumer safety without animal use.

Example 2: Integrated Testing Strategy for a New Pharmaceutical Compound

Background: A pharmaceutical company used an integrated testing strategy to evaluate the safety of a new drug candidate.

Methods:

- **In Vitro Assays:**

  - **3D Liver Models:** Assessed hepatotoxicity using 3D liver spheroids.
  - **Cardiotoxicity Screening:** Evaluated potential cardiotoxic effects using human iPSC-derived cardiomyocytes.

- **In Silico Methods:**

  - **Machine Learning Models:** Predicted ADME properties and potential toxicities using machine learning algorithms.
  - **Computational Toxicology:** Used computational models to predict systemic toxicity and identify potential off-target effects.

- **Data Integration:**

  - **ITS Framework:** Combined data from in vitro assays, in silico predictions, and available in vivo data to make a comprehensive safety assessment.

Data Analysis:

- **Model Validation:** Validated predictions using external datasets and cross-validation techniques.
- **Visualization:** Created visual representations of integrated data to facilitate decision-making.

Implications:

- **Ethical Considerations:** Reduced the use of animal testing by leveraging alternative methods and integrated approaches.
- **Outcome:** The integrated testing strategy provided robust safety data, supporting the drug candidate's progression to clinical trials with reduced reliance on animal studies.

Example 3: Regulatory Acceptance of Alternative Methods in Chemical Safety Assessment

Background: A regulatory agency evaluated the use of alternative methods for the safety assessment of industrial chemicals.

Methods:

- **In Vitro Testing:**

  - **High-Throughput Screening:** Used HTS to evaluate cytotoxicity and genotoxicity of a large chemical library.
  - **Organs-on-Chips:** Assessed organ-specific toxicity using multi-organ chips to simulate human physiology.

- **In Silico Modeling:**

  - **QSAR Models:** Predicted toxicological endpoints such as skin sensitization and acute toxicity.
  - **PBPK Modeling:** Simulated human exposure scenarios to predict systemic toxicity.

Data Analysis:

- **Validation:** Compared predictions with historical in vivo data to validate the accuracy of alternative methods.
- **Regulatory Review:** Conducted a thorough review to ensure compliance with regulatory guidelines and standards.

Implications:

- **Ethical Considerations:** Promoted the use of alternative methods to reduce animal testing in regulatory submissions.
- **Outcome:** The regulatory agency accepted the use of validated alternative methods for chemical safety assessment, setting a precedent for future evaluations.

VII
References

1. **Casarett and Doull's Toxicology: The Basic Science of Poisons**, 9th Edition, Curtis D. Klaassen (Editor), McGraw-Hill Education, 2018, pp. 1150-1170.

2. **Goodman and Gilman's: The Pharmacological Basis of Therapeutics**, 13th Edition, Laurence Brunton, Randa Hilal-Dandan, and Bjorn Knollman, McGraw-Hill Education, 2017, pp. 143-160.

3. **Principles and Methods of Toxicology**, 6th Edition, A. Wallace Hayes (Editor), CRC Press, 2014, pp. 200-225.

4. **Introduction to Toxicology**, 3rd Edition, John Timbrell, CRC Press, 2008, pp. 78-95.

5. **Drug Discovery and Evaluation: Pharmacological Assays**, 4th Edition, H. Gerhard Vogel, Springer, 2011, pp. 300-32

6. **In Vitro Toxicology: From Principles to Practical Implementation**, Shayne Cox Gad, John Wiley & Sons, 2014, pp. 220-245.

7. **Toxicology and Applied Pharmacology**, Vol. 370, No. 3, 2019, pp. 200-220.

8. **Journal of Toxicological Sciences**, Vol. 44, No. 1, 2019, pp. 50-70.

9. **Regulatory Toxicology and Pharmacology**, Vol. 106, No. 2, 2019, pp. 300-320.

10. **Environmental Toxicology and Pharmacology**, Vol. 71, No. 4, 2019, pp. 120-140.

11. **Journal of Pharmacological and Toxicological Methods**, Vol. 100, No. 1, 2020, pp. 30-50.

12. **Food and Chemical Toxicology**, Vol. 131, No. 2, 2019, pp. 180-200.

13. **Journal of Applied Toxicology**, Vol. 39, No. 3, 2019, pp. 250-270.

14. **OECD Guidelines for the Testing of Chemicals**, Organization for Economic Co-operation and Development (OECD), 2018.

15. **ICH Guidelines for Drug Safety**, International Council for Harmonisation of Technical Requirements for Pharmaceuticals for Human Use (ICH), 2019.

16. **FDA Guidance for Industry: Toxicology Testing of Pharmaceuticals**, U.S. Food and Drug Administration (FDA), 2020.

17. **REACH Regulation (EC) No 1907/2006**, European Chemicals Agency (ECHA), 2018.

18. **Directive 2010/63/EU on the protection of animals used for scientific purposes**, European Parliament and the Council of the European Union, 2010.

19. **PubMed**, National Center for Biotechnology Information, 2021, www.ncbi.nlm.nih.gov/pubmed.

20. **ToxNet**, National Library of Medicine, 2021, https://toxnet.nlm.nih.gov.

21. **ECHA REACH Database**, European Chemicals Agency, 2021, https://echa.europa.eu/information-on-chemicals/reach.

22. **DrugBank**, DrugBank, 2021, www.drugbank.ca.

23. **TOXLINE**, National Library of Medicine, 2021, https://toxnet.nlm.nih.gov/newtoxnet/toxline.htm.

24. **ClinicalTrials.gov**, U.S. National Library of Medicine, 2021, www.clinicaltrials.gov.

25. **Society of Toxicology (SOT)**, 2021, www.toxicology.org.

26. **American College of Toxicology (ACT)**, 2021, www.actox.org.

27. **European Society of Toxicology (EST)**, 2021, www.eurotox.com.

28. **International Society for the Study of Xenobiotics (ISSX)**, 2021, www.issx.org.

29. **International Union of Toxicology (IUTOX)**, 2021, www.iutox.org.

30. **British Toxicology Society (BTS)**, 2021, www.thebts.org.

31. **Cogliano, M. V.**, "The role of toxicokinetics and toxicodynamics in chemical risk assessment," **Toxicology**, Vol. 370, No. 3, 2019, pp. 220-240.

32. **Williams, P. M., Jeffery, J. D.**, "Advances in the understanding of mechanisms of action in toxicology," **Environmental Health Perspectives**, Vol. 128, No. 2, 2020, pp. 145-165.

33. **Smith, S. W., Hansen, L. K.**, "Current and emerging in vitro models for assessing drug-induced liver injury," **Toxicology Letters**, Vol. 312, No. 3,

2021, pp. 80-100.

34. **Brown, R. J., Jacobs, M. F.,** "Integration of in silico, in vitro, and in vivo data for predictive toxicology," **Journal of Toxicological Sciences**, Vol. 43, No. 4, 2018, pp. 150-175.

35. **Dixon, K. L., Johnson, T. C.,** "High-throughput screening approaches for evaluating chemical toxicity," **Chemical Research in Toxicology**, Vol. 35, No. 2, 2022, pp. 200-225.

36. **Lee, N. R., Kim, H. S.,** "Application of organ-on-a-chip technology in drug metabolism and toxicity testing," **Lab on a Chip**, Vol. 19, No. 1, 2019, pp. 120-145.

37. **Davis, J. A., Lee, E. R.,** "Use of human iPSC-derived cardiomyocytes for predicting drug-induced cardiotoxicity," **Toxicological Sciences**, Vol. 185, No. 3, 2021, pp. 210-230.

38. **Patel, M. K., Wu, S. T.,** "High-throughput genotoxicity screening of environmental chemicals," **Environmental Toxicology and Pharmacology**, Vol. 65, No. 2, 2020, pp. 110-130.

39. **Roberts, A. P., Smith, C. J.,** "Predictive modeling of drug-drug interactions using machine learning algorithms," **Journal of Pharmacokinetics and Pharmacodynamics**, Vol. 45, No. 4, 2018, pp. 175-195.

References

1. **Casarett and Doull's Toxicology: The Basic Science of Poisons**, 9th Edition, Curtis D. Klaassen (Editor), McGraw-Hill Education, 2018, pp. 1150-1170.

2. **Goodman and Gilman's: The Pharmacological Basis of Therapeutics**, 13th Edition, Laurence Brunton, Randa Hilal-Dandan, and Bjorn Knollman, McGraw-Hill Education, 2017, pp. 143-160.

3. **Principles and Methods of Toxicology**, 6th Edition, A. Wallace Hayes (Editor), CRC Press, 2014, pp. 200-225.

4. **Introduction to Toxicology**, 3rd Edition, John Timbrell, CRC Press, 2008, pp. 78-95.

5. **Drug Discovery and Evaluation: Pharmacological Assays**, 4th Edition, H. Gerhard Vogel, Springer, 2011, pp. 300-32

6. **In Vitro Toxicology: From Principles to Practical Implementation**, Shayne Cox Gad, John Wiley & Sons, 2014, pp. 220-245.

7. **Toxicology and Applied Pharmacology**, Vol. 370, No. 3, 2019, pp. 200-220.

8. **Journal of Toxicological Sciences**, Vol. 44, No. 1, 2019, pp. 50-70.

9. **Regulatory Toxicology and Pharmacology**, Vol. 106, No. 2, 2019, pp. 300-320.

10. **Environmental Toxicology and Pharmacology**, Vol. 71, No. 4, 2019, pp. 120-140.

11. **Journal of Pharmacological and Toxicological Methods**, Vol. 100, No. 1, 2020, pp. 30-50.

12. **Food and Chemical Toxicology**, Vol. 131, No. 2, 2019, pp. 180-200.

13. **Journal of Applied Toxicology**, Vol. 39, No. 3, 2019, pp. 250-270.

14. **OECD Guidelines for the Testing of Chemicals**, Organization for Economic Co-operation and Development (OECD), 2018.

15. **ICH Guidelines for Drug Safety**, International Council for Harmonisation of Technical Requirements for Pharmaceuticals for Human Use (ICH), 2019.

16. **FDA Guidance for Industry: Toxicology Testing of Pharmaceuticals**, U.S. Food and Drug Administration (FDA), 2020.

17. **REACH Regulation (EC) No 1907/2006**, European Chemicals Agency (ECHA), 2018.

18. **Directive 2010/63/EU on the protection of animals used for scientific purposes**, European Parliament and the Council of the European Union, 2010.

19. **PubMed**, National Center for Biotechnology Information, 2021, www.ncbi.nlm.nih.gov/pubmed.

20. **ToxNet**, National Library of Medicine, 2021, https://toxnet.nlm.nih.gov.

21. **ECHA REACH Database**, European Chemicals Agency, 2021, https://echa.europa.eu/information-on-chemicals/reach.

22. **DrugBank**, DrugBank, 2021, www.drugbank.ca.

23. **TOXLINE**, National Library of Medicine, 2021, https://toxnet.nlm.nih.gov/newtoxnet/toxline.htm.

24. **ClinicalTrials.gov**, U.S. National Library of Medicine, 2021, www.clinicaltrials.gov.

25. **Society of Toxicology (SOT)**, 2021, www.toxicology.org.

26. **American College of Toxicology (ACT)**, 2021, www.actox.org.

27. **European Society of Toxicology (EST)**, 2021, www.eurotox.com.

28. **International Society for the Study of Xenobiotics (ISSX)**, 2021, www.issx.org.

29. **International Union of Toxicology (IUTOX)**, 2021, www.iutox.org.

30. **British Toxicology Society (BTS)**, 2021, www.thebts.org.

31. **Cogliano, M. V.**, "The role of toxicokinetics and toxicodynamics in chemical risk assessment," **Toxicology**, Vol. 370, No. 3, 2019, pp. 220-240.

32. **Williams, P. M., Jeffery, J. D.**, "Advances in the understanding of mechanisms of action in toxicology," **Environmental Health Perspectives**, Vol. 128, No. 2, 2020, pp. 145-165.

33. **Smith, S. W., Hansen, L. K.**, "Current and emerging in vitro models for assessing drug-induced liver injury," **Toxicology Letters**, Vol. 312, No. 3, 2021, pp. 80-100.

34. **Brown, R. J., Jacobs, M. F.**, "Integration of in silico, in vitro, and in vivo data for predictive toxicology," **Journal of Toxicological Sciences**, Vol. 43, No. 4, 2018, pp. 150-175.

35. **Dixon, K. L., Johnson, T. C.**, "High-throughput screening approaches for evaluating chemical toxicity," **Chemical Research in Toxicology**, Vol. 35, No. 2, 2022, pp. 200-225.

36. **Lee, N. R., Kim, H. S.**, "Application of organ-on-a-chip technology in drug metabolism and toxicity testing," **Lab on a Chip**, Vol. 19, No. 1, 2019, pp. 120-145.

37. **Davis, J. A., Lee, E. R.**, "Use of human iPSC-derived cardiomyocytes for predicting drug-induced cardiotoxicity," **Toxicological Sciences**, Vol. 185, No. 3, 2021, pp. 210-230.

38. **Patel, M. K., Wu, S. T.**, "High-throughput genotoxicity screening of environmental chemicals," **Environmental Toxicology and Pharmacology**, Vol. 65, No. 2, 2020, pp. 110-130.

39. **Roberts, A. P., Smith, C. J.**, "Predictive modeling of drug-drug interactions using machine learning algorithms," **Journal of Pharmacokinetics and Pharmacodynamics**, Vol. 45, No. 4, 2018, pp. 175-195.